EMPOWERING INNOVATIVE PEOPLE

HOW SMART
MANAGERS
CHALLENGE
AND CHANNEL
THEIR
CREATIVE AND
TALENTED
EMPLOYEES

KARL F. GRETZ·STEVEN R. DROZDECK

PROBUS PUBLISHING COMPANY
Chicago, Illinois
Cambridge, England

ISBN 1-55738-517-3

Printed in the United States of America

IPC

1 2 3 4 5 6 7 8 9 0

With profound thanks, this book is dedicated to

William E. and Janis D. Gretz
and to
Frank S. and Jane C. Drozdeck

from whom the authors obtained their own creativity.

Contents

v

Foreword

by Gary S. Lynn

The Rubbermaid, Inc. Fellow of Innovation at Rensselaer Polytechnic Institute, and author of *From Concept to Market, IdeaLog,* and *Innopreneurship: How to Make Elephants Dance.*

Radial tires were not introduced by Goodyear, Firestone, or Goodrich—they were developed by a small French tire manufacturer, Michelin. Overnight package delivery was not introduced by UPS, or any of the airline companies; it came from Federal Express, an industry newcomer. Digital watches were ignored by the Swiss watchmakers. Mountain bikes did not come from the leading bicycle manufacturers. Light beer was not introduced by Anheuser Busch or Miller; it came from Rheinhold. Both diet and caffeine-free sodas did not initially come from Coke or Pepsi. Wine coolers were introduced by a small start-up company, not by the wine, soda, or spirit companies. Ballpoint pens were not introduced by the leading fountain pen manufacturers; they came from the Biro brothers of Hungary.

History is replete with examples of innovations emerging from industry outsiders rather than from the entrenched companies who were in a much better position to be creative and innovative. Why did the established firms let new competitors in and why didn't the established companies act first on the opportunities? Morita, Chairman of Sony, cites that American executives have become complacent and lazy; this may not be the case. A more plausible explanation is that some American business executives have forgotten that our competitive advantage lies in our people—however our people have grown weary of giving suggestions and being told by their manager "That's been tried before," or, "I'll get back to you" (and they never do). It is no wonder that after experiencing this type of behavior, employees say, "It's not worth the aggravation; I'll keep my ideas to myself."

However, with increased domestic and foreign competition, companies can no longer ignore their greatest asset: people. Who better to offer suggestions on how to improve a welding or machining operation than the individual using the machine day after day? American businesses desperately need innovation today to remain competitive. Innovation is becoming the buzz word for the 1990s. Many companies now use "innovation" in their coporate mission statements; executives of firms large and small promote the virtues of new products, processes, and services to give their companies the competive advantage so badly needed. But innovation does not appear magically; it is the result of creative people developing a vision and then acting to make it a reality.

Who is creative? Recently, researchers tested groups beginning with sixty-five-year olds and continued testing people of all ages. After their testing and analysis was complete, they reached a startling conclusion: the most creative people were five-year-old children. By the time we reach age eighteen, we have already been programmed what to say and what not to say; what questions to ask and which ones get us in trouble. It is no wonder that many of us cease learning at age ten or twelve. This trend is dangerous for our businesses, for our people, and for America.

Empowering Innovative People addresses the issue of how we can become more creative and innovative. It shows how to identify creative people, train existing employees to become more creative, and stimulate creativity by creating an invigorating environment. This book is for decision makers who are faced with competitive challenges and must find new and better ways to conduct business in the turbulent times ahead. The strategy to compete successfully is not with more mergers and acquisitions; companies do not have to look elsewhere for the "secret" . . . the answers are right in front of their eyes.

Preface

In the process of executive coaching and counseling, the authors have worked with many creative individuals whose overall productivity was frustrated because of conflicts with their managers or their general work environment. Certainly employee-manager conflict is often the fault of the employee, but just as often it can be easily remedied by a sensitive manager who understands how to handle such situations without losing a valuable asset.

This book has been written at the request of the many managers and creative employees whom we have trained and counseled. We hope it will help you improve your ability to empower the innovative individuals you manage.

The authors would like to thank particularly the following individuals who provided tremendous assistance (both formal and informal) in the preparation of this book: Cathy Erskin, William E. Gretz, Eugene

Radsepp, James D. McLean, Philip Maloy, David Parrish, Robert Stadoloupis, Fredrick Taylor, Pam van Giessen, and Walter Wiesenhutter.

Karl F. Gretz
Steven R. Drozdeck

Introduction

Traditionally, innovative or creative people have often been thought of as working almost exclusively in departments like Research and Development or Marketing. However, with the advent of books like Drucker's *Innovation and Entrepreneurship* and Peter's *In Search of Excellence*, creativity and innovation are finally being recognized as important throughout a company. In addition, perhaps because of the example provided by the Japanese, more and more managers are beginning to recognize that their most productive personnel are also their most creative and innovative.

This volume is designed to help managers recognize and manage creative personnel and their environment in ways that will help them to maximize their productivity. It does so by answering such questions as: How do you recognize creative people? Where do you find them? How do you communicate with them? How do you lead, train, and motivate them? How do you retain them? And, how do you monitor and evaluate their work?

With the exception of those in charge of research and development or marketing, few of the managers we have spoken to over the years have felt confident of their ability to deal with creative people. In fact, a remarkable number indicated that they felt threatened by employees who constantly offered recommendations for improving the department. As a result, they discouraged the very creativity and innovation needed to keep their departments competitive.

There are three major reasons for this failure to develop and utilize such an important asset:

➡ Leading people—as opposed to just managing them—requires leadership and communications skills, which are not taught in most graduate business schools. According to *Business Week* ("Where the Schools Aren't Doing Their Homework," 28 November 1988), most business schools focus on core subjects like strategic planning and contract law to the exclusion of the people skills needed to motivate and manage personnel.

➡ Managerial bureaucracy is conservative by nature. Unless specifically structured and maintained to seek it out, systems dislike change and fight it whenever they encounter it—and the managerial bureaucracy of any company is a system.

➡ Finally, management is constantly charged with the responsibility to account for and justify every expenditure. This is natural and prudent. Unfortunately, innovation is often hard to justify in its earliest stages, especially in terms of initial Return On Investment (ROI). As a result, it often appears safer to ignore the need for growth and the change that accompanies it in the hope that there will be no negative effects.

Unfortunately, history shows us that companies that do not innovate, die. This innovation must occur not only in the development of the specific products and services they offer their customers, but also in the way each department functions and the way the company seeks finances, does its marketing, and even compensates its employees. While more and more CEOs are beginning to recognize this need, many, if not most, managers still feel some confusion in terms of how to harness the innovative potential of their employees.

In preparing this book, the authors interviewed current and/or former managers of creative personnel at the following corporations:

- American Cyanamide
- Credit Swiss
- Fisher Price Toys
- FMC, Inc.
- IBM
- M & M Mars
- Merrill Lynch & Co.
- Syntex Corp.
- Unisys

For additional information regarding other books, training courses, audio or video tapes, please contact:

Training Groups, Inc.
P.O. Box 996
Newton, PA 18940
Phone: (215) 396-0501 / 639-1922

Recognizing, Obtaining, and Using a Valuable Asset

A frequently wasted asset, creative people can be worth their weight in gold when properly managed. This section will discuss the nature of creativity and how to recognize the creative people who are already working for you. It will then explore where and how to find creative individuals to meet your needs. Finally, it will provide a discussion of the attributes to seek when selecting an effective manager to lead creative people.

1

The Need for Innovators and Innovation

Somebody once said, "The only thing constant in life is change." Once powerful industries such as steel manufacturing and railroads have undergone such dramatic change in the last twenty years that new competition has already driven many of the former giants out of business. Why? Failure to appropriately adjust to changes that should have been readily apparent in markets, production technology, and demand. For example, the failure of railroads to realize that they were in the transportation business rather than just the railroad business.

Throughout industry, changes are occurring each day that will radically influence the way we do business tomorrow. In almost every case, these changes are apparent to those who are willing to look and offer tremendous opportunity to those who are flexible and willing to take the necessary steps to benefit from those changes. However, companies that are locked into specific management, production, or marketing patterns will find themselves outmaneuvered by those that are ready, willing, and able to adjust at *all* levels. This kind of adjustment will require the use of creative innovators at every level of management, production, and marketing.

Every year, over 600,000 new businesses are created in the United States. During the first half of the 1980s over forty million new jobs were created while five million were lost to changing demographics and market demands. It is interesting to note that *the majority of these jobs were created in industries which did not even exist twenty-five years ago.*

For too long, we have depended upon new institutions to provide the necessary innovations in every aspect of business, from the public service sector to major manufacturing. As a result, new companies have risen to take the place of established institutions that were too rigid to change. Yet, established institutions should be far more efficient and effective at taking advantage of innovations than are new, often underfinanced corporations struggling to establish themselves. The established corporation has an experienced management team in place, while the new institution has to develop one. That advantage alone often makes the difference between success and failure. However, unless that existing management team can be made more innovative, they, like the established steel and railroad industries, will find themselves locked in a losing struggle for their very survival.

While some managers may wring their hands and complain that innovation is too risky, others are beginning to realize that there is no strategy that carries more risk than failure to adapt to change. Rather than a risk-seeking missile that threatens the survival of his company, the successful innovator at every level is an individual who has examined the risks inherent in an innovation and found them to be smaller than those risks associated with standing still.

Creativity at Every Level

A popular misconception of creative individuals is that they are limited to the research and development and marketing departments of large, scientifically oriented companies. Of course, there is also the quintessential university scientist, huddled in his lab developing some new scientific breakthrough. Other creative people are thought to be limited to artists (e.g., Mozart, Picasso, or Thomas Mann). However, many companies have benefited from the creative abilities of assembly-line workers, cleaning staff, and secretaries.

Vertical Decision Making versus Group Consensus

It would seem that every time a company fails in the United States, the Japanese are blamed. Whether the electronics, automotive, robotics, or real estate industry, our problem is not our lack of innovation, but the Japanese dumping upon our markets. This has been the rallying cry for every obsolescent industry in this country for the past twenty years. However, a careful comparison of our management system with that of the Japanese might provide another set of answers.

When a market changes or a problem arises in an American company, a fairly rigid series of steps must be followed. The problem is reported up the chain of command and someone "at the top" is charged with making a decision and solving the problem. It is ironic that the individual so charged is often several levels removed from the actual problem. As a result, instead of a solution being sought from the individual who is closest to the problem and most likely to understand it and all of its ramifications, it is handled by someone who is only peripherally involved.

When a problem or a need for change is observed in any area of a company in Japan, management uses a technique called "Ringi." It is a general process and is applied virtually automatically. Once a problem surfaces, the first person to observe it presents it to his or her work team or group. The group members then gather and discuss every aspect of the problem while examining all pertinent data. Each discussion is very thorough and positively oriented. All members of the group are encouraged to participate and voice their opinions and to explore every possible facet of the problem. Once a consensus is reached, any decision about how to solve the problem is referred to the next group of involved individuals (this may be a lateral or vertical referral) for their consideration. By the time they are finished, everyone affected or who may have something useful to offer has been contacted for input. Once complete consensus is reached, the decision is carried out.

This may seem like a long and drawn-out process, but it has had startling results in terms of the development of innovations at all levels. One reason that Ringi is so successful is that it includes several important processes needed to generate creative solutions to problems (these principles will be explored further in the next chapter). It has also been an important factor in the successful development of quality control within Japanese industry years before it became popular in the United States (where it was developed).

Finally, by using the Ringi method, the Japanese involve workers of *every level* in the creative process instead of relying solely upon designated innovators. The purpose of this book is to provide you with the skills necessary to fully utilize the creative ability of all of your employees.

Summary

As managers, we can either act to make the fullest possible use of the resource represented by our creative employees (and to some extent, all employees are capable of being creative), or we can continue to lag further and further behind the competition. There have been many notable instances in which products have been turned around when companies have harnessed the creative potential of their employees. "A mind is a terrible thing to waste," applies to your employees as well as to education.

Chapter 1

What Is Creativity?

creative: 1. creating or able to create 2. productive (of) 3. having or showing imagination and artistic or intellectual inventiveness 4. stimulating the imagination and inventive powers.

creativity: creative ability; artistic or intellectual inventiveness. [*Webster's New World Dictionary of the American Language*]

creativity: the ability to make or otherwise bring into existence something new, whether a new solution to a problem, a new method or device, or a new artistic object or form. [*Encyclopaedia Britannica,* vol. 3, p. 227]

Creativity is like "good" abstract art: we don't know how to explain it, but we all think we know it when we see it (even if we don't agree with it when we do see it). Depending upon the expert you consult, you may be told that creativity is genetic, one aspect of intelligence, a special talent, something that can be learned, something that can't be learned, or even something that takes place solely on the unconscious level.

Are there specific characteristics of creative thinking or the creative process that set it apart from other forms of thinking? One of the great difficulties inherent in understanding creativity is the lack of unambiguous (i.e., specific) research on the subject. Considering the volumes of research published on creativity each year this may appear hard to believe. However, most studies on creativity are very subjective (running the gamut from biographical reports on how individuals like Mozart composed their music to what specific acts a researcher defines as creative, i.e., which acts meet *his* model of creativity). Unfortunately, many of the more objective studies fail to provide adequate and realistic control groups. The result is the current state of confusion and conflict about just what constitutes creativity. Since we need a working definition and understanding of creativity, this chapter will attempt to provide a coherent set of guidelines as well as a summary of some of the arguments surrounding the nature of creativity.

Insight and the Unconscious in Creative Thinking

In his book, *aha! Insight,* Martin Gardner explores the importance of insight to creativity, especially the creativity needed to solve mathematical problems. Essentially, he feels that the creative act owes little to logic or reason and that creative insight, the "aha!" experience, is key to problem solving. In fact, he believes that insights have been closely connected to creativity in science, business, and the arts, and that the great revolutions in science have almost always been the result of unexpected intuitive leaps.

Morris Kline reports that mathematicians have often found that the inspiration they received to solve a problem often had little relation to the work they were doing at the time (they may have been working in the yard, shaving, or thinking about something else). Hence, the creative process is not something under conscious control, but rather the manifestation of something unconscious. Hence, it can neither be summoned at will nor forced. In fact, tension could block it; thus the theory that it functions most effectively when the individuals are relaxed and their minds open.

Kline is not alone in his belief that the unconscious is the primary source of creativity. Whereas he suspects that creativity is an innate talent (and, hence, not available to everyone?) that must be nurtured, William Niederland believes that the creative process is the result of a combination of both conscious and unconscious processes. The crucial unconscious processes, according to Niederland, are the result of early life experiences that provide both information for problem solving and psychological influence, which may either help or hinder the solution of problems. Niederland notes that the nature of the creative process probably varies depending upon the nature, content, and aim of the problem to be solved—for example, the process used by a mathematical genius versus those used by a composer, an author, or a painter.

Finally, there are many studies that indicate that the chief distinction of the creative individual is his reliance upon intuition, an unconscious process. Unlike the average person, the creative individual refuses to allow his intellect to rule.

Gardner reports that many studies of the creative thinking process, while far from conclusive, suggest the existence of some sort of relationship between creative ability and humor. Play is both mentally and physically relaxing, and that relaxation may be key to opening up the unconscious processes necessary for creativity.

Because most humor requires us to look at something unconventionally, humor itself requires some level of creativity. The ability to perceive humor in otherwise humorless situations requires a flexibility of mind and perception that is very important to creative problem solving. This same flexibility of perception is necessary in the creative solution of problems. Searching for innovative solutions also necessitates looking at problems from different angles of perception than may have been previously explored.

Intelligence

Studies have indicated that creative people are usually of above average intelligence. However, above a certain level (an IQ of 120), there appears to be little correlation between creativity and intelligence. In a word, a person can be a genius (as measured by intelligence tests or academic grades) without being very creative. In fact, Buhler, Keith-Spiegel, and Thomas found the relationship between creativity and academic aptitude to be almost negligible. Similarly, creative insight does not appear to be necessarily correlated with quickness of thought. Slow thinkers may be even better at solving problems in an unexpected way than someone who thinks quickly.

Many authorities disagree about the relative importance to creativity of divergent thinking, in which a richness of ideas is produced through a process of broad association, and convergent thinking, the almost straight-line, analytic reasoning measured by intelligence tests. However, the experience of the managers we interviewed, as well as a large portion of the research literature, indicates that both are necessary to creative performance. The degree to which each is necessary appears to vary with the nature of the task or occupation; for example, a mathematical problem may require a more convergent thought process (although not always), whereas a human relations problem may require more divergent problem solving.

Related to the idea of divergent thinking is that of fantasy, in which the creative individual visualizes problems and their potential solutions. Within the fantasy, the creative problem solver explores a challenge from all angles, modifying it over and over until she is able to visualize a potential solution. At times, she may appear to be no more than daydreaming while she is actually developing a highly complex solution to a difficult problem. Ironically, she also may be just daydreaming. Louis Linn states that there are two types of fantasy: creative fantasy, in which the individual prepares for some later action, and daydreaming fantasy, which he feels is little more that the refuge for unfulfillable wishes. The creative fantasy may start in an inspirational moment that is rooted deep within the individual's unconscious. It is then systematically elaborated and translated into a realistic program of action. The daydream, on the other hand, is seen as a tendency toward mere wishful thinking, which tends to diminish with psychological and biological maturing, although to some extent it persists throughout life.

A number of psychometricians have attempted to develop tests that measure creative abilities. To do so, they have developed such test items as unusual or multiple word associations, the composition of fable endings, and the description of unusual uses or improvements for ordinary objects or implements. Unfortunately, the reliability of such tests is still very low. Many people who score highly on them produce little innovation, while many of the most innovative people score very poorly. Hence, the tests' usefulness for industry will remain questionable until they can be made considerably more objective and consistent.

Unconventional Thinking

Some psychologists feel that the unconventionality of thought sometimes found in creative individuals is at least partly the result of some form of resistance to acculturation, which is seen by the creative individual as demanding surrender of one's unique, fundamental nature. Hence, this individual is often perceived as being somewhat rebellious and unwilling to work within rigid societal and corporate rules and policies. As we shall see, they are probably hearing a different drummer.

The Importance of Past Experiences

Contrary to popular belief, far more than heightened creativity is required for the solution of most problems. Robert W. Weisberg states that evidence from research studies indicates that, rather than being independent of past experiences, solution of "insight" problems depends on detailed past experience with such problems. While this seems obvious, many managers forget the importance of adequate preparatory background when assigning projects. Among the managers we interviewed, one of the single most important attributes sought in creative people they hired was breadth as well as depth of experience. In addition, assignments were made to encourage the development of a wide range of experience within their field because of the subsequent enhancement of problem-solving skills.

If divergent thinking is to be of any use to the problem solver, it must be based upon as wide a base of experience as possible. The more varied the information and previous solutions to problems that the mind has to draw upon, the more likely it is to develop a solution based upon divergent thinking. Individuals with narrow experience appear to be limited to solving problems with convergent thinking processes.

Creative Problem Analysis and Solutions

Many of us tend to think of innovation primarily in terms of creative solutions to problems. However, creativity also extends to the analysis of the problem itself. How often have you been faced with a problem that really stumped you, only to kick yourself when someone else came up with a simple solution that was "obvious" once it had been pointed out. At such times, we are often tempted to denigrate ourselves or the problem when, in reality, creative analysis was required to find that simple solution.

Ideally, every problem has a simple, elegant solution. Simple, straight-line thinking often fails to develop such a solution because it fails to explore adequately the requisite number of problem and solution parameters. This brings us back to the need for broad-based experience in order to develop the requisite variety of behavior (solutions) for problem solving. Hence, the broader the base of an individual's experience, the greater his variety of behavior and problem-solving skills.

The creative analysis (or formulation) of a problem requires approaching it in unconventional ways. When a problem fails to fall to standard problem-solving procedures, divergent approaches based upon experience outside that immediately relate to the area of inquiry become important. At this time, experience in solving similar problems in different fields can be of great value.

Similarly, any creative solution to a problem must meet two criteria: it must solve the problem in question and it must be novel in its approach. Some problems are well defined, precisely providing the required characteristics and parameters of the solution from the beginning. However, other problems are poorly defined, and provide no detailed specification of the desired goal. In such cases, the creative problem solver must first determine and specify the criteria that the solution must meet in some detail.

Specific Creative Abilities

One of the best pieces of news to come from the research conducted in creative ability in recent years is the fact that virtually everyone is creative to some extent. Like other talents, some people are more creative than others, but virtually everyone is capable of creativity. The implications of this fact for developing a more innovative department are important. For a long time, many people have considered individuals with lower job classifications, such as blue collar workers or office support staff, to possess little or no creativity. As a result, little use has been made of this tremendous resource to improve overall productivity.

Several factors appear to be critical to just how much creativity an individual demonstrates:

- ➡ The presence and level of actual creative talent.

- ➡ The existence of other mental and physical abilities that may synergistically affect that talent. For example, an artist not only must have the ability to draw or paint, he also must have a strong visual imagination, memory, and ability to conceptualize (see Chapters 7 and 8 for a discussion of the senses and how they affect thought and problem solving).

- ➡ The environment in which he or she was raised. Depending upon the individual and the field of creativity (science versus art versus music, etc.), some environments appear to stimulate the development of creativity while others stifle it.

- ➥ The current work environment. Most research appears to indicate that overly rigid rules and procedures, as well as criticism by peers and superiors, can be very harmful to creativity (see Chapter 6 on establishing an environment that stimulates creativity).

- ➥ The creative individual must be effectively motivated. To an extent, the job environment will provide some of this motivation. However, much of it must be internal. As the manager, you must elicit and use this internal motivation to achieve good productivity.

Motivation and Creativity

Without motivation, no one does anything. Biologists have long proven that natural drives (such as hunger) provide powerful sources of motivation for animals and people. Innovation requires the ability to focus on a problem and stay with it, overcoming all obstacles until an effective solution is reached. Research now appears to indicate that for the creative individual, creation itself is a powerful source of motivation. Weisberg postulates that the degree of commitment to one's work might be an important difference between creative and noncreative individuals. However, he also points out that high motivation alone will not necessarily result in creativity. There are many highly motivated individuals who produce incredible volumes of work without developing anything new. Nevertheless, the pleasure of solving a problem by a shortcut method may even motivate one to learn more about traditional problem-solving techniques, as well as broaden one's experience, making one more effective at divergent problem-solving techniques.

To summarize, differences in the level of internal and external motivation could account for significant differences in productivity and creativity among individuals—even among individuals who use similar thought processes and possess similar levels of talent.

Creativity versus Innovation

Many people become confused when confronted with the difference between innovation and creativity. Harvard's Theodore Levitt makes the following distinction:

> The trouble with much of the advice business gets today about the need to be more vigorously creative is that its advocates

often fail to distinguish between creativity and innovation. *Creativity is thinking up new things. Innovation is doing new things . . .* [italics added]. A powerful new idea can kick around unused in a company for years, not because its merits are not recognized, but because nobody assumed the responsibility for converting it from words into action. Ideas are useless unless used. Until then, they are in limbo.

If you talk to the people who work for you, you'll discover that there is no shortage of creativity or creative people in American business. The shortage is of innovators. All too often, people believe that creativity automatically leads to innovation. It doesn't. (as quoted by Peters and Thomas, pp. 206-7).

As a manager, it is your job to see that ideas become innovations by either personally assuming or assigning responsibility for their development. You may even assign that responsibility back to the individual who produced the idea in the first place. In so doing, you will not only help them experience the costs of following an idea through to fruition, you will also enable them to taste the motivational thrill of having a hand in that process. Thus, because nonproductive ideas are essentially useless, for the purposes of this book we will use the terms "creativity" and "innovation" interchangeably.

Summary

Despite the level of confusion that surrounds the concept of creativity, several points appear to be solidly founded:

➥ There is little question that creativity is an innate talent that most people possess to some degree. However, while there has been little success in developing a test to measure it objectively, creativity appears to be affected by a variety of factors, such as internal and external motivation, the environment in which one is raised or currently works, and the breadth and depth of one's experience in solving problems.

➥ The creative process occurs on both the conscious and the unconscious levels of the mind and may continue within the subconscious once the conscious mind has moved on to different activities. Hence the importance of concepts like aha! insight and intuition.

- Both convergent and divergent thinking are important to creative problem solving. While convergent thinking is strongly influenced by the depth of one's experience in a given field, the ability to effectively produce divergent thinking is dependent upon the breadth of one's experience across many fields.

- Fantasy is the ability to mentally conceptualize a problem, and possibly its solution, so that it can be examined from various points of view. Hence, its importance in terms of structuring a problem to be solved.

- While intelligence is necessary to creativity, it is not paramount. There is no direct correlation between creativity and IQs over 120. Similarly, there is no indication that speed of thought is related to creativity.

- The freedom to look at situations, people, and problems with humor appears to be highly correlated with creative ability.

- Finally, relaxation and flexibility are important to creative efforts. While this is not to say that individuals cannot be creative under pressure, rigid controls and inflexible procedures do more to hamper than to help creativity.

Indentifying the Creative People within Your Company

To an extent, most of us think we can recognize someone who is creative. However, the stereotypes of creative individuals have little to do with reality. Despite their portrayal as such in popular literature and movies, not all great artists live in cold-water flats, wear a beard and smoke "funny cigarettes." At the same time, few people readily recognize the creativity inherent in their own employees, especially if they are office or blue collar workers.

As we mentioned in the previous chapter, most people are creative to some extent. However, almost all of us tend to live up or down to the expectations of our superiors. If we don't expect our employees to be creative, we will communicate our lack of interest in their innovative ideas, thereby costing ourselves a valuable resource.

The purpose of this chapter is to present characteristics of creative people that may make them easier to recognize, not only during hiring, but also among your current staff.

Nonjudgemental

Virtually all of us suffer from some prejudices. For example, we may believe that certain kinds of problems can only be approached in specific ways. Hence, once we have labeled a problem, we have also locked ourselves into a specific way of solving it. Unfortunately, our prejudice may have cost us the opportunity to explore more elegant and less costly solutions.

In his investigations of creativity in science, Donald MacKinnon has found that the more creative individuals are more reluctant to judge what they encounter. Instead, they have a strong tendency to try to apprehend the problem or situation objectively and penetrate its nature. He found that less creative people seemed more prone to evaluate quickly and then turn to other matters (see Chapter 10 for an in-depth discussion). Similarly, Albert Rothenberg reports a tendency of creative people to think in terms of opposites or contraries and unite them in inventive ways. Both MacKinnon and Rothenberg have found that creative people demonstrate a level of flexibility in both their overall thinking and their approach to problem solving.

Reality-Based

Abraham Maslow explored the concept of health through studies of individuals that he considered fully healthy, that is, the most fully developed and creative. According to Maslow, such individuals are characterized by what he called "self-actualizing creativeness," which he considered a broad orientation that leads to health and growth, regardless of the occupation of the person who possesses it. In a word, creative individuals are well rounded.

This theory becomes important because of its implications for selecting creative individuals. Whether or not special creative talents are involved, truly creative people act to grow and be creative in virtually everything they do. Using his studies of creative people, Maslow drew up a list of what he saw as their shared characteristics, which included:

➡ They have a strong reality orientation. Their fantasies are based upon problem solving, not problem avoidance.

➡ They are problem centered. They look at problems as challenges to be overcome, rather than as threats to their safety or sense of self-worth.

➡ They tend to be spontaneous and independent, and they are also generally accepting of themselves and others.

Values and Beliefs

D. N. Perkins found in his work that creative individuals shared several values. The creative individual values originality itself and desires originality in his own work. While cherishing his own independence of judgement, he responds to originality in the work of others. However, highly creative people avoid the rigidity expressed by individuals who appear to feel that if a solution is not original, it is useless (as if there were something inherently wrong with any solution that was simple and had worked before). In a word, they do not seek creativity simply for the sake of change. At the same time, the creative person is likely to perceive himself as being creative and to value his creativity as an important part of his make-up.

Our basic belief systems have a tremendous affect upon both how we approach problems and how we view a problem relative to ourselves. As such, our beliefs can have a tremendous impact upon our ability to solve any given problem. For example, for years, virtually all educated people in Europe believed that the earth was flat and that sailing too far west would result in their falling off of the edge of the world. As a result, their ability to develop creative solutions to finding alternative routes to the Orient was limited. Once Columbus expanded King Ferdinand and Queen Isabella's belief systems to include the possibility of the earth being round, they became open to his creative solution to the problem. Similarly, rigidity of beliefs can even affect the nature of the problem-solving techniques we are willing to explore or the variety of people to whom we consider assigning a given problem.

Creativity Tests

As we mentioned in the previous chapter, the greatest weakness inherent in most tests of creativity is the tremendous level of subjectivity involved in their interpretation. This raises significant questions about their reliability. Most tests involve various aspects of verbal fluency, flexibility, and originality, which are generally subsumed under the heading of "divergent thinking."

Tests constructed to determine the presence of divergent thinking look for the kind of thinking that "goes off in different directions." This contrasts with convergent thinking, which leads to a single right answer based upon the given facts. Typical of these tests is the Torrance series, which, among other things, may ask an individual to think of various ways a product might be improved (e.g., such as asking a child to think of ways a toy might be made "more fun"). Another problem might consist of thinking up unusual uses for common objects—such as a thimble, a milk carton, or a paper clip. Finally, a frequently used type of test, known as "consequences," requires the individual to list all the consequences of a given improbable event. While such tests will stimulate the imagination of almost anyone, scores may be difficult to judge because of the tester's tendency to either look for "cookbook" interpretations based upon the test manual, or to depend upon his own interpretation of which answers should be considered creative.

Summary

Recognizing creative individuals is not as difficult as it may initially appear. Creativity tests are often not useful, and they are also unnecessary in most situations.

- Does the individual have a prior history of creative work (a track record)?
- Does she think of herself as creative?
- Is she flexible and nonjudgemental when confronted with potential solutions to a problem?
- Is he problem oriented?
- Does he look at problems as threats or as exciting challenges?
- Does she have a sense of humor?

Depending upon the answers to these questions, you should have little difficulty in identifying creative people within your department.

Hiring Creative People

The specifics of hiring creative individuals depends to a large degree upon the nature of your business and the needs of your department. George Freedman divides innovators, such those involved in R & D, new product development, and marketing, into two groups, generalists and specialists. These are the individuals who apply inventiveness and creativity to a new idea to turn it into reality. He also divides implementers/innovators into two other overlapping groups, professionals and nonprofessionals (who are also skilled practitioners at what they do).

Generalists. Freedman defines the generalist as someone who works in many different fields simultaneously, as opposed to the individual who limits his expertise (considerable as it may be) to a single field. Each is extremely important to the innovative process. Because of their tendency to simultaneously work at several programs for several different parts of the company, generalists are more commonly found in centers. This facilitates their ability to work with different processes, products, and markets in ways that would be difficult, if not impossible, if they were located anywhere else.

While some managers we spoke to preferred to hire and develop exclusively generalists, they were usually involved in small operations (whether in R & D, new product development or marketing). Managers of larger divisions preferred a mix of primarily specialists with only a few generalists. Each individual specialized in a single product line, market segment, etc., for a given period (perhaps a year, or even five to ten years depending upon the nature of the product and its life cycle). At the end of that period, or at their request, individuals would be rotated to a new area. This helps avoid staleness and provides useful experience for the individual.

To be a generalist, a person must have a solid depth of training and experience in at least one area or field. In addition, he must possess a good breadth of experience in several other fields or areas. Obviously, unless you hire someone who has been a professional student and collected a series of doctorates, you will either be hiring someone who has developed that breadth of experience or you will provide it yourself.

A key quality of generalists is flexibility. While this is true of all creative people, it is particularly true for these individuals. Specialists are expected to be creative within a fairly narrow band of parameters, whereas generalists need the experience and self-confidence to generate ideas and projects across a broad spectrum of your company's products and services. Hence, they must be able to work on several disparate projects from different fields at the same time.

Whether involved in scientific work or marketing distributions, generalists must be competent experimenters. Although the ability to generate concepts is important, it is never enough. A good generalist must have the ability to carry her concepts to the point where feasibility is proven.

Finally, the generalist should be an effective communicator. No matter how effective she is at generating ideas or carrying a concept through to completion, she can't sell it to either higher management or to those who will work on the concept unless she can effectively communicate her vision of it and its place in the company's future. After all, who can convince managers and staff better than the person who had the basic conception and proved it was feasible?

Freedman sees the mission of the generalist as reacting to stimulation from other sources by producing something new that can eventually help the company flourish. The generalist also has the mission of stimulating the creative process in those around her based upon her broad background of experience. This broad experience enables the generalist to bring a wide repertoire of problem-solving skills to play in any situation, which often stimulates a high level of synergy in others.

Technical Specialists. The specialist is someone who has depth of training and experience in a single field and, ideally, enjoys working in that field. He is capable of great creativity and synergy within that field and has solid experience in problem solving in his area of expertise. He can accomplish significant work when teamed with generalists and both have important roles within the organization.

With the exception of broad experience, the same qualifications are required for specialists as for generalists: they must be experts, creative and competent experimenters. The particular nature of your experts will, of course, be determined by the unique blend of your company's culture and needs.

The purpose of the specialist is to provide the required specialized expertise for an innovation team. Hence, the exact number of specialists required will vary according to those needs. However, it is rarely a good idea to have only one specialist in a given field. This is true for several reasons:

- ➡ First, it is important for a specialist to have someone else within his field to interact with if he is to maintain productivity.

- ➡ Second, it may be difficult for one person to keep up with everything new in his field. Being able to share the burden can make this task more stimulating.

- ➡ Third, it increases the chance of synergistic interaction within that field.

When it is impossible to maintain more than one specialist in a given area (either because of geographic or budgetary requirements), you may wish to consider contracting for the services of an outsider on an as-needed basis. Several managers we spoke with told us they provide their specialists with funds to obtain the help of consulting professors from local universities when they are faced with a problem beyond their ken. This has the added benefit of providing helpful supporting funds to universities.

Nonprofessionals. This category includes everyone from lab assistants to model-makers to technicians. Their job is to provide creative assistance to the professional staff. Usually, you should have one for each professional. As they work with creative specialists and generalists, their own creativity blossoms.

Note: It is important to know where to obtain professional and nonprofessional help in your area, e.g., universities, private labs, etc. These resources can often be brought in at a small cost to increase creative synergy and productivity at crucial times.

Hiring Criteria

From where you hire creative individuals and the amount of experience you want them to have will depend upon your particular needs and preferences. However, there are several things you may wish to take into consideration:

➡ Acculturation: Several managers we spoke with preferred to hire creative people (such as designers) right out of school to more easily merge them into their team.

➡ Experience: One manager of a chemical company indicated that he prefers to hire individuals who have at least three years of experience in industry. Those years not only provide a track record, they ensure that the candidate has had sufficient business experience to have taken a product through its entire cycle (whether this required three or even eight years). This experience provides the individual with sufficient understanding of the processes by which a product is developed, from inception to final marketing and customer support.

➡ Flexibility: Self-confidence is critical, but many managers also feel that another important attribute is a certain humility best demonstrated by hard, persistent work; ability and willingness to learn; self-discipline; and adaptability.

➡ Practicality: Are the solutions suggested by this individual reality based, or pie in the sky?

➡ Basic people skills. Can this individual effectively relate to and cooperate with his co-workers?

➡ Team Spirit: The director of new product development for a major toy manufacturer looks beyond raw talent to an individual's ability to add synergy to existing design teams. He indicates that the "creative genius" usually produces less alone than a "slightly less talented" individual who benefits from the synergy of a good team. His department has one of the highest records of productivity and lowest employee turnover rates in the industry. However, while it is important to avoid "prima donnas" and individuals with poor relationship skills, it is also important to avoid individuals who can *only* work on a team. Unfortunately, there may be times when you will have to take a loner and make him into a team player. You need people who can function well on their own as well as in a team.

➥ Does this individual understand innovation and how to get her idea to market?

As one medical research manager pointed out to us, the size of your company may have a great deal to do with who you can hire. Smaller and medium size companies often don't have the research funding to hire Nobel Prize winners. At the same time, you may also find yourself faced with governmental or organizational requirements.

Summary

The criteria you use to select creative personnel will depend largely upon your particular budget, needs and corporate culture. However, a proper balance of professional and nonprofessional generalists and specialists can be very helpful in increasing productivity.

One manager we spoke with described his ideal creative employee as one who had a good sense of humor; who was willing to accept input from others as well as share his own ideas; whose attitude toward "failure" is that it is only temporary, you are on your way to your goal and if you haven't arrived yet, that's okay.

Selecting the Best Manager for Creative People

Managers and department heads that we spoke to universally agreed that a good manager must meet three criteria:

➡ First, she must be able to communicate effectively the concepts and needs of her team or department to higher management, and the requirements of higher management to her team.

➡ Second, she must act as a buffer between her people and higher management.

➡ Finally, she must be a leader who can follow a project from beginning to end and motivate her personnel to give their best.

Some managers felt that a good manager also has to be a good administrator. However, others felt that the administrative aspects of running a team or department—depending upon the size of project, etc.—is best handled by a separate administrator assigned to take care of policies and procedures. Freedman agrees that a combination of an administrator and a manager, with the manager/leader free to lead, works best. He provides the following description of each.

Administrators. The qualifications for any good administrator are few:

➥ First, he must be effective in handling money and hours. He doesn't have to be an accountant but must have at least some understanding of accounting and computer-generated spreadsheets.

➥ The typical administrator is often perceived as something of an unimaginative bean counter. Obviously, the administrator for an innovative project or a creative department must himself be creative. After all, he will have to obtain the resources necessary for the project or department when it may well be the lowest priority among bureaucratic service departments.

The operating rules of any department can either improve or hinder the smooth functioning of that department by affecting morale and general efficiency. Hence, the chief role of the administrator is to establish operating rules and procedures that will increase efficiency and morale. He must expedite actions that will support the role of the manager/leader, leaving the manager's hands free to innovate.

A major problem for R & D (innovative) departments is the tendency of various bureaucratic service departments to consider them the lowest priority. An important job of the administrator is to do everything possible to improve the department's priority status.

The greatest strength of the administrator is his understanding of how to work with the system (the operational and support elements of the parent company). He has the role of protecting the manager from traumatic interaction with bureaucrats in the same way that the manager protects his creative staff. The administrator provides the bridge between the innovators and the bureaucrats.

Another important function of the administrator is to monitor the progress of projects toward assigned goals and to point out where targets are not being met. Depending upon the size of your operation, this role may filled by the manager within a specific set of formal or informal standard operating procedures. For example, Fisher Price Toys has an informal series of "show and tell" meetings in which designers present their progress on assigned projects to peers and superiors. Some of these meetings may occur as frequently as semimonthly, while others will occur every few months, depending upon developmental requirements. These meetings not only give designers a good deal of feedback from several sources, they also force them to think in terms of regular deadlines.

The relationship between the manager and her administrator is very important. They must work as smoothly as a well-functioning athletic team in which success depends upon the work of both. Because the manager holds the ultimate responsibility for the success or failure of the project, department, etc., she must have confidence that she can delegate many of her duties to the administrator. Hence, the manager and administrator present a united front to both employees and the rest of the company.

Effective teamwork between a manager and administrator enables the manager to leave with confidence most of the mechanics of running the department to her administrator. This teamwork then allows her to walk around, providing the kind of leadership and management that is so needed to make a creative department a success. Hence, the staff has a leader that is available when they need her instead of someone who is so tied down with administrative details that she is not there to help solve problems.

Depending upon the nature of your department, you may feel that management by walking around is not feasible. However, many managers use this technique in spite of difficult conditions. For example, despite the incredible geographic separation of individual innovators (field reps) in FMC's AgChem Division, managers (from the director of development through regional managers and supervisors) spend most of their time in contact with each and every one of them.

Managers/Leaders. The manager/leader is ultimately responsible for everything that happens or fails to happen within his department. He must understand the projects he is assigned to manage and he must communicate that understanding to higher management while selling them on the progress of each project.

As obvious as this might appear, it is more complicated than it looks. When managing an existing product line, a manger must understand the product, its markets, and the ins and outs of establishing a good ROI for the company. However, the manager/leader of an innovative project or department has a much more difficult task because he must not only understand the development of his product and its potential markets, he also has to be able to sell it to higher management despite ROI problems (since the lag time between innovative investment and solid return is usually measured in years).

As a result, one of the most important attributes of the manager/leader is bi-directional credibility. The manager must not only have credibility when speaking to higher management about the work of his department, he must also have credibility with his own creative staff. To accomplish this, it is important to find an individual with a proven track record of innovation who also possesses good leadership skills (these skills are discussed in detail in Sections III and IV).

The individual who has been a successful manager is most likely viewed with confidence by higher management as one who can be trusted with important projects. At the same time, his proven record of creativity often enables him to be a useful resource to his staff in solving the problems associated with their assigned projects. In many ways, the ideal manager/leader is a "generalist" (see previous chapter).

In summary, a leader must be both an innovator in his own right as well as an effective manager, as demonstrated by prior performance. If his management skills are only average, it becomes very important to provide him with a good administrator.

A good department head should be a good leader first and a good manager second. The difference between a good manager and a good leader is critical. A leader *leads*. He has already demonstrated his innovative abilities and regularly continues to do so. Creative, innovative people need to be lead to get the best from them. "Good managers" often have excellent skills in terms of strategic planning and handling materials, but poor leadership skills. They are disciplined, orderly, and highly attuned to fiscal matters.

Ideally, the head of R & D should be both a good leader and a good manager. However, if you can have only one or the other, select the leader and compensate for his management weaknesses with a good administrator. It is better to make an occasional error in management than to fail to develop the new ideas and programs the company needs to grow and succeed.

Good leaders are optimistic and have a positive attitude (see Chapter 24). They take it on faith that they will succeed in whatever they are working on and that they can eventually solve virtually any problem. This confidence is critical because if a leader doesn't believe in what he's doing, it is doomed to failure from the start. The worst possible manager/leader for creative people is the pessimist. His lack of faith in himself, his people, and the future is one of the greatest possible blocks to creative achievement. How can anyone who doesn't really believe in success motivate a staff to overcome obstacles? In addition, a manager/leader's job includes selling his programs to the higher-ups. Pessimists make poor salesmen. "You wouldn't really like to buy this lemon, would you? Its kind of expensive, but I suppose it could make the company money eventually, if no more problems arise."

However, being optimistic does not mean being blind to reality. A manager *must* be very competent in his own field because this experience enables him to recognize the limits of any project. Otherwise, optimism can run amok while the manager wastes large amounts of capital pursuing the impossible.

A manager/leader must have effective people skills. In addition to being an excellent communicator, he must also understand creative people and know how to motivate and even inspire them with a sense of their mission (much of this book is devoted to these skills). He must be creative himself with a good imagination. In addition, he must be secure enough to be receptive to the ideas/concepts of others without feeling threatened. Hence, he needs to be able to be as enthusiastic about other's ideas as he is about his own. In a word, he must be both open-minded and flexible.

Finally, a good leader has to have a real vision of what he is trying to accomplish. At the same time, it must be understood that vision goes far beyond having a good idea, or even having a good concept of how to develop and implement that idea. Vision requires that the manager/leader fully understand the idea and its ramifications for his company and even the industry. This kind of leadership requires an emotional commitment to the program, idea, etc., that will carry the manager through to its completion.

Summary

Selecting the best manager for something as important as your creative departments is never easy. To help, Raudsepp and Yeager have provided a checklist of some of the more important personal attributes to look for when choosing a manager/leader of creative people.

- ➡ Is tactful and insightful
- ➡ Respects individual differences
- ➡ Understands creative problem solving
- ➡ Is professionally competent

- Knows how to communicate
- Leads by suggestion
- Feels secure
- Takes calculated risks
- Knows how to assign responsibility
- Criticizes tactfully
- Provides inspiration
- Gives recognition
- Is receptive
- Knows when to use an idea
- Knows how to identify the problem
- Bolsters self-confidence
- Keeps top management informed
- Insists on flexible organization

On Becoming
Even More Creative

One of the most frequent criticisms of creative people is the inconsistency of their creativity. Whether you work with scientists or marketing specialists, an individual's ability to be creative affects their value to the firm. The way that we see, hear, feel, and interpret events around us has a great deal to do with how we create. This section introduces the concepts of sensory modalities, submodalities, and behavioral modeling as applied to increasing one's own and one's employees' creativity. Each is then explored in greater detail.

Establishing an Innovative Environment

The establishment of an environment that is fertile for innovation must be done on two levels: first, on a company-wide basis and, second, department by department. Failure to establish an innovative environment on a company-wide basis can lead to the eventual failure of the company to remain competitive within its industry, while failure on a departmental basis can result in failure of the manager in question to demonstrate the efficiency and effectiveness of both his department and his own management skills.

The Innovative Company: Policies and Procedures

Although this book focuses on managers improving individual creativity within their department, it is important to digress long enough to explore the affect of corporate policies upon the overall creativity of individuals throughout the company. This is important because any corporation is a system and all systems automatically resist change. In his excellent book, *The Pursuit of Innovation,* George Freedman makes the critical point that the corporate culture in which you work is one of the most important factors in determining just how innovative you can be. Whether you manage R & D, marketing, training, or even housekeeping, the culture produced by the chief executive officer and the executive offices will ultimately determine the level of innovation and creativity you can achieve.

When you consider the typical management matrix, the lines of interdependence between individuals and departments become clear, and it can be seen that a change in one department or project affects all of the others. A simple proof of this can be seen in the fact that a limited budget means that any increase in projected expenditures by one department means a reduction in expenditures by another. In addition, that reduced expenditure may also mean a reduction in the power and authority of that department manager and his employees, possibly affecting their career tracks. With that in mind, it is easy to see why managers tend to be conservative by nature.

However, since (as Freedman points out) it is the executive office which provides the ultimate source of support for innovation in any company, the executive office has both the authority and the responsibility to overcome the natural conservatism of managers and empower innovators, giving them the credibility they need to achieve their goals. Unfortunately, it also has the authority to unconsciously undermine the spirit of innovation so necessary for any company's survival.

In *Innovation and Entrepreneurship,* Peter F. Drucker suggests that there are certain policies, practices, and structures necessary for any company to encourage innovation. He begins by stating that managers have to be made hungry for new things and ideas by establishing policies that clearly reward innovation and innovative thinking and that "punish" stagnation and reliance upon maintaining the status quo. One way to do this is to periodically put every product, process, technology, and market, as well as every internal staff activity, "on trial for its life."

Drucker reminds us of the importance of reviewing everything we are involved in by asking the question, "If we were considering this product, staff activity, market, etc. for the first time, would we feel it was worth the investment of the money, manpower, and material currently being expended upon it?" If the answer is no, we must ask ourselves how to stop wasting resources on it. Note that he does not advocate outright abandonment of every product and procedure that receives a "no" answer. Sometimes, that just isn't feasible. But at least such questions get the mind moving.

Another important policy suggested by Drucker is to avoid wasting your best people and resources on trying to resurrect products or areas that no longer perform up to expectations. Once managers realize that "the dead will be left to bury their dead," they will be ready and willing to embrace innovation. Until the executives recognize that organizational survival depends upon overcoming the desire to wallow in past failures, successes, and near successes, they will resist any serious effort to move their best people and resources towards innovation.

Drucker reminds us that any product or service has a limited life cycle. By reviewing each and every product or service and its markets, a company can project that product's life cycle and its place within that cycle. This review enables the company to project where it will be if it merely continues to manage to the best of its ability what already exists. This information will enable a company to predict the gap between where it can realistically expect to be and where it needs to be to meet its objectives.

Since innovative efforts carry no certainty of success, Drucker suggests that any company should have under way at least three times the number of innovative efforts needed to fill the gap between realistic expectations and objectives.

Finally, an entrepreneurial plan must be developed that includes the commitment of sufficient resources and individuals with proven performance capacity. Once this is done, those individuals must be provided with unambiguous guidelines regarding what is expected of them, including specific deadlines.

Fostering an Innovative Management Attitude

Because of the reactionary nature of any system, it is natural for a manager to spend more time trying to maintain what he has and understands than to take risks with something new. Hence, when employees, or junior managers offer innovations to procedures, policies, or products, they are often perceived as a threat rather than as a resource. While this defensiveness is natural, managers we interviewed recommended several steps for overcoming resistance and fostering innovative attitudes in department directors, managers, and staff.

➥ General George C. Marshall once said, "There is no limit to the good you can do if you don't care who gets the credit." Although this is certainly true of all managers, it is especially so for those who are creative. Freedman correctly points out that for the innovator, the most important part of compensation for her work is recognition of what she has done.

➥ Make it a company-wide policy to reward ideas that save the company money, improve or find a new use for an existing product, or find a new market for an existing service. Provide recognition for the innovative individual, regardless of her position or department. A surprising number of excellent product and marketing ideas have come from individuals who were "only" support staff.

➥ Teach managers to seek out positive opportunities as well as problems that have to be overcome. In Chapter 24, we'll discuss in detail the impact of constant emphasis on the negative on creative thinking. While it is natural to want to stop the ship from sinking, if you spend all of your time worrying about plugging leaks, you may also sail right past a port of opportunity.

When you meet with your managers to hear their reports on their operations, have them first emphasize what things are going better than they expected. Then have them explain what they are doing right to perform so well. Follow up with any "problems," and explore solutions. By emphasizing the positives first, you remind each manager of her abilities and resources. When problems are discussed, she will be able to explore them from a position of confidence (this attitude is far more likely to lead to solutions).

➥ All of the managers we spoke to emphasized one point above all others: Where possible, when an employee/manager offers an innovation give her the responsibility for developing that innovation or idea and see that she gets the resources she needs. Then hold her accountable for it.

➥ Get senior executives involved in the creative process. This is relatively easy to do and lends credibility to the work done by innovators. Periodically have a senior executive meet with groups of junior engineers, executives, marketing people, managers, etc. to discuss their vision of where the company is going, what it is doing right, and what it is doing wrong. This gives the senior manager an excellent opportunity to obtain effective insight into the thinking of his next generation of management.

It also gives him an opportunity to meet and select creative individuals for future opportunities. And, it gives the junior people a better understanding of management's objectives for the company.

➡ Encourage managers to sponsor innovative concepts, products, services, etc. within their departments and areas of responsibility. In *In Search of Excellence,* Peters and Waterman point out that one of the things that sets truly "excellent" companies apart from their competitors is the sponsorship of innovation by internal "champions."

➡ Finally and perhaps most importantly, foster the understanding that in innovation, failure is not a sin. As Freedman points out, if your efforts at innovation succeed only 10 percent of the time, you are still doing better than the national average. People who are afraid to fail won't take the calculated risks inherent in innovative thought and action. Instead, they take the far greater risk of trying to maintain the status quo in an ever-changing market environment.

The Innovative Department

If the executive offices set the culture for the entire company, you, as manager, have a tremendous impact upon the culture within your own department. Even if the corporate culture is supportive of innovation, you can unwittingly squelch that innovative spirit in your department if you communicate defensiveness when new ideas are presented. Fortunately, the reverse is also true.

Hence, to an extent, the same formulas provided for company-wide innovation can be applied at the departmental level. No one knows their jobs better than the people doing them. They know the problems, and they often have excellent practical suggestions for solutions. Given half a chance, almost any secretary could tell her boss several ways to increase the efficiency of information flow within the office. The same is true for virtually every job.

➡ Encourage your employees to make suggestions for ways to improve the efficiency and effectiveness of their area of responsibility. Whether you ask for all suggestions in writing, or encourage individuals to bring them to you in person (there are pros and cons to both), take a few minutes to review them carefully and always let the individuals who submitted them know you appreciate their efforts.

➡ Even when an idea suggested by an employee is not useful, recognize the individual's effort and encourage her to continue. Take a few minutes to listen to her idea and clearly communicate your understanding and appreciation even if you can't implement it. You will be communicating an important message about how important you consider that employee's efforts, which will often increase her productivity and job dedication. Note: This can be particularly true of jobs that are repetitive and boring, such as some assembly-line work. The Japanese have used this technique to significantly reduce production costs and errors and increase productivity.

➡ Once an employee has presented a viable idea, make her responsible for its development, providing the necessary resources for success. Example 1: A secretary demonstrates an idea that can save time and energy in the processing of information within the office. Have her develop a plan to implement her idea. Once you've reviewed it and determined its feasibility, put it into practice and try it out. If it doesn't work, thank her for her efforts and encourage her to keep trying. If it does work, make an announcement to the rest of the staff and give her credit for it.

Example 2: An assembly-line worker presents an idea that will increase the life of the belt motor. Have him demonstrate how his idea should work and provide him with whatever technical assistance he will need to implement it (engineering, machining, etc.). The Japanese found some time ago that the individual doing the work usually knows his area and what makes it work better than anyone else.

➡ Finally, when an employee ("creative" or not) brings you an innovative idea about something outside your own department that you think has serious merit, take the "risk" of rejection and sponsor it. Become her champion. If necessary, fight to obtain additional champions higher in the corporate structure. The rewards you'll obtain in terms of the work atmosphere in your department and the loyalty of your staff will more than compensate for any inconvenience. Remember, loyalty has to work both ways.

Summary

One of the single most important factors in determining the level of innovation and creativity in any department or company is its culture, or atmosphere. The company culture is determined in the executive offices, but you determine the atmosphere in your department. Supporting the creative efforts of your staff can significantly increase their productivity as well as their overall job satisfaction.

Sensory Oriented Language and Experience

The way we process information and the sensory emphasis that we apply to that information has a large impact upon our ability to create. The skills taught in this chapter are based upon principles of cognitive behavioral psychology developed by Richard Bandler and John Grinder, and will teach you how to recognize your own and others' sensory orientation as well as how to enhance it.

Components of Thoughts, Memories and Experiences

Everything that we experience comes to us through our five senses—sight, sound, feeling, taste, and smell. We process information (think and remember) by using mental equivalents or representations of those five senses; that is, most of us think by using pictures and/or sounds and/or feelings. For instance, before you read any further, take a moment to remember, or to re-experience, a situation from your past that you remember as a positive experience. Close your eyes and remember it now.

What aspect of the memory did you recall first? Did a scene flash into your mind first? Or, was it a sound or a feeling/sensation? Perhaps

43

even a pleasant odor, or a taste. Were you aware of all the visual, auditory, and feeling components? Or, was one aspect not immediately available to you? Think about something at the office or at home. Replay it in your mind. Which aspect—sight, sound, feeling, smell, or taste— were you first aware of? Which aspect were you most aware of? Least aware of? This experiment demonstrates three things:

1. Thoughts are composed of sensory components. Psychologists call these sensory components "modalities."

2. Our minds tend to recall one particular modality first.

3. Even though most experiences contain all five sensory components, certain components may be initially unavailable to our conscious mind.

As you further review our experiment, did you notice that each sensory component could be broken down into further subcomponents? For example: the visual sensory component/modality could easily be broken down into various subcomponents such as color, focus, brightness, size, etc. These subcomponents are called "submodalities," and have a tremendous impact upon our feelings and the ways in which we process and assign meaning to information. Submodalities will be discussed in greater detail in Chapter 8.

This dependency upon one or two primary sensory modalities occurs for several reasons. One of the most important reasons deals with our five senses and our experiences as we mature. Although we are born with five senses, as we mature we begin to rely upon one or two more than the others. One result of this is a tendency to remember that aspect of an experience more completely than the others. Hence, if we tend to rely upon our sight, we are more likely to remember the visual aspects of an experience.

Of course, some experiences will dominate a specific sense regardless of which one we tend to rely upon. For example: a cold shower would dominate the kinesthetic sense, while a symphony would compel the auditory, and a rainbow, the visual.

Once we begin to rely upon one sense over the others, the data received through that sense would tend to dominate our thought processes. As a result, we may even begin to "specialize" in that sensory mode in the way that we think. What this means is that if you tend think by making pictures, you are probably someone who also tends to rely upon your sight and to be most aware of the visual aspects of your experiences. Of course, this doesn't mean that you aren't able to remember the sounds and feelings associated with an experience. They probably just aren't remembered as being as "obvious" as what you see. This can result in our using some of the other senses so infrequently that we can actually become confused when we receive too much information through them. Psychologists refer to this as sensory overload.

The sensory components of our thinking process have a tremendous impact upon our ability to solve problems and to be creative because they determine how we process data. While each of us tends to think and conceptualize predominantly in one component, we also use others. Some people have developed each of the sensory components equally, but most of us have a secondary and tertiary component. For example, if you are an individual who thinks primarily in terms of pictures, you probably remembered the visual aspect of your pleasant memory first. If your second most dominant component was kinesthetic, you probably also automatically associated certain feelings with those pictures. Because the auditory component was third, it may at first have been difficult to remember any sounds associated with the pictures of your pleasant memory.

Individuals who predominantly remember the visual component of most memories generally tend to think in pictures and to process data visually. That means that they tend to process information by establishing a series of mental pictures, or images, to enable them to manipulate and give meaning to the data presented. It also means that they will most easily and clearly understand data presented in a visual format. Depending upon the depth of their reliance upon the visual components of thought, they might even find it difficult to understand or relate to data, or even directions, that are presented verbally. This individual will be most effective when dealing with problems and concepts that can be manipulated visually, such as architectural and engineering problems, how a new product will look, etc.

Individuals who rely most heavily upon the audio component of thought tends to process information verbally to *"hear* how it will *sound."* They will tend to *discuss* ideas and concepts internally and with others to gain a greater understanding of them. Hence, they may *repeat* the same idea several times with slightly different wording just to *hear* how it *sounds* before deciding it sounds right to him. They are most effective when creating auditory-related concepts such as speech writing, advertising copy, presentations to the board of directors, etc. Depending upon how much they rely upon the auditory component of thought, visually oriented data, such as charts and graphs, may not be their forte.

Finally, individuals who rely upon the kinesthetic components of concepts process data and information by how it "feels." When presented with an idea or problem they will give you a gut reaction to it. They are often very good with their hands and are often very effective at making models of a new product or concept. They are often athletic and tend grasp physical movements and processes very quickly.

Summary

The mix and dominance of our sensory modalities have a tremendous effect upon the way we process information and conceptualize problems. Do we create a mental picture of a problem and manipulate it until it looks right? Or do we talk it over, with ourselves or others, until it sounds right to us? By recognizing and understanding which modalities an individual employs, we can better understand what processes he uses to solve problems. This information can aid any manager in building a more effective and productive creative team. We have included a brief list of submodalities in the next chapter.

Submodalities and the
Process of Creative Thought

In his book, *Using Your Brain For A Change,* Richard Bandler defines submodalities as sub components of sensory modalities. Simply put, submodalites are the parts that make up a sensory experience. For example, color, brightness, clarity, and size are just a few of the submodalities of any visual sensory memory or experience. As you will learn, submodalities affect the impact that experiences, thoughts and memories have upon us. By learning to recognize and manipulate our own submodalities, we can increase or decrease that impact. In a sense, submodalities can help give conscious control of unconscious processes.

There are two very important aspects to submodalities:

➥ First, they can have a tremendous effect upon the impact of feelings that we associate with memories or experiences.

➥ Second, it is possible to consciously control them.

Before we discuss submodalities any further, we'd like to take you through a brief exercise that will demonstrate to you your own ability to control your feelings by modifying the submodalities you associate with a given memory. In this experiential exercise we'd like to figuratively take you for a ride. Take your time with this next exercise to experience its results as fully as possible. We think you'll enjoy it.

Directions: Pick some enjoyable ride that you have taken (car, roller coaster, motorcycle, airplane, bicycle, etc.) and mentally pretend that you are *watching yourself on a television screen*. Be aware of your feelings as you observe yourself going through the experience and the changes in your feelings as you try the various suggestions. Note: At this point, the important idea is whether your feelings change intensity, not whether the changes are more or less pleasurable. Now:

➡ Make the television screen the size of a large movie screen. Did your feelings change as the picture became larger?

➡ Imagine that you are sitting very far from the screen so that it is no larger than a postage stamp? Does that effect your feelings?

➡ Return the picture to the original size and make the picture very bright, then very dark. Again, was there a change in the intensity of your feelings?

➡ What if you make the memory a single snapshot or a moving picture? How does each act on your part effect the intensity of your feelings?

➡ This time, try changing the components of sound—making any sounds much louder, then much softer, then shut off the volume entirely. Were there any changes in the feelings attached to this memory?

Note which changes, if any, modified your feelings. Now try stepping through the screen and into yourself in the picture and *reliving* the experience as if it were happening to you right at this moment—reseeing it now, rehearing it now, and feeling these feelings again. Re-experience it as fully as possible.

What was the difference in your feelings' intensity between watching yourself on television and reliving the experience? For most of us, the intensity of experiences tends to increase as we relive (become "associated" with) a memory. The "dissociated" state (watching oneself on television) tends to be less intense for most people. Remember, the differentiations in the pictures or sounds (light/dark, near/far etc.) are called "submodalities."

In a moment we'll ask you to step into the past and make another series of submodality changes as you relive a pleasant memory. Once again, the purpose is to verify in your personal experience that certain changes in submodalities result in a change in feeling intensity. These simple changes should be made in the midst of the experience (making modifications of what you saw or heard); that is, you will be changing the components of a memory. Finally, for each modification, be aware of the change in feeling intensity that may occur.

Directions: Recall a *pleasant* experience, perhaps a particularly enjoyable conversation with someone you enjoy being with.
Visual changes in the remembered experience: Be aware of changes in the intensity of your feelings as you do each of these.

➡ Make what you are seeing much darker, then much brighter.

➡ Make certain aspects more or less focused.

➡ Try zooming in on a part of the scene, then zooming out.

➡ Make the movie much faster, then much slower.

➡ Make any visually oriented variation you choose.

Auditory changes in the remembered experience: Be aware of any feeling-intensity changes as you do each of these.

➡ Make any sounds much louder, then much lower.

➡ Change the direction that the sounds are coming from—in front, behind, from the left, then the right.

➡ Change the tempo so that it is much faster, then much slower.

➡ Make any auditory-oriented variation you choose.

Feeling changes in the physically (or "kinesthetically") remembered aspects of the experience: Be aware of any feeling-intensity changes as you do each of these.

➡ Make the environment much warmer, then colder.

➡ Have the entire feeling be located in only one part of your body, then have it spread throughout your entire body.

➡ Become more aware of any tactile aspects, then less aware.

➡ For the sake of simplicity, we'll include taste and smell within the kinesthetic aspects. Are you aware of any odors or tastes associated with the memory (for instance, if the remembered conversation was held over a malt)? Strengthen, weaken, or change them and notice the change in feeling intensity. Note: smells associated with memories often have an extremely powerful effect on the feeling intensity of a memory.

➡ Make any kinesthetically oriented (physically oriented) variation you choose.

Having gone through this phase of the exercise, you were almost certainly able to change the intensity of the experience as you made some of the suggested changes. The key point to realize is that you can change your feelings by changing the way you remember (or anticipate) events. To a very large degree *many of your feelings are subject to your conscious control!*

The final aspect of this exercise is to relive the experience one more time, making a series of changes that enhance the pleasure of the experience. A brief listing of some of the submodality changes is provided below. Remember, you can take this or any other pleasant experience and make the memory more intensely pleasurable. Vary each of the components and, as you vary it, leave it at the point that gives you the best feeling. Note: Some of the variations will result in large intensity changes while others will provide no conscious effect. Interestingly, in the future, whenever you recall a memory that you have modified, you will recall it in its modified rather than its original state.

Visual	Auditory	Feelings
color	volume	temperature
focus	pitch	location
speed	direction	pulse
contrast	rhythm	pressure
brightness	tempo	texture
distance	tone	intensity
clarity	frequency	movement

The submodality listing above represents only a few of the more than fifty variations that can be made. Variations of these techniques can allow you to *neutralize unpleasant memories* and associations. By modifying how you remember something you modify the feelings associated with it. This alone can give you more control over your performance. In addition, you can now modify how you internally conceptualize and manipulate data by modifying the submodalities associated with that data. By changing the brightness, color, loudness, or texture of concepts, you can modify the creative process you use to develop an idea or solve a problem.

Before going further, try this experiment, which will be explained later. For the moment, please think of your enhanced pleasurable experience while carefully looking at the symbol immediately below:

#1

Anchors

The #1 symbol above represents a visual "anchor." In his book, *Applications of NLP*, Robert Dilts defines anchoring as "The process of associating an internal response with some external trigger (similar to classical conditioning) so that the response may be quickly reaccessed." [p. 61] Hence, "anchor" is a term which represents the stimulus in a conditioned response. To be technical, it's similar to the Stimulus—Response (S → R) phenomenon of the behavioral schools of psychology. Perhaps the easiest way to think of an anchor is as a reminder bell or wrist alarm for thoughts or feelings. Setting the wrist alarm reminds us to do something, or feel something, whenever the bell is sounded. Once we have set the alarm, we go on to other jobs until the alarm goes off. Whether it be minutes, hours, or weeks later, the sounding of the alarm triggers a memory of what needs to be done. If we really thought about the item when we set the alarm, that alarm will remind us of the task.

Similarly, an anchor acts as a reminder of a particular thought or emotional state. Once established (installed), an association occurs between the outside stimulus (the symbol or anchor) and the memory or feeling. When "set off" (triggered), the memory or a minirepresentation of it, is automatically played back. Consequently, an anchor allows us to "capture," virtually at will, the essence of a memory.

A feeling that occurs in one context of your life can become associated with another situation. For example, look carefully at the symbol below and remember what it represents:

$$\boxed{\text{\#1}}$$

As you looked at the symbol, did a certain pleasant experience almost immediately come to mind (perhaps only fleetingly) with a few pleasant associations? If so, you've just experienced what psychologists call "anchoring."

Anchoring and Creativity

The concept of anchoring is very important to our understanding of the process of creativity. Just as the symbol #1 above acted as an anchor for the pleasant feelings that you associated with it, other stimuli often act as anchors that enhance or even hurt our creativity. For example, certain phrases, such as, "Lets get out there and win one for the gipper," may be a motivational anchor for some, increasing their feelings of enthusiasm, self-sacrifice, and willingness to work harder on a team effort. However, for others, the phrase may be an anchor for feelings of frustration and hopelessness in the face of an impossible task. In the one case, the enthusiasm necessary for optimum creative performance will be increased while, in the other, it is almost eliminated. Recognizing your own anchors can help you to overcome those that may act as blocks to your own creativity.

Summary

The subcomponents of sensory inputs, or submodalities, have a tremendous impact upon the way we conceptualize and manipulate data. Just as sounds, such as certain words or voice tones, can affect behavior, so can visual and kinesthetic anchors. By modifying these submodalities you can enhance your creativity and overall productivity.

In Chapters 10 and 11, we will discuss techniques to establish and program your own optimum state of creativity by using the concepts of submodalities and visual, auditory, and kinesthetic anchors presented in this and the previous chapter.

Strategies and the
Creativity Model

Often, we admire someone's charisma, intuition, natural way, or special talent. Creative people seem to have that certain "something" that really can't be defined or replicated. *Or, can it?*

Until recently such abilities could not be easily replicated. These talents were considered "gifts," which you either had or didn't have. We could try to imitate, but the imitation was probably going to be ineffective because it would require the mimicking of thought processes that are not normally available. The external behaviors of an individual are relatively easy to copy—that is what all children do naturally when learning to run, ride a bike, or play ball. The internal thought process has been another story because, until now, you could only obtain the information of which the creative person, the "model," was consciously aware.

Now it *is* possible to model a person's thought processes as well as their external behavior. Although inappropriate in a general sense, such modeling can have tremendously beneficial effects on specific skills such as problem solving. For example, wouldn't it be worthwhile to replicate the specific and exact thinking process of an Albert Einstein? How about just the thinking strategy of the most creative person you know, or a high achiever in any field?

Using some of the techniques derived from a discipline of cognitive psychology called Neuro-Linguistic Programming[1] (NLP), such internal processes can be precisely defined and taught to other people. Will they automatically become another Einstein? Of course not. However, they would be working with a thinking sequence that has already proven effective for theoretical physics. Their individual background knowledge and experiences would form a different base and therefore they would produce different ideas. Albert Einstein's strategy can, unfortunately, only be partially captured from his writings. Yet, there are thousands of other people whose creative thought processes and problem-solving strategies should be modeled.

Learning an effective strategy is analogous to learning to ride a two-wheeled bicycle. If you have never ridden a bike before it takes some time and effort to learn to steer, balance, pedal, etc. There will be a period of time in which you make lots of mistakes and, if you have to do it all on your own, you may or may not eventually learn to ride the bike. However, if you are provided a bicycle with training wheels you will be able to start riding almost immediately. You need only concern yourself with steering and learning to pedal. The balancing will come naturally. You will also save yourself a lot of falling down, and you will be able to use the bike more quickly and efficiently. In a word, using training wheels will make your learning process much easier.

This chapter will provide you with techniques to learn another person's internal problem-solving (or any other) strategies. By utilizing their strategies for yourself, you will give yourself the benefit of a set of mental training wheels.

Theory

The theory is quite simple. As indicated in Chapters 7 and 8, we all receive information through our five senses (sight, sound, touch, smell, and taste). This sensory information is stored within our memory as a miniature representation of the original experience. As previously discussed, we then manipulate this stored sensory data, which includes symbols and words, in the process called "thinking."

---

[1]Early applications of modeling, modifying and creating strategies can be found in Dilts, et al., *Neuro-Linguistic Programming Vol. I: The Study of Subjective Experience.* Cupertino: Meta Publications, 1980.

When we engage in problem solving, we mentally undertake a trip from point "A" (the problem) to point "B" (the solution). Like any trip, this process can be mapped. When we want to take the same trip someone else has taken we ask them to draw us a map of their trip and give us directions, making notations of landmarks, places where we need to turn, etc. Thinking, creative or otherwise, is no different. *Thinking is a systematic process which can be notated.* Psychologists call this process of mapping thinking and behavioral processes "modeling."

Most of our thinking is done below the level of conscious awareness. Yet, even this unconscious portion can be discovered if there is a careful application of the correct technique. Note: At this point, please accept on faith that this can be done. The exact procedure requires more data than is provided here. Please refer to Chapters 7 and 8 on "Predicates" and "Submodalities" for more detail. Once a strategy is notated there are numerous applications. The next few paragraphs explore some of them.

Personal Performance

Each of us has had occasions where we performed at our peak, able to accomplish our tasks easily and effectively. We have also experienced days where we couldn't seem to get out of our own way. The difference between these two days is probably due to the use of efficient or inefficient thinking sequences. The off days may be the result of skipping of a critical step. It may be because a particular mental image, for whatever reason, is fuzzier than it needs to be. Whatever the reason, a key difference determines the change in performance levels. Because this occurs below the conscious level of awareness, it is difficult to understand what's "wrong" with us. This leaves us with a feeling of being out of control, and, normally, we'd just wait until we returned to our normal selves.

However, if your efficient strategy had been previously elicited, whenever you had an "off" day, you would be able to check the sequence of thoughts that led to your inefficiency and reprogram yourself by consciously following your own efficient sequence. Most likely, your personal efficiency would become significantly better.

Mapping the sequence of your thoughts can be applied in many types of situations—from mental to physical proficiency. Each of us has a strategy for literally everything we do. Refer back to the earlier comment on creativity (which was based upon an actual example). The individual was able to modify his mental image of an idea (the procedure for this is found in Chapter 8) and the idea became "crystal clear."

One client was a marathon runner whose strategy for peak performance was to mentally rehearse the first few steps, which mentally "got her going." This always puts her in the best frame of mind and enables her to perform at her best. However, she occasionally used to forget to rehearse those first steps. At those times, she performed poorly in the run. When her strategy of prerace mental rehearsal was elicited, she was taught how to *always* put herself in the best mental frame possible. Now, whenever she doesn't feel just right before a race, she knows to mentally rehearse. The result? She is now much more consistent in her running performances. Differences like these can and do make all the difference in the world!

Business Applications

This modeling process has been extended to many areas of business. Over the last few years there have been numerous articles indicating how certain major companies and organizations were trying to "computerize" the thinking strategy of their top people. After all, if an "essential" individual is unavailable at a critical time, who can take their place? Who can "think" like them? The companies are spending thousands of hours and millions of dollars trying to place the thinking sequence of these key individuals onto a computer. An entire industry has developed around this process.

The idea is that if any one person's brain is irreplaceable, perhaps it should be "copied" so that the organization is not too severely hurt by the loss of any one individual. These projects have met with a limited amount of success. However, the procedure used to discover and then teach a person their own patterns of effectiveness has been very successful.

Specially trained personnel can elicit information from valuable people about both the conscious and unconscious steps that make up the strategies they employ to make decisions, solve problems, or develop new products or services. Once a strategy is elicited, it can be taught to another individual (or even programmed onto a computer) so that the organization can now have two or more individuals who use the identical strategy for decision making, creativity, and so on.

If you have a particularly talented individual in your organization, perhaps it would be worthwhile to get a second one in case the first one has to be replaced. This safeguard is important for sales and management as well as innovative people.

Scientific Applications

Consider how useful it would be if your top scientists were consciously aware and in control of not only their own strategies, but of *someone else's strategy* as well! If their strategy couldn't solve a particular problem, they could "try out" an alternative thinking process, which might be more advantageous to whatever they were working on. At the very least, the use of the new thinking process would give them a new perspective on the problem. They would have an additional procedure to employ whenever they became "stuck" or "blocked."

Medical computers are being developed to diagnose a patient's condition. So far, the computers can handle certain tasks: They ask precise questions, always remember to make certain tests, and check references for all illnesses that are correlated with specific symptoms. However, they do not have the ability to make "intuitive diagnostic leaps" like humans can. Much time, effort, and money has been spent programming those medical computers—money ultimately well spent. The computer's main lack is its inability to replicate the unconscious, creative process called "intuition."

Creative intuition consists of a strategy and, like any other strategy, it can be mapped. Unfortunately, to date, the programmers have not had the skills necessary to delve into this level of thinking. As a result, the processes used to obtain the required information from their models have been cumbersome and exceedingly expensive.

Beyond placing a strategy on a computer, consider how useful it would be for medical researchers (or any other beginning professional for that matter) to have access to efficient strategies. Mapping successful strategies allows us to decipher a mental process. Once the conscious *and* unconscious aspects of an efficient mental process are diagrammed, it becomes easy to teach that process to someone else. They can quickly "make it their own" by including subtle, personal changes that they need to feel comfortable. This method enables them to become proficient faster than learning by trial and error.

Thus far, we have explored only a few of the general applications of this method. *There are many, many more.* Anything that can be done by a human being can be "modeled" via strategies and then taught to someone else.

Think for the moment about the potential applications of this technique for yourself and your organization. Whatever you do or wherever you work, there are times when having the ability to map thinking strategies would be very helpful.

There are seven primary strategies that act as "basic" programs. They are:

➡ Motivation

➡ Belief

➡ Creativity

➡ Memory

➡ Learning

➡ Reality testing

➡ Decision making

Motivation Strategy

An individual's motivation strategy consists of the specific steps he takes when motivating himself or when being motivated by others. Its importance is readily apparent. A brilliant person without an effective motivation strategy might never put ideas into action. We all probably know someone who fits into this category. Or, how about the person who just can't seem to get out of bed? Or, the person who barely utilizes his or her potential?

In each of the above situations, the individual's motivation strategy is ineffective, broken, or bypassed. *Each of these problems can be resolved!*

Belief Strategy

A belief strategy is an internal program that "convinces" us to do or accept something, for example, determining whether or not something is valid or correct.

A belief about ourselves or others can be either advantageous or disadvantageous. A rigid belief could result in being closed to new ideas. Even if we want to be more receptive, we can't. On the other hand, there are individuals whose belief systems are so tenuous that they will believe anything and everybody. An example of a belief is our faith that something can or cannot be accomplished. "Whether you believe something to be possible or impossible, you are right," is a well-known quotation. Think of the self-imposed limitations caused by negative beliefs. Fortunately, beliefs can be changed. Belief strategies can be enhanced or modified to the advantage of an individual.

Creativity Strategy

A creativity strategy is the process we use to generate new ideas. Some people seem to be able to take the same information available to everyone else and generate new possibilities. Inventors, writers, product developers, innovators in any profession are just a few. Because they manipulate data differently than most people, they obtain a broader range of interpretations or solutions. What is the difference in the way they manipulate data that enables them to generate ideas?

Many innovative people have particularly productive periods, like "creative streaks." Instead of randomly getting these streaks, they can now plan to have them.

Memory Strategy

Similar to a learning strategy, a memory strategy is the process by which information is sorted and stored in the brain for later retrieval. Our favorite example of a memory strategy may assist your understanding.

A subset of the memory strategy is the "Spelling Strategy." Cognitive psychologists have discovered that people who are good spellers create a mental picture of the word they are attempting to spell. Somewhere in their "spelling strategy" they develop a visual image of the word (i.e., as if it were written on a blackboard). When they need to spell the word, they remember the picture of the word on the board and can literally read it off—frontwards and backwards. Poor spellers do not have this effective visual check. Rather, poor spellers tend to spell fonetikally (the way it sounds), like most of us were taught to do. Unfortunately, English is not a phonetic language.

Did something disturb you about the spelling of one of the previous words? It doesn't look right, does it? How did you know that? If you say it out loud, it certainly sounds right. (Note: The correct spelling is phonetically.) It is apparent that effective spellers must have some way to verify the correct spelling of the words. How can this be done except via a memory of what the word should look like? Just like you knew "phonetically" was incorrectly spelled. It is quite simple to teach a poor speller how to access his or her visual memory.

This technique has been successfully taught to hundreds of school children, who immediately started to get excellent spelling test scores instead of constantly failing. This technique has also been taught to adults with the same rate of success. The spelling strategy is also related to *learning strategies,* which will be explained later.

The example of the spelling strategy illustrates the earlier point that the way we process information determines the effectiveness and results of both our thinking and responses. In a word, each of us has a series of individualized strategies that we use for virtually everything we do, whether that be learning a foreign language, solving a problem, or knowing when to become angry. For example:

> Remembering your name and address isn't structurally different from remembering a telephone number, a mathematical formula, or a person's name. Some people have great memories for some things and poor memories for others. The difference results from the use of different strategies to remember essentially similar things. Once the differences in those strategies is identified, they can be eliminated. This then gives the individual a more effective strategy for remembering anything.
>
> Note: Numerous memory books on bookstore shelves provide excellent memory-enhancing techniques that require learning new strategies that can be employed by most people. However, because of individual differences in the way we process sensory information, no single strategy will be effective for everyone. Fortunately, it is relatively easy to learn how to modify a strategy to meet your individual needs.

Learning Strategy

A learning strategy is just what it appears: the process we use to learn to do anything. The fifteen to forty-five minute task of teaching a poor speller how to be a good speller is both simple and fun. The recipients of this strategy are constantly amazed at its simplicity. After modeling effective spellers, it was discovered that there was a common element shared by them (visualization) that was not employed by the phonetic spellers. Adding the additional step of remembering what the word looked like and reading it off a mental screen provides the ex-poor speller with the needed key ingredient. Once installed, the new strategy becomes an automatic part of their thinking process.

Effective learning strategies enable us to learn efficiently any new material because they provide us with the necessary procedures to do so. The mental correlations involved in learning are joined together so that the material is learned much more easily and effectively than before.

The elicitation of a learning strategy also allows us to define the differences in thinking between a subject that we easily learn and one that is difficult. Because of the different processes involved in handling various subjects (e.g., chemistry versus a foreign language versus dance), a learning strategy that is effective for learning music (which would probably stress auditory components) would probably differ significantly from one used to learn how to throw a baseball accurately (which might stress kinesthetic and visual components).

Reality-Testing Strategy

This strategy consists of the internal processes that allow us to differentiate between reality and imagination. For example, schizophrenics have either an ineffective strategy for testing reality or an effective strategy which is only occasionally applied.

It's interesting to note that most studies on schizophrenia study current schizophrenics. It might be more effective to study those who have been "cured" and find out how their reality-testing strategy was changed.

Decision Strategy

A decision strategy consists of the sequence of thoughts by which we decide to do, or not do, something. Discovering a customer's decision-making strategy would be a tremendous benefit for anyone involved in sales. A sales presentation (or for that matter, any idea) could then be presented in a way that replicates the way the person normally makes a decision—greatly increasing the probability of acceptance. The same is true for selling an innovative idea to higher management.

Another application for decision strategies would be assisting people who never seem to be able to decide anything. All they might need is some sort of "ending sequence" so that they can come to a "closure."

The preceding information was designed to show the potential of learning strategies. Literally everything we do—from tying our shoes to making a major decision—has a strategy associated with it. When our strategies are working effectively, we are able to perform the required functions. When strategies are deficient, misplaced, or random, we are working significantly below our peak performance.

In summary, learning the strategy of someone who is already proficient at what you want to learn is akin to getting that set of training wheels we mentioned earlier. You gain a method that gets you where you want to go faster by avoiding many of the mistakes that you might otherwise make. New thought sequences allow alternative solutions that would otherwise be unavailable due to the inherent limitations in any one process. In the end, learning new strategies automatically increases your variety of behaviors, giving you access to greater combinations of solutions.

The preceding discussion identifies what strategies are and how they can be used. The next pages will provide a more detailed explanation of how these processes actually work.

Components of Strategies

At the beginning of the chapter, we explained the concept of a strategy by comparing it to a map or set of directions. Like any good map, each strategy requires notations to guide the individual through the mental processes involved in the strategy.

Note that the concept of modeling, or mapping a strategy, is technical and can be confusing to a nonspecialist. It is presented here for your information. However, a full understanding of the technical aspects of modeling and strategies is not necessary to benefit from them (for example, the spelling strategy is taught to young children with no understanding of strategies). The following notational system will be useful as the concept of strategies is further explained.

Sensory Data

You will remember from Chapters 7 and 8 that each of us tends to represent data and memories in terms of sensory patterns associated with them (visual=V, auditory=A, and kinesthetic=K). For example, our mental representation of a cold shower would probably consist of kinesthetic sensations. Sensory data can be created or recalled in six primary ways:

Vr = Visual remembered: Any mental image that we have that is based upon something we have actually seen.

Vc = Visual constructed: A mental image that we have created in our heads. For example, what would an elephant with a dog's head look like?

Ar = Auditory remembered: Similar to Vr above, although with sounds.

Ac = Auditory constructed: Similar to Vc above, although with sounds.

Ad = Auditory dialogue: Mentally talking to yourself. Mentally debating or processing an issue or conversation.

K = Kinesthetic: Any internal or external sensation or feeling.

All internal representations are represented by an (i), whereas all external representations have an (e). Thus, K(e) represents touching something, while K(i) would represent a feeling or a memory of touching something. V(e) would represent something that we see, while Vr(i) represents something that we remembered seeing.

Using this basic notational process and through the use of additional techniques, we can notate the sequence of a person's thought processes and the subcomponents of each thought. For example, it might be important to a process to note whether a person uses a focused, bright image when Vc (visually constructing) or a partially focused, dim image. For the purposes of our example, using a clear image will facilitate a creative process, whereas the creative process might fail if the image is "fuzzy."

Exploring Strategies

Most readers will be familiar with the traditional "stimulus-response" [S → R] model made popular by B. F. Skinner and behavioral psychology. More current understandings of this concept indicate that there are many internal sequences that occur between the S and the R. The model might be more appropriately diagrammed like this:

$$S \rightarrow [1] \rightarrow [2] \rightarrow [3] \rightarrow \ldots \rightarrow R$$

The boxed numbers represent smaller mental sequences that determine which "R" will occur. You might think of these smaller mental sequences as a kind of decision-analysis tree in which many alternative responses are possible.

Box 1 might be expanded to include the various components of a sensory-based thought with one of the senses (in this case "V") having greater weight than the others, such as:

| VAK |

Where V, A, and K are the sensory components of the microprogram.

This could be further expanded to include an entire thinking procedure, which is summarized by V A K.

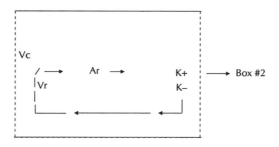

In this sequence, a constructed visual image is compared to a remembered visual image, which leads to a remembered sound or comment. This then gives either a positive or a negative feeling. If positive, the strategy then goes to step 2 (which can be more or less complex). If negative, then the strategy loops back to a new comparison of constructed and remembered imagery. Note: Each of the above can be further differentiated using submodalities.

The time required to discover a strategy depends upon its complexity and the total number of choice points within it. A strategy like the one above might take a half an hour to fully elicit and verify.

If any of the component parts of the strategy are changed, then the response also changes. In effect, you have a new program, which will therefore yield different results. The ramifications of this are critical. If you have a self-defeating strategy, such as blocking when faced with certain types of problems, you can now examine your blocking strategy and modify it to automatically lead you into your problem-solving strategy. Below is an example of the steps involved in one doctor's diagnostic strategy:

A doctor examining a patient makes a diagnosis following her own personal strategy for diagnosis. Her strategy might include the following steps: the doctor reads the patient's chart—looks at the patient—listens to the patient tell about the symptoms—examines the patient—makes a mental image of the patients condition—talks to herself about diseases that have those symptoms—compares the images of the patient's symptoms with internal images of possible diseases—identifies the disease or more than one possible disease—continues the examination or orders tests.

Each segment of the strategy above would have multiple internal sequences of thought—many below the conscious level of awareness. Any medical student can be told the general procedure. However, on a statistical basis, only a few would create an internal thought process similar to one of a great diagnostician. Most will have to learn to do it through trial and error. They'll have to intuit the type of image to be made of the patient, know what to say to themselves about the symptoms, know which information to retrieve and how to categorize the relative importance of the information, and finally how to know when to continue the examination or to order additional tests. The job becomes infinitely easier when the student has an efficient thought process already in place.

Discovering a Strategy

A variety of techniques are employed to discover an individual's strategy for doing something. Because of the complexity, we will limit ourselves to providing the basic questioning process. This should furnish enough of the critical information for a manager to assist his creative staff.

The primary question that sets the frame for strategy elicitation is: "How, specifically, do you do that?" Suppose you have to take your staff member's place for some procedure and have to exactly replicate his or her thinking process. You would begin by using this question.

Your staff member will provide you with information that is *consciously* available. Consider this to be the first level of information. Next, take whatever they provide, and for each item ask the following questions:

➥ "What do you do immediately before X?" And,

➥ "What do you do next?"

Note: Always warn the individual that you are going to request a lot of detailed information to enable you to create a mental road map. By so indicating, you'll be more likely to obtain their cooperation.

We have included the following form to assist you in the process of eliciting from individuals the unique mental processes involved in their particular strategies. An effective strategy has visual, auditory, and feeling components which you will need to discover. However, the specific sequences of these components will vary from person to person. Similarly, each person should have some steps that have a visual, auditory, and feelings orientation. A sample elicitation is provided immediately after the blank form.

Testing a Strategy

The way to test a strategy is to simultaneously engage yourself and the model (the individual with whom you are working) in an identical situation and end with an identical response or answer (verified with submodalities and specific performances). You should be able to mentally replicate their thinking process. If, when you review the process in your mind, there's a step missing, then ask a few more questions regarding that piece of information until any gaps are filled in.

Create a situation, then mentally speak out loud as you follow the model's progress. He or she will then be able to correct you and enhance the procedure even further. The net result is that you have a map of the model's thought process. This process can be refined much more fully, but right now you know enough to assist the person. For example, if they are having a bit of difficulty with something, you would be able to ask them to conceptualize the problem again and determine whether they employed all the key aspects of their own thinking process. Often, you will find out that they have left out a component and can be put back on track by reinserting that component.

Summary

Each of us uses mental strategies for everything we do. A strategy is a form of mental road map that contains a series of both conscious and unconscious steps that we follow to complete an action. The ability to elicit a strategy can provide us with the means of modifying not only how we perform any act, but to learn new and more efficient ways to perform that act. The ramifications for the use of strategies in creative work is almost limitless. Most importantly, it can enable us to become both more efficient and effective by working with both the conscious and the unconscious components of creative problem solving.

Basic Strategy Elicitation Form

When you first think of the problem, you:

Visualize something	Hear something	Feel something

Then you:

Visualize something	Hear something	Feel something

Then you:

Visualize something	Hear something	Feel something

Then you:

Visualize something	Hear something	Feel something

Then you:

Visualize something	Hear something	Feel something

Then you:

Visualize something	Hear something	Feel something

You know you are completed when you:

Visualize something	Hear something	Feel something

Basic Strategy Elicitation Example

When you first think of the problem, you:

Visualize something	Hear something	Feel something
	Mentally ask myself what is missing from the process.	

Then you:

Visualize something	Hear something	Feel something
Visualize how the machine would look if it had that part.		

Then you:

Visualize something	Hear something	Feel something
		If it feels right then I know I'm on to something. If not, I continue playing with the picture.

Then you:

Visualize something	Hear something	Feel something
	Debate whether or not it would be economically feasible.	

Then you:

Visualize something	Hear something	Feel something
I see a number of end-user applications and a picture of how the product would be used.		

Basic Strategy Elicitation Example (continued)

Then you:

Visualize something	Hear something	Feel something
		I just get a sense as to whether or not it will work. Once I get that good feeling then I know I'm on to something.

Then you:

Visualize something	Hear something	Feel something
	Imagine talking to some of the other guys to find out what they think about the idea.	

You know you are completed when you:

Visualize something	Hear something	Feel something
		I can mentally see them getting excited. If I don't envision this then I know that it's back to the drawing board.

Verbal Reframing and Creativity

"Reframing" is a concept originally developed by Bandler, Grinder and Dilts, based upon the work of Milton Erickson and Viriginia Satir. It is no more complicated than changing your perspective of a situation or problem. However, despite its simplicity, the effects of reframing can be dramatic, especially when used in creative problem solving. It is a technique that has two distinct applications to managerial science, which will be explored in this chapter: personal and interpersonal issues and creativity enhancement.

Personal and Interpersonal Issues

Many times an individual can be upset with something that has happened at home or the office. It might have been a confrontation with a friend or co-worker, or something else. Although it is usually the result of a simple misunderstanding, the individual can be mentally fuming, depressed, or experiencing a host of other mental states that are decidedly unproductive. What can or should you do?

Many of the managers that we have interviewed, as well as much of the existing literature, suggest that you let it go for a couple of days and the problem will usually resolve itself. We agree. Most managers make a specific point of staying away from an individual's personal business. "I'm not a therapist or a counselor," we were told. "I'm there to manage, not babysit." This, for the most part, is an appropriate attitude. Most people do work things out for themselves and many would resent what could be thought of as interference or meddling.

In reality, such situations are rarely brought to the manager's attention. Of course, there are going to be numerous exceptions to the rule. These exceptions usually fall into the following categories:

1. The affected employee who wants to get something off his chest and uses either other co-workers or the manager as a sounding board.

2. The socialite co-worker (see Chapter 16) who has a psychological need to smooth things over and make things as pleasant as humanly possible.

3. The manager who invites his employees to discuss any and all problems with him.

Each of these three situations will be briefly explored. Then, specific reframing techniques will be discussed.

The affected employee who wants to get something off his chest and uses either other co-workers or the manager as a sounding board is a common situation in corporate America. The number of productive work hours lost each year because of this situation is incalculable. While this can be expected of almost everyone at some point, there are certain people who abuse the privilege.

The individuals who abuse this privilege need to be informed, gently at first, that time cannot be spent during the day attending to such personal issues. Most people usually respond favorably when this is brought to their attention. The chapter on coaching and counseling offers specific suggestions for dealing with those who do not respond to your initial request.

The socialite co-worker who has a psychological need to smooth things over and make things as pleasant as humanly possible. These people are often great to have around, but seemingly involve themselves so much in other people's business that they do not get their own job done. Often these people, in an attempt to "help," compound the problem by making it a departmental issue. Here, letting the person know that their assistance is counterproductive may slow them down. However, if they have strong socialization needs, they may have to understand that their "smoothing" attempts actually cause more problems than they solve.

The manager who invites his employees to discuss any and all problems with him. This is fine as long as you have plenty of time to do something other than managing. When a manager becomes involved in a personal problem involving two or more employees he risks a very dangerous situation that can result in an unfortunate, long-term departmental problem. This occurs for two reasons. While your job requires that you occasionally be a part-time counselor and listen to your employees tales of woe, that's not your profession and you can't spend all of your time at it. Similarly, there will be times when you must become involved in a problem between two of your employees because the problem will affect the working atmosphere of the team. However, every time you do become involved you risk alienating one or both of the offended parties by your handling of the problem.

Verbal Reframing of Personal Issues

When an employee comes to you with a personal issue, you may want to suggest different interpretations. This usually allows the individual to take a second look at the situation in question and admit the possibility that he might have to reevaluate his perception of it.

For example, one manager we spoke with discussed how an employee had a sense of humor that was laughed at behind his back by people who had an Ivy League upbringing. This individual didn't understand why he was not accepted by the group and became more and more withdrawn. The manager, an excellent observer of group processes, spoke to the employee's co-workers and discovered their concerns about him. They responded that his "street humor" might be appreciated on the streets of Brooklyn (where he came from), but they felt that it was totally out of place in the office.

The manager was faced with the task of telling his employee about the inappropriateness of his humor without making him even more withdrawn than he was already. The manager used a very simple approach by demonstrating how humor varies from one geographic region to another. He did it by telling a couple of would-be Southern "knee slappers" that didn't even get a chuckle from his employee. He also told a cowboy joke, which similarly failed to draw a smile. When asked why he didn't laugh, the employee said he neither understood nor appreciated the jokes.

The manager then took the opportunity to explain that the individual's co-workers were having the same reaction to his jokes. Because they came from a different background, they couldn't appreciate his jokes. The employee was quite relieved when he realized that it wasn't something about him that they disliked, it was their lack of understanding and appreciation of his style of humor. As a result, he took his manager's suggestion to integrate himself in the group in a different way.

Reframing, then, consists of enabling someone to see something from a different point of view. When you think about it, virtually all humor is based upon reframing situations that might otherwise be very unfunny. One key technique of reframing is to provide the individual with an example of an equivalent experience (e.g., such as telling a joke that won't have meaning, as in the example above) and then indicating that the experience was analogous to the situation you are dealing with.

Another approach might consist of actually stating how something could be interpreted differently. Very often, the mere possibility that there is an alternative explanation is sufficient to diffuse a situation. It causes the individual to wonder whether he was right in the first place and allows for the possibility that his interpretation was only one of many possible explanations. More often than not, the person just wants to hear that their interpretation was incorrect, and they are hoping that you will provide the "real" explanation. They are usually pleased that their fears were unfounded. Intuitively, you know that one of the best approaches to this situation is the "Just maybe . . ." approach. "Just maybe he meant this," you say. "Just maybe the issue can be resolved if we. . . . "

Another example can be derived from the common linguistic error known as an overgeneralization. In overgeneralization people exaggerate the problem in their own mind and then make statements like:

"They *never* give me a hand."

"*Everything* is going wrong."

"*Everyone* thinks I'm the bad guy in this situation."

At that moment in time, the person usually believes that the statement is true. In fact, the statement is often a dependable reflection of their feelings at the moment. However, it is very rarely an accurate representation of the situation as judged by an outside observer. The most effective way to deal with an overgeneralization is to question it and search for the one exception to the rule. Using the previous statements as examples, the manager might ask:

> "They have never, *ever* given you *one degree* of assistance at anytime in the past?"

> "*Each and every single* thing in the entire project has backfired? Isn't there anything at all that has gone right?"

> "You mean that *every single person* in the company blames you?"

Once these questions are asked, the person will usually be able to find the exception to the rule, which significantly modifies his feelings and opens the problem up for discussion. Remember, the purpose of the questioning is to get the person thinking again. You are trying to have the person think about the situation from a different perspective than they had previously.

One of the most dramatic examples of a change of perspective can be seen in Exhibit 10-1.

Exhibit 10-1

AN OLD WOMAN?

A YOUNG WOMAN?

Most people see either a young girl or an old lady. Whichever they see, it usually takes a decided shift of mental perspective to perceive something different. Our minds are predisposed, or "prejudiced," to seeing things in the expected way. The phrase, "We see what we expect to see," is an excellent description of our mental "sorting" process.

Most people seem to be locked into a particular mode of thinking—a sort of habitual thinking pattern. Creative people regularly break out of that habitual mode by examining things from a different point of view. Most of the books that teach people how to be creative use a process similar to what is being described here. What the creativity books lack is introduced in our chapters on "Strategies," "Submodalities" and "Personal Excellence."

Until now, people have relied on a hit or miss approach to teach individuals how to be more creative. The techniques presented in this book demonstrate that much of the process can be proceduralized so that creativity is taught with purpose (rather than just with hope) and that creative states can be accessed at will by any individual who knows how.

Once you've given them the chance to do it their own way, there are usually a number of things that you can suggest to assist a person to break out of a rut. Often, merely giving them another task will allow them to take their minds off of the original situation and allow their unconscious mind to work on it. This is the equivalent of sleeping on it or just letting the mind daydream and waiting for something to pop out. As you know, that is frequently what happens.

For the purposes of this example, we will assume that the traditional methods haven't worked and that an individual is stuck in one frame of mind. When this occurs, you may be able to employ one of the following methods to help them get going again. Note: While these techniques will not necessarily solve the problem, they are designed to reactivate the natural creativity process and can be very effective. The three techniques to consider are:

1. Look at the problem from someone else's perspective.

2. Change the submodalities you use when conceptualizing the problem or situation.

3. Try an alternate strategy.

Look at the Problem from Someone Else's Perspective

Virtually any product or service can be used by a variety of people. Think of five or six different customers and mentally step into their shoes. Then view your potential product or service from their perspective. For example, how will a doctor use a laptop computer? An engineer? Will an attorney have different needs? If so, what might they be? What about a high school student? What design modifications might be necessary for a factory or hard-hat worker? As these questions are asked, different software and ruggedness requirements become immediately evident. What would happen to the computer if it *had to* fit inside a jacket pocket?

The concept is that if you can get someone to consider a situation from several points of view he will automatically engage the creativity process and get himself going again. Of course, it may be helpful to actually ask a variety of customers about their anticipated needs. Let them create a wish list, which might spur another good idea.

An interesting variation on this approach is to pretend that the project has been cancelled. It can no longer be produced for the intended audience because a competitor has captured the entire market. Now, make design changes to allow it to be used in a different way or by a different group, that is, a different market. Some very interesting innovations have occurred because of such situations. The authors would appreciate your writing to us about such occurrences—good, bad or indifferent—so that your situation may be included in a future book.

Changing the Submodalities

The chapters on submodalities describe various mental shifts that can be accomplished as you change the components of the picture, sound, or feelings that make up your concept. Necessary background is provided there and should be thoroughly reviewed before continuing.

For the purposes of reframing and starting the creative juices flowing again, we find that the following submodality shifts often result in new insights:

➡ Mentally view the project from different visual angles, such as from the top, looking up through the floor, or from the inside out. Each alternate perspective gets the person thinking again.

➠ Change the focus so that certain parts are seen clearly while others are diffused. Mentally enlarge certain pieces until they become huge. Often, when viewed this way, design flaws are easily seen.

➠ Change the sounds, if any, associated with the product/problem. Then determine what internal changes would have to occur to produce this new sound.

➠ Change the weight and size of the product so that it becomes significantly larger or smaller.

➠ Change the materials that it will be made from so that variations must be made to accommodate this new requirement.

➠ Add bright colors to the picture and mentally see a movie of the product being used over time.

These are just a few changes. The modifications you select are limited only by your imagination and your knowledge of submodalities. Each change of a submodality will result in a shift in perspective that can stimulate the person you are working with. Of course, each of us is different, and the impact of any particular change of submodality will vary with the individual. So use your imagination and try lots of changes. Note: The submodality chapters contain a more complete listing of changes that can be suggested. Does this procedure always work? Of course not. However, it works often enough to make it a standard piece of your repertoire.

When this approach works with a particular individual, make a note of the submodality modifications that made a difference for them. The chances are that the same shift will provide similar results in the future. Hence, you will want to try those submodality modifications first should a situation requiring your assistance arise again.

Trying an Alternate Strategy

This is a rather unique approach which requires you to have previously discovered the individual stategies of other members of the group. We realize that this may not be possible for many of the managers reading this book. However, the concept is intriguing since it entails people literally trying alternative thought processes.

As described in Chapter 9, strategies represent a thought sequence habitually employed by an individual. Both the conscious and unconscious components of a strategy can be discovered, enabling any person to become more consistently effective. It also provides the opportunity to teach others the specifics of how a particular individual thinks or solves problems. When someone needs a different perspective, when they can't see the forest because of the trees, one effective approach is to let them try on one or more strategies used by other people.

Summary

Reframing is a powerful technique for helping creative individuals overcome blocks to their creativity. The process of reframing consists of changing the perspective from which we deal with a given situation. It can be done v bally or internally. Regardless of how we reframe something, the change in perspective changes the nature of the problem or situation and opens new ways to deal with it. In the next two chapters, we will demonstrate ways to utilize strategies and reframing to improve your own and others productivity by placing yourself into your most creative state at will.

Putting Yourself and Others in a Creative State

Recently, there has been an increasing emphasis on helping employees and managers achieve states of personal excellence in their work and individual lives. To a smaller extent, some have even attempted to teach others how to achieve states of creativity. Techniques ranging from meditation to jogging have been introduced and vaunted as the key to personal growth and creativity. Yet, despite the "pop psych" attention that the concept of improved creativity has attained, few people seem to really understand what a state of creativity is or how to achieve it.

Perhaps the best way to define a creative state is as a combination of psychological and physical states that enable us to perform creative tasks at optimum levels. These peak creative performances are often remembered as times when we approached our maximum performance in a problem-solving situation—when everything just clicked and we "had the world by the tail."

The difference between average, or even good, performers and the "superstars" of any profession, is that the superstars achieve and maintain a state of excellence on a regular basis. In a word, they have a higher batting average. Their performances are *consistently* excellent rather than just occasionally, or randomly so. For them, maximum or near maximum performance is a way of life. These people have an unconscious mental program for efficiency and effectiveness that they habitually employ. The same is true for creativity. Virtually everyone has moments when they are creative. Some people have even achieved temporary or lasting fame as a result of a brief flash of real brilliance. However, the truly innovative individual is one who is capable of being creative whenever she is faced with a challenge or problem.

The purpose of this chapter is to provide you with a method of 1) accessing memories of previous creative flashes; 2) capturing the unconscious "mental attributes" of the physical and psychological states associated with those creative moments; and 3) establishing an automatic response to specific future situations that will include these ideal mental and physical states.

Although this may seem to be a large order to fill in a limited number of pages, it is actually quite easy. The techniques that you are about to learn are derived from applications of Neuro Linguistic Programming.

Why Control the Creative State?

As a manager of innovative people, your overall productivity and general effectiveness depend upon your employees' abilities to develop creative solutions to problems on a consistent and regular basis. However, even a "brilliant" scientist is of little value if he develops a flash of insight only once every few years. The techniques we will present have helped individuals achieve outstanding results in a wide variety of activities. For example:

➔ A *product development engineer* uses this technique to overcome technical obstacles when developing the manufacturing processes for new products.

➔ An *Olympic swimmer* uses this mental conditioning process to prepare for swimming meets. She has conditioned herself to automatically feel great as she leaves the locker room and approaches the pool. Her results have become so much more consistent that the coach is having this process taught to the other team members. The same technique is used in other sports.

- *Scientists* use this technique when faced with the requirement to develop new chemical processes for creating ecological pesticides.

- *Salespeople* automatically feel motivated, confident, enthusiastic, etc. when beginning a sales presentation. As a result, their sales ratios are consistently high and "off days" have become a thing of the past.

- Broadway *actors and actresses* use this technique to re-create their best performances each time they go on the stage.

- An *advertising executive* considers this knowledge to be his "secret weapon" that keeps him a step ahead of the competition in developing new marketing campaigns.

- A successful *attorney* we know uses this technique to accesses a state of excellence before walking into the courtroom.

These people have trained their minds to automatically tap into mental and physical resources that enable them to maximize their creative performances. In addition, each person has carefully predetermined when, where, and under what specific circumstances these creative states will occur. The balance of this chapter will provide you with the skills to elicit at will your own personal creative state.

A summary of the "creative state" process is provided next to enable you to understand how the various concepts and techniques fit together. Although helpful, it is unnecessary to read the entire chapter before doing the various exercises. There are three broad steps:

First, you'll determine when and where you want your creative state.

Next, you'll decide what mental attributes or resources would be most useful and then insure that these mental resources will automatically occur when you need them.

Finally, you'll use the procedures that combine all of the previously taught techniques to achieve your own creative state.

In order to obtain maximum benefits you are encouraged to follow the directions precisely. Try all of the suggested experiments and answer the various questions. The highly sophisticated techniques presented will allow you to obtain precisely what you want. The results you obtain will depend upon careful and thorough progress through each recommended step.

Before you begin, it is very important to carefully consider exactly what achieving a creative state means to you. Each of us has our own unique definition. This becomes particularly important because, like any goal, achieving a creative state has to be specifically meaningful to you.

Please take a moment and think of a situation in which you would like to be consistently at your creative best and write it down on a separate piece of paper or on the line below. For reasons that will be given later, it is important to determine precisely where and when a *particular* creative state would be useful.

A situation/time in which I would like to be more creative is:

_____

Associated with times of peak creative performance are specific mental and emotional states. For example: the product development engineer needs to simultaneously have confidence, eager anticipation of solving the technical problems she faces, and enthusiasm. She also perceives each problem itself in a certain way when she thinks of them. These mental and emotional states are necessary ingredients for her creative state.

Considering the situation that you indicated above, what mental states or resources (confidence, motivation, relaxation, enthusiasm, etc.) are needed or would be useful for this situation? Write them down on a separate piece of paper, or on the lines provided.

1) _____   5) _____

2) _____   6) _____

3) _____   7) _____

4) _____   8) _____

More Completely Defining the Resources Needed

The next question is very important because your creative state will be partly a result of the answers you provide. What does each of the words you listed on the resources list mean to you as an individual? In a moment we'll provide you with a series of questions to ask about each feeling, which will help you more clearly define its meaning for you.

As you take a moment to consider the meaning of each of the resources that you've chosen, make note of a particular time in your life when you experienced that particular feeling very strongly. Be as specific as you can and answer each of the following questions in as much detail as possible. Remember, this is essential because, by doing so, you will "capture" the essential components of the resources you've selected and incorporate them into the creative state toward which you are working. During the process you will be working with and "installing" each individual resource feeling so that when they are fully combined their collective power will be felt. By carefully recalling and defining the essential physical, mental, and emotional aspects of the listed resources now, you will be assured that you can access it correctly later. *Lack of specificity will lead to poor results.*

Use a separate sheet of paper or an index card for each of the resources you've listed as necessary or useful for attaining the specific creative state you wish to achieve.

Resource wanted: _____

How do you know when you have it? How do you stand, sit, hold your body? Recreate the exact physiology. If you stand/sit like that right now, do you recapture that feeling? If not, what must be done to capture the feeling?

How do you look? _____

How do you sound? What, if anything, are you saying to yourself? _____

How do you feel? How would you describe the feeling to someone else with enough detail so that they could replicate all the nuances of the feeling in themselves? _____

How do you differentiate this feeling from other feelings?
_____

What in you allows you to know that you are having this particular feeling and not another? Briefly describe a past situation/event when you had it:_____

_____

_____

Now that you've determined which resources would be the most useful, as well as defined the specific aspects of each resource selected, you should explore the submodalites of each resource. When you look at the visual aspects, experiment with the submodalites of size, clarity, color, movement, etc. to see how modifying them affects the power of the resource. Now explore the submodalities of the sound and feelings components.

Defining My Outcome

These techniques are effective and powerful when correctly employed. Because of their power, it may be worth briefly repeating the legend of King Midas. King Midas loved gold and prayed to the gods that everything he touched would be turned to gold. He was granted his wish and, as is often the situation in life, got more than he bargained for. Everything he touched turned to gold—including his wife, children, and food.

The old adage "Be careful of what you wish for, you may get it," applies here. Your outcome from this procedure should be very carefully defined because *you will get exactly and precisely what you want.*

As a result, it is important to examine just how your creative state should be contextualized. When do you want it and when would it be inappropriate or undesirable? After all, think how much better off King Midas would have been if he could have turned his "golden gift" on and off as needed. Hence, it is usually wise to play "devil's advocate" with yourself and really think about the times when this particular state of mind would be inadvisable or undesirable.

As you carefully define your desired outcome, follow these simple rules of thumb. Carefully consider each of the following questions, then write the answer down on a separate piece of paper or in the space provided below.

➡ What do I want to do, achieve, be? (How would I like to be different?)

- Is my outcome stated in positives so that there is something specific to move toward, rather than simply something I don't want? For example: "I want to be more enthusiastic" rather than "I don't want to be bored."

- Is the outcome within my control? (Is it something that I can individually accomplish? It should not require the actions of somebody else.)

- How will I look, sound, and feel once I have my outcome? For example: I'll stand tall with my shoulders back. My voice will sound confident. I'll feel good about myself when I'm like this.

  - How will I look?

  - How will I sound?

  - How will I feel?

- When, where, and with whom do I want this outcome or behavior?

  - When?

  - Where?

  - With Whom?

- Under what circumstances?

- When would I NOT want this outcome? When would it be inappropriate? There are almost always circumstances or situations when a particular behavior would work to your disadvantage. *Think carefully about this.*

- How will I know for sure that I have achieved it? What will be the proof that I have it? Be certain that you have defined your outcome specifically. Very often people will say "I want X," but if you haven't defined what that means, how are you going to know when you have achieved it?

- How will getting this outcome affect other areas of my life?

  - Social?

  - Mental?

  - Emotional?

→ Spiritual?

→ Family?

→ Professional?

➡ Will getting this outcome help me achieve other things in my life?

➡ Is this outcome really worth getting?

Having defined your outcome, please review the personal resources you listed at the beginning of this excercise and add or subtract mental resources to help you achieve that outcome. Remember, you will need to precisely define them visually, auditorilly, kinesthetically, and psychologically because of the way that the mind and body work together. You have already experienced this as you completed the exercises above. In addition, these exercises have prepared you to implement the final set of procedures, which will culminate in your specific creative state. However, there is one more component for you to understand before establishing your creative state.

Anchoring the Creative State

In Chapter 7, we discussed the process of anchoring given feelings or states to specific contexts. For example, we might anchor a time when a person was unusually efficient in doing a task. Then, "attach" the efficiency anchor to a situation where additional efficiency is desired. In this way, the situation itself triggers the desired mental state associated with efficiency. That "state of efficiency" causes a higher level of effectiveness to occur in that new context. The same thing can be done with heightened creativity by attaching the creativity anchor to situations in which additional creativity is desired.

You will be using anchors to develop your creative state. You may use a visual, auditory, or kinesthetic anchor for your creative state. However, for the purposes of this exercise, instead of a symbol we'll be using a key word or phrase as the anchor. To do this, we'll use anchor words associated with times when you demonstrated the desired resources in the past. Then we'll significantly intensify these resource states through manipulating their submodalities and by actually adopting the posture, tone, physiology, and psychology that you associate with each resource.

At this point it would be useful to review the resources that you want to have and prepare a separate index card or sheet of paper for each of the resources that you list. The format is repeated for your convenience. This time, however, pay particular attention to the event in your life when you really had that specific resource available to you. It is very helpful to recall events that have had a similar context to the one you are about to work with. That is, if you want more enthusiasm in a business situation, try to remember any previous time when you were enthusiastic in a business context. If no specific instance comes to mind, remember any time when you were enthusiastic, perhaps about reading a book, an idea you had, etc.

Desired State Questions

Resource wanted: _____

How do I know when I have it?

➡ How do I look?

➡ How do I sound?

➡ How do I feel? If I were to describe the feeling to someone else with enough detail so that they could replicate all the nuances of the feeling in themselves, how would I describe it to them?

➡ How is this differentiated from other feelings? What in me enables me to tell that I am having this particular feeling and not another?

➡ A past situation/event when I had it?

➡ A key word/phrase which I can use to recall this situation or event?

Establishing Your Mental Resources

For each of the past situations in which you had this resource, enhance the memory as much as possible using submodalities. Take your time with this. As you enhance the resource memory so that you feel even better about it, think of and mentally listen to the key word or phrase that represents that event. This key word or phrase will itself become an anchor for the enhanced feelings. Finally, these anchors of key resources will be used in developing your creative state.

Summary

You have just completed the preliminary work for creating, enhancing, and anchoring a new creative state in your life. In the next chapter, you will learn how to install this state so that it may enhance your functioning in any desired situation.

Installing Your Creative State

Now that you've completed the preliminary work, you are ready to "install" your creative state. To do this, we'll utilize a two-step process which will give you added behavioral flexibility and resources in specific future situations.

The Behavior Generator

The Behavior Generator is a technique that allows us to predetermine how we will act in an anticipated situation. It insures that our automatic responses will be the ones that are most appropriate and beneficial in that context. A broad summary of the process follows.

➡ First, review your answers to the "Determining My Outcome" questions so that you are clear about the times and places when you want the new responses to occur.

- ➥ Now, mentally "try out" the new behaviors by imagining how you would look and sound as you act in this different way.

- ➥ Add any resources that would be useful.

- ➥ Finally, once you determine the new behaviors you desire, mentally rehearse how you will react with a certain person, complete a performance, or be the absolute best you can be in that situation.

Follow the directions precisely in order to receive the full benefits of this technique. When, and only when, you have completed each of the preliminary exercises, the Behavior Generator will insure that your creative state becomes a reality.

The Behavior Generator is divided into three primary steps:

1. Determine how you would like to act in a given situation.

2. Modify the new behavior until you are completely satisfied.

3. Install the future behavior.

Because this procedure creates an automatic response, it is very important to thoroughly consider the potential side effects of your behaviors—something already done by answering the "Defining My Outcome" questions. As you generate the desired new behaviors, you'll automatically create a set of alternative responses that will enable you to appropriately react to variations of the selected circumstances. This is because your new behaviors will be flexible and adaptive, rather than "locked in stone."

The procedure for the Behavior Generator is as follows: [Note: Please read this thoroughly before you begin so that you will be familiar with the terminology and procedures and will be able to utilize the process effectively.]

1. Determine what behaviors you would like to have and review the Defining My Outcome questions. This step is very important because it will insure that you obtain precise results at the needed time.

2. Determine whether you know what to do or how to act in the situation. If you know exactly how you would like to act then go to step 3. If you're not too sure exactly how you would like to act,

you might wish to "model" or emulate someone. If so, go to step 2a.

2a. Choose a person that you would like to model or emulate. That is, think of someone who already elegantly demonstrates whatever behavior you are trying to learn. You can model someone you know or know of. For example, many people model a TV or movie personality. Remember, the person you select should elegantly demonstrate the behavior you would like to add to your repertoire.

2b. Create a mental movie and watch and listen to the individual you've selected to emulate as they perform the desired behavior. At this point you are their "understudy." Carefully memorize how your mentor acts and reacts to the situation you have selected.

2c. Decide whether or not you would like to act in this manner. If yes, then go to step 3. If not, redirect the scene or decide upon another model and return to step 2a. Note: this recycling procedure is part of the "checks and balances" built into the process, which further ensures its effectiveness.

3. Create a mental screen on which you may *watch and listen to yourself* try out the experimental behaviors that you've selected. It is important that you be able to watch yourself role playing in this mental movie; that is, that you are dissociated while trying out the new behaviors.

4. Observe and listen to the movie carefully. Do you like your actions? Feel free to modify your actions, reactions, responses and so on. Experiment. Enjoy the process.

   In addition to modifying your own actions, posture, and statements, modify the movie "effects": that is, modify the visual and auditory submodalities of the imagined experience until you are completely satisfied. Review the list of submodalities already provided for ideas.

   Change any of the components that would make your movie script look or sound better. Make note of which changes create a positive or negative reaction and keep the effects that you like.

   If you had previously determined that certain additional personal resources would be helpful, add them now, one at a time, by looking at the key word or phrase you wrote down, thereby triggering the anchor. Be aware of any changes in your feelings as you do this. Also be aware of your changes in posture or speech pattern as you add these new resources.

If you are less than totally satisfied or slightly uncomfortable watching and listening to your image, then change the script by going back to step 4, adding additional resources, modifying your physiology, and making additional submodality changes. You might also decide that you would like to see how someone else might do it by returning to step 2 and further observing the same or a different role model.

5. When *totally satisfied* with the movie script, mentally step into the picture so that you are momentarily "living" the movie. The purpose of this is to determine whether or not the new behavior actually "feels good;" that is, whether or not you really like the new behavior. You'll get a positive or negative feeling at this point. If it feels good, then you have a potential new behavior and can go to step number 6. If not, then step out of the picture and return to watching yourself on the screen again. Then go back to step 4 and make any necessary additional modifications. Note: at this point, you might wish to concentrate on the "effects" and additional resources.

6. Having found one or more alternative behaviors, it is important to "future-pace" yourself. To do this, imagine a time in the future when you will be in that situation or a similar situation. Note: this is sort of a mental rehearsal in which you condition yourself to employ the new responses or behaviors at the time that you want it. Imagine yourself on the mental screen in that future situation. If it still feels good, go to step 6a. If something doesn't look, sound, or feel right, return to step 4.

6a. Imagine what it would look, sound, and feel like if you were "living it" (the new behavior) now: seeing through your own eyes, hearing through your own ears, and being aware of your feelings. If you like your new responses, especially the feelings, continue to the next step. If not, it is important to return to step 4.

6b. If you are fully satisfied with step 6a, mentally rehearse your new behaviors in at least two additional future situations—that is, repeat step 6 for additional future-pacing for times or situations when you want these new behaviors. This insures automatic implementation of the new actions at the appropriate time.

7. Congratulations! You have completed the process and have installed additional behavioral responses. This process can be continued with additional refinements as your needs change. *Because we cannot control other people and their actions and reactions, it is wise to work on different scenarios so that you have a variety of responses.* This technique can be applied to many areas of your life. While the technique may at first seem somewhat complicated, thousands of people have found that they can change their lives by simply following the procedures exactly as they have been provided. If you later decide to make modifications or enhancements to a behavior, merely repeat the process.

The Behavior Generator can be utilized for virtually any situation in which you would like to perform more elegantly and comfortably. *The key is to modify the script until you are completely satisfied with the entire performance.* A thorough reading of the previous material will allow you to use easily the following summarized procedure.

Summary of the Behavior Generator

1. Decide what you want.

2. Do you wish to "model" someone?

➥ No, go to step 3.

➥ If Yes, (a) choose the person, (b) understudy that person, (c) decide if you like what he or she does and either go to step 3, or choose someone else to model.

3. Observe yourself on a mental screen.

4. Change the script, the submodality "effects," and add resources until totally satisfied, or choose another model and return to 2a.

5. Momentarily "live in" the movie. Check your feelings. Continue or return to step 4.

6. Imagine three future situations by first observing yourself and then "living it." If satisfied, you have completed the procedure. If not, go back to step 4 and continue until you are satisfied.

It is important to note that you can now exercise conscious control over previously automatic reactions. You can now mentally program personal excellence with this process.

Stepping into a Creative State

This is the final process required for establishing your creative state. This process is made up of five easy steps in which you will use the results of all of the exercises that you have completed thus far.

1. You have already created a series of resource anchors and placed them upon index cards. Next, you must determine what external stimulus you wish to use as a trigger anchor for your creative state. A golfer might choose picking up a club at the first tee; a salesperson may choose putting her phone to her ear; a musician might choose the first note used to verify the key in which he is playing; while another person might choose the doorway of an office or another location as the thing that triggers the creative state. Since you already know in which situations you want this state, choose something that you would definitely see or hear to serve as the anchor.

2. After choosing the anchor, mentally pretend that you are about to enter into the situation—in fact, it is just one step away from you. As you mentally see, hear, or feel that anchor, look at each of the index cards carefully and allow the resource anchors to be triggered. Take your time. Add in the resources one at a time, feeling yourself become more and more excellent. Just as the intensity of each anchor is being felt, say out loud the word "excellence" in voice tones and qualities that represent how wonderful you feel. The word "excellence" then becomes an anchor for the combined resources.

3. After you have mentally "revved up," physically "step past" the imagined initiating anchor while mentally repeating the word "excellence" using the exact voice tones and qualities that you had just finished using. That physical step is a representation of your stepping into your excellent state and has been found to be an excellent enhancement to the state.

4. As you make that step, allow the feelings of excellence to swell up within you.

5. After a minute or so, repeat the physical step procedure. Do this a minimum of three times. Essentially, you are training your mind to automatically re-create this creative state whenever you step into the anticipated situation.

CONGRATULATIONS !!! You have completed the process and now have insured that a "creative state" occurs at the time desired. You have learned to direct your mind in such a way as to insure that you are regularly using more of your inherent potential. Welcome to the ranks of the habitual star performers.

Summary

In this chapter, you have literally learned the secret used by so many of the world's most successful scientists, business people, performers, and athletes to achieve consistent, outstanding performance. By practicing it, you can virtually guarantee that your performance during sales meetings, with customers, and with your superiors will be superlative. You'll increase the effectiveness with which you utilize your current resources, as well as add the additional resources you need to make it to the top.

Note: In Chapters 10 and 11 you first completed a thorough process of preparation before stepping into your new creative state. It is imperative that anyone who attempts to install such a state complete each of the outlined steps and precisely define things for themselves. These skills are also provided in our tapes and workbooks.

III
Managing the Creative Individual

Both creative individuals and their managers have one thing in common: much of their success depends upon their ability to convince someone else to do what they want. As manager, you must convince your staff to dedicate themselves to the company's goals and the latest project. Your creative employees must convince you to support their ideas of how to complete that project and reach those goals. You must then convince your superiors to fund the research and development.

The art of winning your employees' loyalty and cooperation will depend to a large extent on your ability to communicate your desires and your understanding of and concern for their needs. The ability to communicate effectively, build rapport, and quickly determine an individual's psychological make-up can be powerful qualities in management. They enable you to step inside of an employee's or customer's world and demonstrate how he can meet his needs by accepting your idea or program.

YOU *CANNOT* NOT COMMUNICATE

For the purposes of this book, communication will include all of the behaviors, feelings, and expectations that you bring to your relationships with your peers, customers, employees, etc. In management, as in marriage, it is impossible not to communicate. Unfortunately, the extent of the information we exchange in any relationship, as well as the expectations that each individual brings to the relationship, can make effective communication very difficult. For example: If your employees believe that your *only* interest in them is to make you look good with their individual efforts, this could significantly reduce their enthusiasm for your ideas and programs and, hence, their productivity.

In this section you will learn techniques that will enable you to examine your own psychological profile and style of management, as well as psychologically profiling other managers within the first few minutes of speaking to them. In addition, you will learn how to use this and other information in selecting managers to work with your creative personnel. You will also learn techniques for establishing goals and setting limits for innovative people.

Personality Traits and Manager Effectiveness

During the last thirty years, psychologists have developed a variety of techniques to help understand people by profiling their behavior. Early pioneers in the development of uncomplicated, psychological profiles included Myers-Briggs, Satir, Buzzotta et al., Berne and others. As a result, there are many methods available for classifying individuals according to behavioral traits, even to the extent of psychiatric evaluation. In this book, we will provide a simplified system of evaluating and categorizing the behavior you see in others in order to help you communicate more effectively. This system will also assist you in selecting which management techniques best fit your own personal style. This book will work with some primary behavioral attributes, which are listed below, and then consolidate them into a psychological profiling system.

Before we present the basis of this psychological profiling system, take a moment and think of people you know, or know of, who fit some of the elements of the following descriptions:

➡ Harry is a person who is *very dogmatic and always has to be right*. When he is wrong, he tries to bully his way through, often at the top of his lungs. He always wants to be in control, and is often contemptuous of others. His three most frequently used words are *I, me,* and *myself.*

➡ Roberta always *goes by the book* because she believes *rules were made for good reasons.* She rarely takes chances and does not wish to stand out from the crowd. She does not wish to be the leader, but resents whoever does take the lead. She will frequently gossip about people, but will rarely confront them to their face. If a new idea is suggested, she usually has some reason why it won't work and shouldn't even be attempted.

➡ John is always *hanging out with the crowd.* He bases his sense of self-worth on other people's reactions and perceptions of him. Hence, he is eager to please, and may even appear to be a *social butterfly.* He is very garrulous, and tends to be very conscious of the latest fashions and trends.

➡ Sandy is *an independent thinker who is respectful of other's feelings and opinions,* then makes up her own mind. A natural leader in any group; she is social, polite, and friendly, but not insincerely so. When necessary, she is able to set limits on herself and others.

The chances are that you are already thinking of other managers, employees, and even customers who fit quite well into some of these categories. Most of us demonstrate at least some of the traits of each of these characters at one time or another. However, we tend to predominately resemble one. Think of some television or historical figures that might fit into each group. The purpose of the above exercise is to demonstrate how true-to-life psychological profiling can be.

Primary Personality Traits

For the purpose of our profile, we have selected two basic personality types, the **Leader** and the **Follower**, and two modifying characteristics, **Hostile** and **Friendly**. These term—**Leader, Follower** and **Hostile, Friendly**—have many more connotations than their dictionary definitions suggest. They imply general orientations regarding how individuals deal with others, and will be explained in detail on the following pages.

Leaders have a drive to take control in personal encounters and a desire to be paramount. This may manifest itself through a cluster of traits such as initiative, decisiveness, forcefulness, and independence. They are goal-oriented and self-motivating.

Followers have a disposition that tends to let others take the lead and make decisions in personal encounters. This may manifest itself in traits like dependence, indecisiveness, lack of assertiveness, and passivity. Followers usually demonstrate a willingness to be controlled, to avoid personal confrontations, and to comply with other people's wishes. Both their goals and their motivation must often be imposed from the outside.

Hostility is generally manifested by a lack of regard for others and a concentration on self. Hostility demonstrates the attitude that other people have less value than oneself, and therefore deserve less care. It implies indifference to others, insensitivity to their needs and ideas. Hence, it often results in resistance to collaboration and, in some cases, outright animosity. Hostile people are often cold, emotionally insensitive, and generally manipulative. Hostile people demonstrate a *self-oriented, win-lose,* or an *I'm OK, you're NOT OK* orientation.

Friendliness on the other hand, is basically one's concern for others. It involves recognition of others' value and dignity and a sensitivity to their needs. Friendliness might be defined as the extent to which one is involved with people and is sensitive to their needs. It implies a realization that we can only achieve our own goals by helping others (e.g., our employees and peers) to achieve theirs. It demonstrates a *win-win* or an *I'm OK, You're OK* orientation.

The personality each of us shows others is a combination of the traits that we've just discussed, and can be demonstrated on a simple grid. Which traits predominate in any given situation are usually determined by the context of that situation. To enable you to understand the grid system we will be using, we have divided the traits along two axes. See Exhibits 13-1 and 13-2.

Now let's merge these traits and see how they provide an easy-to-use psychological profiling system. In Exhibit 13-3, we have combined the trait lines to show the interrelationship of the primary traits. As we discuss each type of personality, we will show only that portion of the grid which applies to that type and show how the combination of traits leads to the personality types, which we have labeled for easy identification. In Chapters 14 and 16-19, we will include the rest of the traits, further describing the personality types.

Exhibit 13-1
The Vertical Axis

This axis deals with the LEADER- and FOLLOWER-oriented traits.

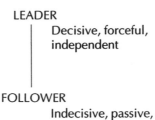

LEADER
Decisive, forceful, independent
FOLLOWER
Indecisive, passive, dependent

Exhibit 13-2
The Horizontal Axis

This axis deals with the traits of HOSTILITY and FRIENDLINESS.

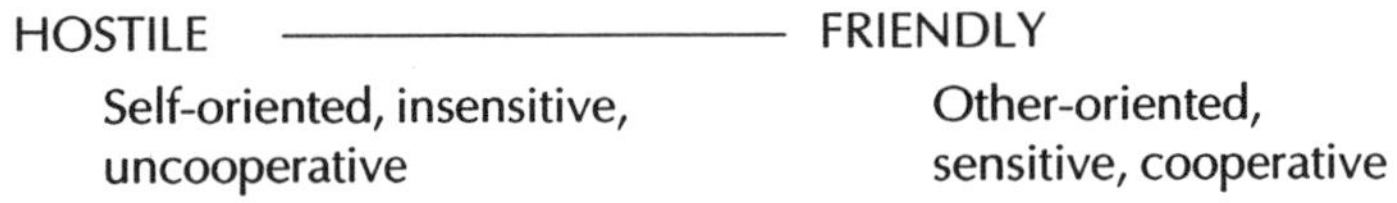

HOSTILE
Self-oriented, insensitive, uncooperative
FRIENDLY
Other-oriented, sensitive, cooperative

Exhibit 13-3

LEADER
HOSTILE
FRIENDLY
FOLLOWER

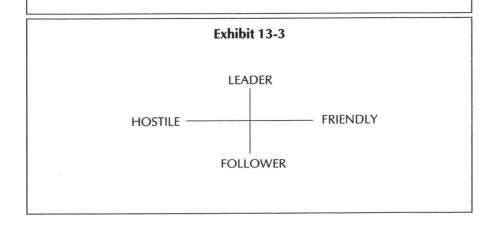

The four extremes of leader, follower and hostile, friendly, presented above, form a grid. When the various combinations are considered, we find that these four categories produce a system that will enable us to easily recognize common personality types. In the next few pages, we will briefly outline each of the categories, then more precisely define the prospect or client characteristics associated with each primary type.

As a manager, the **Dictator** Harry (Exhibit 13-4) is an individual who is often very dogmatic and always has to be right. When he is wrong, he tries to bully his way through, often as loudly as possible. A Dictator-type manager insists on being in control, and often communicates contempt of others, especially subordinates. His most frequently used words are *I, me, mine* and *myself.* His hostile and unresponsive nature often causes the Dictator manager to be labelled as aggressive (often with negative connotations). The Dictator feels that, *I'm OK. You're NOT OK.*

Historically, the Dictator has been the most common type of manager in many industries. This is hardly surprising when you realize that, during the 50s and 60s, most entry level managers were hired because of their aggressiveness in solving problems and "getting the job done." An outgrowth of the Second World War and the Korean Conflict, this aggressive attitude in management was seen as an example of American competitive spirit. It was generally assumed that only someone who was naturally aggressive could survive. However, even though that attitude has been modified somewhat in the last ten years to reflect a growing emphasis on customer and employee relations, it is still a powerful influence in the selection of management personnel.

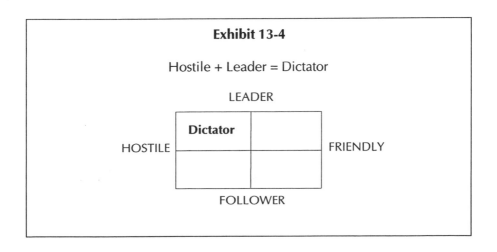

Exhibit 13-4

Hostile + Leader = Dictator

LEADER

	Dictator	
HOSTILE | | | FRIENDLY

FOLLOWER

One reason that this attitude has persisted has been the continued emphasis on "the bottom line" and short-term profitability that has become the mark of American industry. Since people are most comfortable with individuals they perceive as being like themselves, aggressive executives have continued to hire new executives and managers who demonstrate the same style of management as their own, even while giving lip service to the importance of leadership and personal management in employee and customer relations. Hence, Dictators make up a large portion of today's management. In addition, because many senior managers are themselves Dictators who have achieved their own success through their emphasis on bottom-line productivity, they often appoint Dictators to be in charge of R & D and marketing departments (both of which are often seen as stepping stones to top management).

The quintessential Dictator has a tendency to try to push his way through situations and to demand loyalty and total acceptance of his dictates because, according to him, he is the manager and therefore probably not only has more business experience but is also better, smarter, and so on, than anyone working for him. Unfortunately, his *I'm OK, you're NOT OK,* hard-nosed attitude does little to engender the loyalty and dedication that he both needs and seeks, especially from creative personnel.

The extreme Dictator tends to assume that the two main ways to motivate employees is with a carrot or a stick. The stick varies from public sarcasm and humiliation to threats of firing. The carrot is usually limited to financial rewards such as raises in pay, bonuses, "perks," or public recognition, such as a title or attendance at some recognition function. Unfortunately, these common techniques really only account for about 30 to 40 percent of what really motivates people.

Because of his need to be better than everyone else, the Dictator manager often has ambivalent feelings about his staff. To the extent that it reflects upon him, he is proud of their performance. However, he may also feel threatened by the thought that they are more creative, smarter, or better in any way than he is or the fact that much of his performance depends upon theirs. This dependency can be a serious threat to his position. Ironically, his aggressiveness and hostility are often also very stressful to himself and frequently result in family problems and health difficulties. We'll deal in detail with specific recommendations for handling that stress in Chapter 28 when we discuss stress as a powerful demotivator.

When working with creative people, the Dictator is often threatened by their creativity, fearing that they will appear to be smarter, better, or more effective than he. As a result, he will often publicly denigrate any idea that he didn't personally develop, then introduce it later as his own. When criticized by higher management he will usually blame his staff or circumstances. If his department is praised, he will accept it as *his* due without sharing it with his staff. When he is supportive of his staff, it is in order to insist on total loyalty and productivity upon demand. In fact, bottom-line productivity is often his watchword.

In summary, because of his aggressiveness and rigidity, the Dictator makes a poor manager for creative people. His hostility often makes employees hesitate to suggest innovations and new concepts because they fear rejection and possible public humiliation. As a result, R & D departments that are run by Dictators rarely produce completely new concepts, preferring instead to offer modifications of existing ideas or products (either yours or the competition's) to achieve the productivity they seek. Because these managers stifle the very creativity upon which their department depends, they are poor motivators. As a result, they often have a high rate of employee turnover.

Extremes

In a sense, the Dictator really represents something of an extreme, since we all demonstrate the tendencies of this type (as well as the others) at some times. Actually, if we were to look at a scatter diagram of behaviors, we would notice that for a real-life Dictator, the weighting occurs predominantly in one area. See Exhibit 13-5.

Bureaucrat manager Roberta (Exhibit 13-6) is a person who always *goes by the book* because "rules were made for good reasons." She rarely

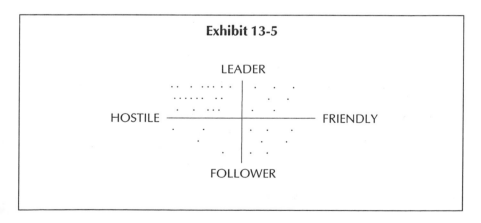

Exhibit 13-5

LEADER

HOSTILE ———————————————— FRIENDLY

FOLLOWER

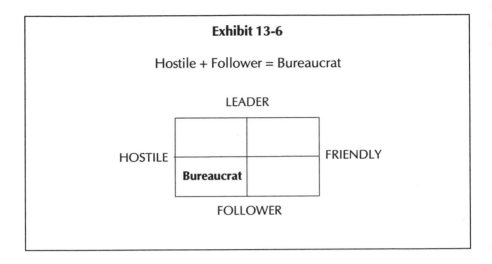

Exhibit 13-6

Hostile + Follower = Bureaucrat

LEADER

HOSTILE   FRIENDLY

Bureaucrat

FOLLOWER

takes chances and does not wish to stand out from the crowd. Although she enjoys the power and prestige of being a manager, she does not wish to be the leader. Yet, she resents anyone appointed over her. She will frequently gossip about people, but will rarely confront them. If a new idea is suggested, she usually has some reason why it won't work and shouldn't even be attempted. When faced with someone whom she considers more powerful than herself, she will usually take orders without disagreeing. However, she may also attempt to undermine those orders if she can do so without being blamed. When faced with a subordinate or someone she considers less powerful, she will usually appear to be a Dictator. Of course, like the Dictator, the Bureaucrat is an extreme representation. She has an *I'm NOT OK, You're NOT OK* orientation.

Because of her lack of flexibility and need to go by the book, the Bureaucrat makes a poor manager of creative people. Her unwillingness to attempt anything new results in a stifling of any creative efforts on the part of her staff. In the end, the most she will allow is the development of small innovations on already existing products or services. In terms of management, she is best suited to the role of devil's advocate, someone who can look for reasons why a new concept or product won't work before funding its further development.

Socialite John (Exhibit 13-7) is a friendly follower: someone who is always hanging out with the crowd. He bases his sense of self-worth on other people's reactions and perceptions of him. Hence, he is eager to please and may even appear to be a social butterfly or a good-time-Char-

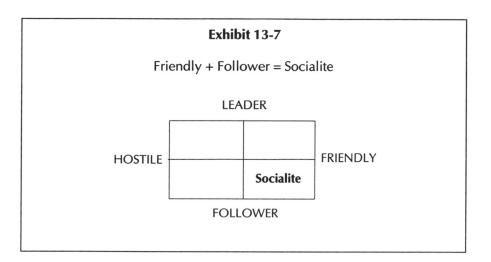

Exhibit 13-7

Friendly + Follower = Socialite

LEADER

HOSTILE ――――――――――― FRIENDLY

Socialite

FOLLOWER

lie. He is talkative and tends to be very conscious of the latest fashions and trends. Because he tends to subordinate his goals to the desires of the group, he rarely takes the initiative. He sees the world from a *You're OK, I'm NOT OK* orientation.

The Socialite's greatest strength as a manager of creative people derives from his desire for teamwork and harmonious relations within the department. Because he is gregarious himself, he tends to encourage the interaction and cooperation among his staff so necessary for the development of creative synergy. Unfortunately, his desire to please everyone often makes it difficult for him to maintain firm limits and goals with his staff, or to defend adequately their projects to higher management. If he is to be used as a manager of creative people, the Socialite should be backed up with "Executive" subordinate managers who can maintain limits without discouraging creativity.

The **Executive** Sandy (Exhibit 13-8) is an independent thinker and is respectful of other's feelings and opinions, but makes up her own mind. A natural leader in any group; she is social, polite, and friendly, but not insincerely so. When necessary, she is able to set limits on herself and others. The warmth of the Executive's dominant behavior often causes her to be seen as assertive by others. She thinks, *I'm OK, You're OK.*

The Executive is the ideal manager of creative people. She most closely matches the criteria listed in Chapter 5 for the ideal manager. Her warmth and friendliness enable her to work with all kinds of innovative individuals without stifling their creativity. At the same

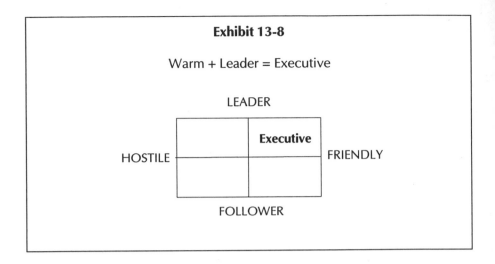

Exhibit 13-8

Warm + Leader = Executive

LEADER

HOSTILE | Executive | FRIENDLY

FOLLOWER

time, her self-confidence enables her to explore and even support views and ideas that may be radically different from her own. Finally, her assertiveness enables her to establish goals and set limits with her staff to maximize her department's productivity. As a result, she is able to build the necessary creative synergy among her staff, while keeping them focused on the company's desired outcomes.

Summary

In this chapter, we have presented a broad summary of four personality types, which each of us demonstrates to some extent. Each of these personality types reflects a specific set of emotional needs, and each can be not only appropriate but actually useful in certain contexts. For example:

➡ The Executive's self-confidence and leadership skills make her the ideal manager/leader for creative people.

➡ Because of his desire to relate to others, the Socialite manager frequently makes an excellent public relations executive.

➡ The Bureaucrat is often utilized most effectively in overseeing corporate expenditures or the legal department, where their "by-the-book" way of looking at things can save the company legal and financial headaches.

➥ Even the Dictator's aggressive attitudes can be very useful in overcoming engineering problems in the field that might daunt others more willing to give in.

By recognizing which type of individual we are dealing with at any one time, it is possible to assign projects to them appropriately and to motivate them more effectively by recognizing and responding to their emotional needs.

In Chapters 16-19, we will use the same grid system to explore how you can expect your employees to react to you, based upon their psychological profile. Later, in Section VI, we will deal with how to motivate and quickly build an effective relationship with any of these four types.

Relationship Styles

We've already pointed out that no one is always a Dictator, a Bureaucrat, a Socialite, or even an Executive. After all, an individual who is a Dictator at the office will often be a Socialite when playing with his infant child at home. This concept is important, because we all demonstrate each of the personality types at different times, depending upon the context. And each can be useful. For example:

➡ When brainstorming, the open positiveness of the Socialite's style is often very effective in stimulating creative interaction.

➡ However, once the brainstorming is over, the down to earth, by-the-book attitude of the Bureaucrat can be very useful for weeding out ideas and concepts that are unrealistic or overly expensive.

➡ When trying to overcome an obstacle in the lab or an engineering problem, the aggressive approach of the Dictator can be just what's needed.

➡ Finally, the warm assertiveness of the Executive can be most effective when attempting to get a team of individuals to work together to solve a common problem.

The key to relating to others, especially creative people, is flexibility. When we relate to someone the same way each time we encounter them, regardless of the context, we become locked into a rigid system that can be very self-defeating. Yet, in management, we frequently run into employees or customers who relate to us in a rigid style, always coming from the same personality type. If we are not flexible in our response to them, we risk ending up in that rigid, self-defeating pattern, which may eventually force them or us to end the relationship. For example:

➡ Have you ever had an employee that always wanted you to make the decisions, but always found some reason for not going along with your idea?

➡ How about the opposite, the individual that always insists on doing things his way, even when you know he's wrong, and then blames you when his idea doesn't work?

➡ Customers can be that way, too. We've all had at least one customer who "knows exactly what he wants" and doesn't want to hear anything different. However, he then blames us when things don't work exactly as he thought they would.

Frustrating, isn't it? How do you respond to these employees and customers? When the first individual left all of the decisions to you, did you make the decisions or try to involve him? When the second individual tried to dominate you, did you give in and let him, or did you fight back? Psychologists [Satir Watzlawick et al., Scoresby, Harper et al., and others] have found that when we get locked into any relationship pattern in which we continually dominate while another submits (or just the opposite), we have developed a "relationship style" with that individual that will be frustrating and self-defeating at best.

The **relationship style** is basically a way of describing the way two people commonly communicate within their relationship. The way that most of us relate usually varies with the context and the person to whom we are relating. However, it can become common to all contexts with a given person or even to all of our relationships (e.g., the rigid patterns of relating often seen between a teenager and his parents). When this happens, problems almost always occur. In this chapter, we will describe three basic styles of relating: complementary, symmetrical, and parallel.

The Complementary Style

The complementary relationship is one of opposites (e.g., dominant-submissive, introvert-extrovert, hostile-warm, healthy-sick, and so forth).

The most common form is the dominant-submissive mode. This is a rigid mode in which one person is *always* in control while the other is *never* in control. Conflicts are generally resolved by either the submissive person withdrawing in defeat, or by the dominant person handing down an edict. You will see this type of relationship whenever a Dictator relates to a Bureaucrat or a Socialite. For example:

➡ The aggressive administrator from the head office and the pliant, eager-to-please director of research and development; or, the dominating manager and the pliant, eager-to-please employee (employees certainly need to be teachable and to accept direction and instruction, but they must also be able to think for themselves).

➡ The dominating manager and the resistant employee who is finally won over, but who never sends back the necessary paperwork to pursue the required product development; or, the dominant manager and the apparently cooperative employee who speaks badly about the manager behind her back.

➡ The hostile administrator and the overaccommodating manager (who can't seem to maintain productivity); or, the hostile prima donna in research and the manager who can't get him to cooperate.

You should recognize that your submissive employees and customers receive a great deal of *payoff* for maintaining their submissive role and will therefore try to maintain that role in your relationship. Don't let them. Move into the Executive mode and lead them into making their own decisions, and then support their decisions (even if they are not the ones you wanted). As you do so, they will begin to see you as a source of support instead of a threat and will begin to take more responsibility for their decisions.

In addition, submissive employees and customers carry an all-powerful veto—they need only to appear to surrender, seeming to go along with what you wish, and then fail to follow through with whatever was agreed upon. This could place you in the position of having won without obtaining your goals anyway. Deal with potential problems before they occur! Remember, dominating your employees and customers can become very self-defeating.

The Symmetrical Style

This style may be found in situations and relationships in which both individuals respond identically, such as both are dominant or both submissive. When power or control is sought, neither gives in and the struggle escalates until serious difficulties may arise. Neither feels sufficiently secure in himself, the other person, or the relationship to relinquish control voluntarily. As a result, power becomes the primary source of validation in the relationship. In the dominant-dominant context, each effectively thinks, "If I were really okay, I'd win." In the submissive-submissive context, each effectively thinks, "If he were really okay, he take responsibility for this situation and let me off the hook."

When you run into aggressive employees or customers, do you find yourself confronting them and trying to overpower them? Or, when you work with passive employees or customers, do you have difficulty gaining their cooperation because you can't make yourself ask for a commitment? In both situations you and the other individual are responding identically to each other, and nothing is getting accomplished. Frustrating, isn't it? Ultimately, in both cases, the other individual holds ultimate control because of his veto. All he needs to do to win is *nothing*.

Whenever you meet a Dictator, Bureaucrat, or Socialite employee or customer in their mode, you risk a symmetrical interaction. Move into the Executive mode and show the Dictator that you are not threatened or defensive, but that you also do not need to threaten. Show your interest and confidence and he will change his mode. When working with the Bureaucrat or Socialite, use your Executive skills to support them and help them make decisions. If neither of you takes the lead, nothing can be accomplished.

The Parallel Style

The parallel style of relating is the healthiest and most effective of the three because it is the most flexible. As a result, it is also the most effective when working with creative employees. It's a style in which neither you nor your employee is anxious in your dealings with the other, and you both feel able to express yourselves without a struggle developing. In addition, you both decide the issues of power and control by the needs of the situation rather than by arbitrary or conflicting expectations. Remember, you may be the manager and have the power to hire and fire; but your own success depends upon the willing cooperation of your creative staff.

In practice, as the Executive in the relationship you are able to maintain the necessary flexibility by supporting your employee's needs for self-esteem while providing the necessary leadership to help solve problems. It is a relationship in which neither of you has to win all of the time, and it consists of honesty, openness, trust, and cooperation.

In the creative relationship, the parallel style occurs when you and your employees work together to solve problems and develop new products and services. In most cases, a parallel relationship will result in your taking the lead in seeking and proposing potential goals and problems to be solved, but in every case, it allows your staff to accept responsibility for the final decision.

There are four common elements that occur in all three relationship styles, namely, the processes of control, communication patterns, change, and decision making. It is the variations among and within these four areas that determine the style of interaction or relationship.

➡ *Control* is the way each person in the relationship attempts to manipulate or coerce the other in an effort to maintain control of a situation or the relationship itself. This process can be seen whenever either you or your employee or customer attempt to manipulate the other to obtain your own ends. (Note: Attempts to manipulate are almost always construed as negative by the person being manipulated.)

➡ *Communication* is each person's willingness to participate in two-way communication between peers rather than attempting to control the flow of information between them. Are you perceived as someone who communicates freely with your employees, or who only speaks to them when you have a new program to sell or are unhappy with their work? Do you perceive your employees as clearly sharing data about their needs, goals, and concerns, or as people who only come to you when they have a problem?

➼ *Change* is each person's willingness to risk altering their own behavior as well as the relationship itself without being threatened. An example of this is when you feel the need to suggest a change in research strategy. How well do your employees handle the change?

➼ *Decision making* is each individual's ability and willingness to place the needs of the relationship above his own desires relative to the decision at hand. You are the manager. It may seem that this means that you get to make all of the decisions and your employees should cheerfully support them. For example, at times, you may feel that a particular strategy is exactly what is needed to increase production or relieve pressure on you from upper management. However, your creative staff, who may be more closely involved in the problem than you, may know their area or responsibility better and have a more effective strategy. If one of them suggests a different strategy, are you willing to follow their inclination rather than risk damaging the relationship by insisting on your own point of view? Are your employees willing to trust your judgment?

The elements of control, communication, change, and decision making will vary from relationship to relationship. As a leader, rather than a driver, you will find that by relating in a parallel style, with both you and your employees taking turns at decision making at the appropriate times, you will achieve a great deal more of *your* goals. The dominance, or overuse, of any of these characteristics is usually less effective than a more or less equal mix of them.

Summary

The concept of relationship styles will help you to be sensitive to the need for flexibility in your communications with your creative employees. Without flexibility, innovation is impossible. Examine some of your current relationships and ask yourself if you are getting into a rut with any of them. If you are, note situations that always seem to start and end in a predictable manner and think about new responses that you can try. You'll be amazed at the results.

Setting Goals for Creative Personnel

One of the most difficult tasks in managing innovative people is establishing performance goals for them. This task is also one of the most important because it influences how you will measure their productivity (Section VII).

The problem inherent in setting productive goals for creative individuals is that they are not performing routine tasks that can be quantified incrementally by time. Thomas Edison had to do over 10,000 experiments before he "discovered" the first effective filament for an electric light. Was he productive? If he was working for you, how would you have handled the assignment from headquarters? "Find a cost-effective filament for electric light bulbs." How would you have established performance goals for that task?

Innovative personnel are often assigned the task of developing a process to solve a problem, or to develop a new product or service to meet a consumer need. In each of these cases, the problem or need presented to the innovator carries within it the parameters of its own solution (once you know the parameters of a problem, you know the parameters of the

121

solution). Knowing these parameters can provide a starting point for productive goal setting. However, how do you set goals for individuals who are expected to develop useful innovations on their own (e.g., the product development engineer who is expected to develop ideas for toys on his own, in addition to projects he is assigned to work on)? The answer to both of these problems will be presented in this chapter.

Eight Steps to Goal Setting

While each of us needs to establish goals for our personal lives, our personnel, and our own career development, most goals are handed to us from higher authority. As managers, we have to translate those "corporate goals" into departmental and individual goals that we can assign to specific persons or teams. Before a goal can become a motivating, dynamic force, it must meet several criteria:

1. *Establish the parameters of the problem to be solved.* Explore the problem or need that you are addressing until you have thoroughly established its parameters. Once you have the parameters of the problem, you can derive the parameters of your solution to the point where you should already have some conception of your goal. Before Edison began his experiments on the light bulb, he knew the performance parameters of the filament he wanted. As a result, he was able to recognize it when he finally "discovered" it. Note: The initial parameters will often be somewhat vague. However, the more specific you can make them, the easier your task will be.

2. *Goals must be written.* While this is probably already obvious to you because of internal company auditing requirements, we are amazed at the number of people who do not write down their goals. "I have it right here," they say, tapping their forehead. "I know exactly what I'm looking for." Unfortunately, they often don't, and, as long as the goal is only in *their* head, no one else can really help them with it.

   Providing your subordinates with goals in written form is particularly important to avoid later misunderstandings. Once the goal has been agreed upon and recorded in writing, you may wish to have them sign it.

3. *Goals must be stated positively.* Concentrate on what you want to achieve, rather than on what you want to avoid. For example:

"I want a filament that can be produced for less than $.10 a piece, that will produce 750 lumens when drawing 100 watts of power from a 120 volt line, and to increase sales production by 30 percent in the current fiscal year" (positive), rather than, "I don't want the bulb to be expensive or inefficient" (negative). The importance of stating things positively is further explored in Chapter 24.

Positively stated goals are particularly important when working with innovative people because negative statements often result in narrowing, rather than broadening thought patterns. Negative thinking, as well as negative attitudes, are extremely self-defeating when it comes to innovation. Each member of the department must believe that the assigned goal can be accomplished. It is very hard to maintain the kind of faith and energy level necessary to achieve success if negative thinking is allowed.

Note: In Chapter 29, we will discuss the difference between people who are motivated by moving towards something and those who are motivated by moving away from something. Both can be trying to accomplish positive things and should be encouraged to state their goals in positive terms.

4. *Your goals must be within your control.* As a manager, you will be held personally responsible for the completion of any goal placed upon your department. This responsibility can be frustrating for two reasons: first, almost all of your goals are presented from higher authority (over whom you may have little or no control) and, second, because reaching virtually all of your goals depends upon what *someone else* does. After all, that is the function of management. For example: Marketing says that their research indicates that there is a real need for another toy truck. You are already doing well in toy trucks and it is clear that to maintain your edge in market share you need another toy truck. The goal of developing another toy truck is placed upon you by the president. You, in turn, direct your design team in charge of toy trucks to come up with something new. The key to your success will depend largely upon how much of the process you can manage.

Remember, too, that goals need to be reasonable and attainable. Goals that are overwhelming become discouraging and can sap an individual's will to continue. At the other extreme, goals that are too easy are boring and quickly lose their ability to motivate. When assigning goals, select some that can be achieved only by stretching. If you find that an individual is achieving your goals too easily, make the next one harder. If you find someone becoming too frustrated at the difficulty of a goal, consider first if they are working efficiently toward achieving it. If they are, break it down into smaller pieces and reexamine the time frame you've established to achieve it. When you meet with employees to review their goals and their progress, help them set challenging but achievable goals that you can both feel good about.

5. *Each goal must be testable* in some objective manner. This is true regardless of the nature of your goal and derives from the parameters established in step 1. For example: Your goal is to develop a new chemical process for retarding corrosion in ferrous metals. Based upon the parameters you established in step 1, how will you test your process to determine its effectiveness? Unfortunately, the development of requisite testing equipment and procedures often becomes an important secondary goal in itself. However, unless you can test your results, you run the risk of having something that may "appear" to work without really understanding why it works or recognizing potential problems. This is a common problem in the medical industry where some medications were in use for years before anyone understood how they worked or their negative side effects. Remember, when you establish criteria for testing each goal, the criteria should be sufficiently objective so that an observer could tell if you have achieved your goal. Note: Section VII will deal in detail with measuring and monitoring productivity within the creative process.

6. *Be sure that you really understand each goal.* What technical obstacles do you face in achieving the goal and what resources will you need to overcome those obstacles? What *specific* steps must you take to help your staff overcome those obstacles? Note: Remember the concept of control, again. If achievement of your goal depends upon someone else's behavior, what steps do you need to take in terms of motivation and support to help them help you achieve your goal?

Remember, the process of goal setting described here will work whether you are setting a goal for someone else, or establishing a personal development goal of your own. However, when working on personal goals (yourself, or with one of your staff), you should ask yourself the following series of questions to explore your understanding of the goal.

a) Is this *your* goal, or something that you think is expected of you by your peers or society? Granted, you must fulfill the expectations of your company to remain employed. However, trying to live up to other people's expectations has caused more stress and more burnout than almost any other factor. What, if any, goals are you imposing upon your employees? How will the imposition of those goals affect their levels of stress and efficiency?

b) How will you know when you have achieved your goal? (tests?)

c) When, where, and with whom do you wish to attain your goal?

d) What will change in your life if you obtain your goal? For the better? For the worse? Always remember that every goal carries a cost. What will happen if you don't achieve it? This is particularly important because the way that we define the results of not attaining a goal are a large factor in how stressful a goal becomes. It also determines how effective this goal will be in motivating you. And, of course, if you attain the goal, will what you receive be worth what it costs?

e) Related to the last question is: How do you know if your goal is really worth obtaining? Did someone else tell you? How do they know?

f) What is stopping you, or what might stop you from obtaining your goal? What obstacles do you face?

g) What personal resources will you require to overcome these obstacles and achieve your goals? Which of these resources are already in your possession?

7. *A goal should maintain the positive aspects of the current situation.* This is another of those obvious precepts that so many managers forget when setting goals, especially in terms of the functioning and productivity of their department. For example: Your department may currently be working on a series of short-term projects that bring quick and measurable results. One of

the nice things about quick and measurable results is that they provide everyone with immediate feedback about their performance. They can be very helpful when measuring overall productivity to determine raises and promotions. It is also often very motivating for the staff involved. However, if your goal is to expand your department's capabilities to handle long-term projects as well, you may need to find a way to provide regular feedback to your staff about their performance or risk losing much of their motivation.

8. *Your goal should be worth the effort.* As obvious as this may appear, every year companies spend prodigious amounts of capital on research to develop completely new ways of doing something, when a smaller investment in improving the existing system would be much more practical (of course, the opposite is also true).

This criteria can be demonstrated in terms of your own personal and career goals. For example: Let's say that your goal is to triple your personal income during the next fiscal year. You may be able to accomplish this, but it may also cost you your family, your integrity, your best employees, and/or your health. Would it be worth it?

If You Can't Measure It, You Can't Manage It

So much of your success as a manager of innovative people depends upon factors that are outside of yourself. Yet you are expected to set and achieve goals that are affected by these factors. Consider the impact of the following factors:

- → Employee turnover (not just creative employees, but support staff as well).

- → Your "critical few," that is, those critical items for which you will be held accountable by higher management, such as number of new products developed over time, response to a given marketing campaign, etc.

- → The performance of your department compared to others in your region and industry.

- → Delivery of critical equipment.

How will each of these influence your success, and how will you control or deal with them? The reality is that you will be held accountable for the effects of these and many other factors upon the productivity of your department. However, if you can't measure something, you can't manage it either. Once you stop managing, you are a failure waiting to happen. You must be able to measure and test not only your goals, but also the factors that influence them.

How To/Chance To/Want To

As you set goals (technical, innovative, or personal) for yourself and for each member of your department, it is important to answer three questions about each goal:

➥ Do you or your employees know **HOW TO** achieve the goal? Do you have the technical skills necessary?

➥ Do you or your employees have the **CHANCE TO** achieve the goal? Is it possible to achieve this goal with the resources at hand in the time required? At what price? (Will you have to stop work on other projects of equal or greater priority to complete this one in the time allotted?)

➥ Do you or your employees really **WANT TO** achieve this goal? Is this your goal or someone else's? Does this goal motivate you enough to give it the necessary effort to achieve success? In a word, do you really believe that this goal merits the time, attention, and resources that will have to be allotted to complete it?

Even before you begin, these questions will enable you to determine the feasibility of your goals. If you're going to modify or eliminate a goal, do it before you've made a significant commitment to it.

"Chunking Down"

Many people tend to think in terms of the "big picture." Unfortunately, creative projects frequently have a habit of becoming overwhelming when dealt with as a whole. For example: The design of a aircraft wing can require a great deal more than a computer model and wind tunnel studies. Often, entirely new composite materials have to be created before the design of the wing itself can be implemented. In addition, projects are often so long term that intermediate and short-term steps have to be programmed into the work to enable you to keep track of any progress.

Remember the old riddle that asks, "How do you eat an elephant?" The answer is, "One forkful at a time." Developing a new aircraft wing is no different. However, even by the forkful, eating an elephant can be a bit daunting. But, how about the elephant's leg? That's only one chunk of elephant. Given enough time, it's easy to believe that anyone could eat just the leg. That's how we divide a project into subprojects, as well as establish intermediate and short-term goals; we "chunk down."

Chunking down is the process of breaking a large project or goal into pieces that are small enough to handle. Large pieces become subprojects that can be assigned to different individuals or project teams. These projects represent one form of intermediate goal for the overall project. Their development is then broken down into further milestones, or intermediate goals, which mark significant progress toward the long-range goal. Smaller pieces of each subproject become short-term goals, and indicate the level of progress toward the intermediate goals. Each bite could be a daily goal.

However you break a goal down, it is important to do so in a manner that will motivate you and your staff and demonstrate your ability to eventually achieve your desired result. If your chunks are too small, you risk boredom or overattention to detail, which results in losing sight of the end goal or big picture. If they are too large, you can become frustrated and discouraged and fail to properly allot the necessary resources. Ideally, you want to break each project into the kind of chunks that will allow you to feel satisfied with what you have accomplished each day. Do the same with your employees. Be sure that their goals become achievable by helping them to break them down into manageable chunks that still require a little extra effort.

Once you have divided a project into manageable chunks, remember to allot your resources accordingly. In fact, the availability of resources may have an important impact upon the way you divide a project. Finally, resources often include far more than just equipment, bodies, and finances. It also often means knowledge or skills. Does your staff have the knowledge or skills necessary to complete the task? If not, you must either get them trained or hire a consultant to fill the gap. Make the obtaining of those resources (skills and knowledge), goals in themselves. Then break them down into manageable chunks, as well. Remember, their success is your success.

Setting a Time Frame

The most effective way that we know to determine if you are on track is to monitor your progress relative to the completion of your project. We've already discussed the importance of placing milestones on the road; now let's look at setting up a time frame for accomplishing each goal.

To establish a goal without setting a specific time within which to accomplish it is to give it the lowest of priorities. After all, if you don't set a time requirement, you have "all the time in the world." How much effort do you put into something *now* that has no time requirement? We need that sense of urgency to help motivate us and to help us determine which tasks must be completed first.

The problem with long-range goals is that they are exactly that—long range. They are so far in the future (for some industries they are at least a year, and frequently five or more years) that there appears little reason to put one first, today. By establishing intermediate and short-term goals, we increase not only the sense of urgency, but also the sense of accomplishment and movement toward that long-term goal. Hence, whenever you set a goal for yourself or for an employee, establish the time frame in which you wish it to be accomplished, and then follow up! Whether for yourself or for an employee, no time frame has credibility unless someone is held accountable for the goal's attainment.

Long-term goals usually imply completion in five to ten years, while intermediate goals can stretch from six months to five years, and short-term goals occur within six months to one year. However, even a short-term goal can, and probably should, be broken down into monthly, weekly, and even daily chunks.

It is important to be aware of lag time. You already know that, depending upon the nature of your business, it can take an average of three weeks to three months to develop a project plan and determine the necessary resources. In addition, there may be an additional lag between completion of the plan and allocating the personnel and resources to begin work. If not handled well, these lags can become a source of frustration and demotivation for those assigned to a given project.

Daily Focus

When working on your own personal goals, set daily objectives for yourself and keep track of them (this is also discussed in the chapters on managing stress). For example, each day, make a list of things you wish to accomplish. Prioritize them and do not begin work on the lower priority items until you have completed those with the highest priority. As you set goals of specific tasks to complete each day, keep track of how many you accomplish. Remember: If you don't have a goal, any direction you go is as good as another.

Overcoming Fear of Failure

In his excellent book on leadership, *The Ten Most Wanted Men,* Paul H. Dunn suggests that many of us have been raised to be so afraid of failure that we drive through life with our brakes on. Not only is this exhausting, it keeps us from reaching our fullest potential. In fact, fear of failure is the single greatest reason why so many people never even attempt to reach for their dreams. The great psychiatrist Alfred Adler called this "assumed disability." Essentially, this means we'd rather not try than try and fail. But what is "failure" and why are we so afraid of it? As someone who is already a success, it may be difficult for you to understand and empathize with that fear in others. But your ability to do so will greatly enhance your ability to help your employees overcome it in themselves.

For most of us, failure means not living up to somebody's expectations of us and being rejected as a result. For any manager, failure means producing less than is required of us. Statistically, most innovators fail many times more than they succeed (e.g., Thomas Edison's 10,000 failures with the electric light). As a result, for the creative employee, this means that the more conscientious he is, the more he will fail. That's terrible! Or is it?

A well-known motivational expert, Art Mortell, likes to point out that failure (or negative feedback) is the only way that we ever try something new. As long as what we've been doing works even a little bit, we will continue doing it rather than risk trying something new that could be even better. Simply put, we need to fail if we are ever to ultimately succeed.

We've already mentioned Thomas Edison's 10,000 efforts to invent the electric light bulb. When asked how he felt about failing 9,000 times (he still hadn't "succeeded" yet), he said that he hadn't failed at all. He had succeeded in finding nine thousand ways that didn't work. This is an important attitude to have when working with innovative people. Those who cannot handle "failure" will never be able to cope with the stresses of creative work. Remember: Failure has two sides, one is instructive and even motivational, while the other is discouraging and exhausting.

Do It and Review It!

Goal setting is not to be treated as a long-term goal in itself. If you haven't already done so, begin today and write down your long-term goals for your career, your personal development (physical, intellectual, emotional, and spiritual/character), and your family. This may take some time, and you may wish to discuss it with your spouse or a close friend, but do it!

Once you have established major objectives in each of these areas and they have met the criteria discussed in this chapter, break them down into intermediate and short-term goals, until you have a daily program to achieve each goal. Once you've accomplished this for yourself, have your employees do the same for their goals. People need to feel good about doing things on a daily basis so that they can go home with the satisfaction that they have made some headway toward their intermediate and long-term goals.

Finally, remember that experience and circumstances tend to change one's outlook on things. Whether dealing with project or personal goals, review your goals regularly. Short- and intermediate-term goals should be reviewed at least monthly, and long-term goals need to be reviewed quarterly. Have your personnel review theirs regularly as well. You'll find it worthwhile to review each employee's goals at least semiannually and, probably, quarterly. Keep a copy of their goals to review with them.

As you review each goal, also review your progress toward achieving it. Where you have met or exceeded your expectations, congratulate yourself and keep up the good work. Where you have not met your expectations, try to determine why, then reassess your plan for achieving that goal. Ask yourself, "What have I learned?" This step is particularly important when reviewing your employees' goals. Let them know how pleased you are with their progress if they have met or exceeded goals. If they haven't, review the possible causes and work with them to overcome anything that is holding them back. If you determine that an individual's goals were too big, help him to bring those goals closer to reality so he can experience success. Reaffirm their goals and their motivation for accomplishing them. We'll review key motivations in Section VII.

Keep Your Balance

Make sure that you haven't made great strides in one area by sacrificing growth toward your other goals. Lack of balance in our goals is one of the greatest causes of failure further down the line, and a major source of stress and eventual burnout. Are your employees' goals balanced? Are they leaving enough time for their family? Remember, if an individual's personal needs aren't being met, they will eventually interfere with the quality of her work.

Another source of problems is the failure to budget the time necessary to meet a goal. Be sure that you leave both enough days and enough time in each day to accomplish any task that you set for yourself or for someone else. Even three projects that each take only four hours can be overwhelming if we expect someone to accomplish them within one day.

Other Employees

Because your innovative employees obtain much of their satisfaction from the nature of their work, it can be easy to forget that the same may not be true of your support staff (secretaries, stock personnel, etc.). However, without their help, your creative staff would accomplish little. Ironically, these support staff are usually the lowest paid employees in the company, but one clerk can completely destroy the work of years with a single slip of the pen. You may find it very helpful for either you or one of your managers to meet with these support staff and discuss their career and financial goals. Meet with them selectively to discuss things that are going right and things that could be improved. By doing this, they can help identify problem trends quickly and can often make excellent suggestions to increase overall office efficiency and profitability.

Help them establish and attain goals of their own, and reward them for good work. Their pay may be set by the company, but as a manager you have many ways of recognizing their work and showing appreciation.

Summary

Setting individual as well as project goals can be one of the most important and challenging tasks you face as a manager of innovative people. However, the efficiency of your department, as well as the overall effectiveness of the individuals within it, depends to a large extent on how well you do this. Without clear goals and milestones to measure progress, no project has much of a chance for success.

How to Communicate Effectively with Creative Personnel

Every individual has emotional needs that can act as a hidden agenda and affect his work. Being able to recognize those needs and meet them can radically increase the productivity of creative and noncreative employees alike.

This section provides a series of simple skills for increasing trust and leadership by communicating with people on their deepest levels.

➥ It includes a simple grid system for quickly categorizing and handling the hidden emotional agendas of both creative and noncreative personnel. (See Chapter 13.)

➥ It explores the importance of maintaining effective rapport through both conscious and unconscious communication with your creative employees and provides a series of techniques for building that rapport.

➥ It also explores the importance of thinking positively, a concept with far greater ramifications than just self-help.

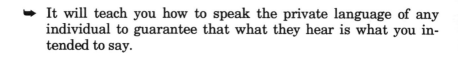 It will teach you how to speak the private language of any individual to guarantee that what they hear is what you intended to say.

Handling the "Prima Donna"

Like managers, creative employees can be divided into each of the four primary personality traits. By understanding which personality trait each employee exhibits, you can increase productivity by meeting your employees' emotional needs.

The Dictator/Prima Donna

According to some stereotypes, the antisocial prima donna (Dictator) represents the classic creative genius (Exhibit 16-1). In the movies, this individual prefers to work alone because lesser minds inhibit his creative flow. All he really needs to solve all of the world's problems is sufficient money and equipment and a slavishly loyal support staff to do his bidding. Note: To him, support staff includes his manager, whose sole responsibility is to provide funds and equipment when ordered by the creative genius. This individual thinks of innovation as a win-lose situation. As a result, he perceives management and other creative staff as prepared to resist his ideas and feels that he must overwhelm that

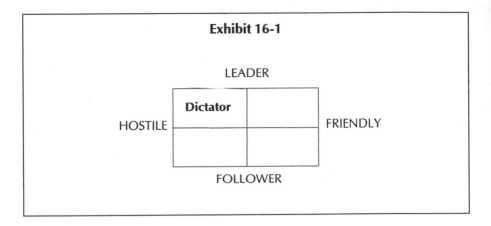

Exhibit 16-1

LEADER

Dictator

HOSTILE | FRIENDLY

FOLLOWER

resistance. He relates in an adversarial way and tends to use force and manipulation to obtain his desire, believing that *the end justifies the means.*

In the long run, his relationship style is at best self-defeating. While he may temporarily appear to succeed, his inability to work in concert with others robs him of the synergy that is generated when cooperating with other creative individuals. He is often hired because of some initial, well-publicized innovation (which itself is often the result of some synergistic collaboration with another individual) and then fails to produce any significant new idea thereafter.

Several directors of research and development at Fortune 500 companies have discussed this problem with us. They have communicated a strong sense of frustration over having built their R & D teams around well-vaunted creative geniuses fifteen years ago and obtained little in terms of new ideas since. It is this individual's credentials rather than his latest accomplishments that help him maintain his position. Because his credentials make him appear to be the logical choice for R & D, managers often assume that his failure to produce is their fault for not providing sufficient financial support. It is not surprising that this individual is rarely missed once senior management decides to reduce the R & D budget because his relationship style does little to build rapport and support the team effort.

This individual is often difficult to work with because he naturally assumes that he is more important than other members of the team. Hence, his needs should always be placed first, even over the needs of the group. If he is not given what he wants, he may make veiled threats about upcoming breakthroughs that will be hindered if he doesn't get his way. If he perceives weakness in a manager he may be openly disrespect-ful.

General Guidelines

There is little difficulty in dealing with *new* Dictator employees. Because they tend to be authority-oriented themselves, most Dictators will often respect and bend to any authority that they perceive as being greater than their own. A firm, friendly, no-nonsense stance will usually result in conformity to your standards and wishes. When a problem occurs, simply use the communications and rapport skills discussed in Chapters 21 to 24 and the counseling skills in Section VII.

The problem in dealing with the *successful* Dictator stems from the hesitation some managers feel about risking the loss of any prima donna because of his reputation and "past success," as well as any relationship he may have developed with other senior managers. In reality, there are several things that can be done to make life with such an individual less stressful. These will be repeated in greater detail in Chapters 28 and 29.

➤ When this individual is upset, establish rapport and use *fogging techniques* (found in Section VII) to calm him down and deter-mine the nature of the problem.

➤ Remember that the Dictator is motivated by a series of strong emotional needs. Look for ways to meet those needs that will allow him to feel special without threatening the smooth func-tioning of your department. In addition, utilize the motivational techniques found in Section VI.

➤ Remain firm and friendly. Dealing with a Dictator who is an employee isn't really that different from dealing with one as a peer or customer.

➤ Use the counseling techniques found in Section VII to correct his behavior and bring him into the team.

➤ If possible, assign him projects on which he can work indepen-dently.

Summary

The Dictator is the individual that most of us have liked the least. Overbearing and occasionally obnoxious, we tend to deal with him by avoiding him or giving in to his desires. It is now possible to work with him and to turn him into the most loyal and hard-working employee simply by meeting his needs.

Dealing with the
Bureaucratic Employee

In almost every organization, there seems to be at least one individual who is always prepared to tell you why something can't be done, or won't work. She may even have articles and books to prove that what you want to do is impossible. Unfortunately, she rarely seems to have any constructive ideas to offer as alternatives. However, despite her apparent negativity, this individual can be quite creative and is often trying to help. Who do you think comes up with all of the government's red tape? Encouraging that creativity is possible if you understand what drives this individual and how to use it to motivate her.

The key to working with this employee is to use her apparent rigidity in constructive ways, such as testing the feasibility of concepts or projects raised in an idea-generating session.

The Bureaucrat

This kind of creative employee is relatively rare. She does not relate well to others and resents authority, yet she will rarely buck authority openly. The Bureaucratic employee (Exhibit 17-1) is passive-aggressive in the way that she relates to people, and her resentment is frequently transparent within a short time. For example, when a requirement for a completely new product or approach is inaugurated, she has all the reasons why it won't work.

She feels that management and customers are like herself and don't trust really new ideas. She believes that they will move only when they are ready, and, hence, that there is little that she can do to influence them in favor of the new product or service. As a result, she resists completely new approaches to problems, whether they are marketing, engineering, production, or human resource problems.

Because of her distrust of radical changes, she is slow to make decisions, but will follow orders to the letter to avoid criticism. Often, the closest that she comes to success is in following specific directions to explore innovations within a very narrow area. However, if given very specific instructions and guidelines about what is desired, she can be very innovative in developing modifications of existing techniques or procedures. Because her innovative skills are best used only within very narrow frameworks, she appears to demonstrate little creativity or leadership and, in the end, is often relegated to being little more than someone who blindly follows instructions to the letter. Her behavior parallels that of the classic bureaucrat.

General Guidelines

While few managers are motivated to hire someone who demonstrates the characteristics of our Bureaucrat, it should be remembered that

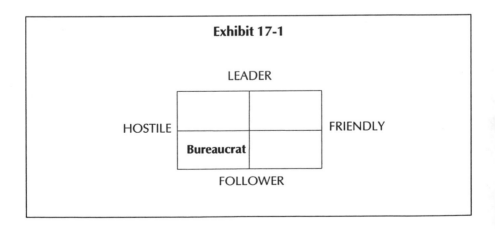

Exhibit 17-1

none of us has a personality that is always one way. During an interview, the Bureaucrat may have been enthusiastic and even appeared to be something of a Dictator, with an aggressive, gung-ho attitude. However, under pressure, many Dictators revert to bureaucratic behavior—and vice versa. Hence, the office Bureaucrat can become something of a bully to new employees or support staff that are unsure of themselves.

Let this individual know, early on, that a negative attitude is neither helpful nor acceptable in the department. While she is not expected to support every new idea or project, she should keep her negatives to herself unless specifically requested. Because this person does tend to look for the negative in situations, make use of this trait. During brain-storming sessions, have her remain silent during the generation of ideas because her negative attitude may discourage others from coming up with of ideas. However, when the generation period is completed, have her speak last and bring up all of the potential problems in each idea that has been discussed. Then, once a decision has been made, let her know that she will be expected to support it wholeheartedly. In this way, you can use her conservative attitude positively.

Be sure to give her firm goals and specific plans to attain those goals in each area of her work. Then follow up on a regular schedule. The regularity of the schedule will be important because it will provide a sense of security for her and enable her to plan for each deadline. Then be sure that you let her know how well she is progressing. If she is not making progress, use the tips given in Chapter 32, "Counseling Creative Employees," to give very specific advise about how she can improve. Make sure that she accepts responsibility for the changes she needs to make, as well as for her current failings.

Summary

The Bureaucratic personality is rarely perceived as being very creative. However, when given specific parameters to work within, she is capable of remarkable productivity. In addition, while often considered negative, she can become very enthusiastic about and loyal to projects on which she is participating.

The Socialite

18

Creative people are often characterized as being hardy individualists who work best alone in an isolated laboratory, but there are many who function effectively only when they are actively involved in a team effort. They are often very garrulous, and it may sometimes seem as though they spend more time socializing than working.

Because of their apparent need for interaction, these individuals are often labeled unproductive. They may even be seen as distracting others in the department from their work. However, their enthusiasm, as well as their apparent tendency to distract others, can be a valuable asset in developing synergy within any R & D team. In fact, of the four personality types presented, they are the ones most likely to successfully stimulate cross-pollination of ideas.

The Socialite

The Socialite (Exhibit 18-1) is an easy employee to hire. He is enthusiastic, warmly agreeable, friendly, and has great social skills. In fact,

143

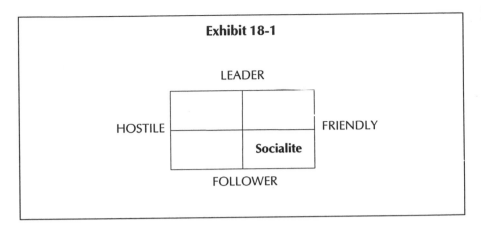

Exhibit 18-1

LEADER

HOSTILE

FRIENDLY

Socialite

FOLLOWER

during the hiring interview you may find that he is extremely enthusiastic about your company and the programs that you offer. He speaks easily and is very likable, generally making a good impression on everyone he meets.

When he first begins to work, he usually does so with gusto, anticipating success because he enjoys working on a team with his friends. He attempts to make friends with all of his co-workers. He is cheerful, congenial, and well liked around the office. His Socialite tendencies make him initially popular with management, his co-workers and customers because he appears to put their interests before his own. However, because he dislikes unpleasantness, he has a tendency to avoid making decisions or confronting a co-worker when he disagrees about a project. For example, he fails to point out errors or problems in a project for fear of offending other members of the team.

He often does not accept responsibility well and is also particularly vulnerable to rejection. As a result, he may avoid making presentations in which he will be expected to defend a project against strong resistance in higher management. At the same time, his relationship skills make him an excellent individual to work with customers or marketing. For example, one large chemical firm we spoke to sends its scientists to the field on a regular basis to work with customers on bringing new products to market. The socialite works particularly well in this kind of situation.

Most managers we spoke to emphasized the importance of providing private offices or work areas for creative personnel so they can avoid distractions. An excellent case in point, the Socialite needs easy access to others to meet his social needs, but too many distractions will have a greater negative impact on him than on any of the others.

General Guidelines

Work with him to establish specific daily and weekly performance goals for any project. Remember that his self-image is strongly dependent upon the opinions of others. Praise him when he meets the goals you've established together and encourage him to continue. Avoid publicly humiliating him if he fails to make the goals you have agreed upon. When making goals with him, remind him that you are asking no more of him than of *everyone else*.

Do not take his enthusiasm at face value. When you have completed a discussion with him, have him summarize what has been said, or ask him questions to determine whether or not he really understood you and accepted the goals. If not, probe to determine the nature of his doubts and deal with them. Keep him focused on the point being discussed since he may jump ahead of you as he becomes enthused with the topic being discussed. Use some of the other ideas provided in the section on motivation. He will need particular support when projects fail.

Remember that he needs to socialize. Because this can be very useful for stimulating creative interaction with other members of your staff, meet this need, but do not allow it to override productivity. When providing guidelines for new projects, be as specific as possible in giving their parameters. Firmly guide him through your expectations and be explicit in your recommendations. Don't take his enthusiasm and easy acceptance of the project at face value. Probe for underlying doubts.

Summary

Although warm and friendly and a pleasure to be around, the Socialite shares, with the Bureaucrat, the frustrating inability to make and act quickly on a decision. Hence, some planning and regular supervision is necessary to obtain his best work. In fact, this individual responds best to superiors who manage by walking around.

By appealing to their emotional needs for security and group approval, it is easier to gain their cooperation. Despite his weaknesses, this individual can not only be very productive himself, he can also increase the overall productivity of your department as he provokes synergistic interaction with other members of the staff.

The "Ideal" Creative Employee

In almost every creative team, one individual stands out as the natural leader. She seems self-confident, has lots of ideas, and seems naturally goal-oriented. Even better, she works well with others, listening to their ideas and asking and offering help as needed. She seems to have little difficulty convincing others of her ideas and makes an excellent team leader.

The Executive

This type of person may be the ideal creative individual. Essentially, she is self-confident and believes that virtually any problem can be solved if one applies enough effort and creativity to the task. The Executive (Exhibit 19-1) is likely to probe and explore each new project, problem, or assignment to understand and define all of its parameters before she begins to work on solutions. She works well with others and tends to take the lead in any discussion of a problem, providing ideas herself as well as listening to and building upon the ideas of others.

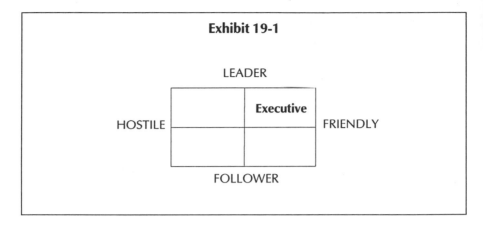

Exhibit 19-1

LEADER

HOSTILE   Executive   FRIENDLY

FOLLOWER

She is generally supportive of other members of the staff or team and shares her ideas freely with them. At the same time, she is not afraid to ask for their ideas for improvement of concepts or projects for which she is responsible. She is a good team player and makes an excellent and natural team leader.

These individuals expect you, their manager, to understand them, to meet their needs, and to communicate to them specifically what you expect and what support you will provide them in their efforts to meet your and their goals. In terms of receptivity, they are willing to listen and are open to new ideas and projects, but will often be impatient with vagueness. Do everything possible to involve them in the decision-making process while using open probes to determine their interests and concerns about any project.

Be assertive and walk them through the available parameters of new projects, answering their questions and explaining how the project or product on which they are working is expected to meet the specific needs of clients. These individuals will respond to respect and will return it with loyalty. They are also goal-oriented and can make decisions. They are emotionally secure and have a positive self-image that allows them to be open to others (*I'm OK. You're OK.*). As a result, they are often successful when working directly with a customer or even noncreative executives and managers within your firm.

General Guidelines

Again, always emphasize the end benefits of their efforts by showing how a project or product will help the company. Involve them in as many decisions surrounding a project as possible. In many ways, the Executive is, clearly, the easiest individual to work with. Once she is convinced of the benefits of a course of action she is well motivated, organized, and able to make and act on decisions.

Summary

Whether you are dealing with a Dictator, Bureaucrat, Socialite, or Executive, knowing the personality types of your employees can make life a lot easier for you as a manager. By meeting their emotional needs, you will find that it requires less effort to motivate them to cooperate with your goals. It will be much simpler to keep them happy and, as a result, more creative and productive. Now explore the mastery exercises below.

Mastery Exercise 19-1: Personality Traits

Read each of the following statements, and decide which psychological profile the individual speaking would fit into: Executive, Socialite, Bureaucrat, or Dictator. The answers can be found on the next page.

"We all know just how important it is to do exactly what is expected of you—no more and no less. A company ought to get what it pays for, and it doesn't pay us to make up new company policies."

"A department is run efficiently if all of the people are working in accord with one another. This virtually insures that the company is getting optimal performance."

"The company requires that you pay attention to both the needs of the individual and the objectives of the department. Neither is always right."

"There can be one leader on a project and one leader only. When I want your opinion I'll ask for it. Till then, just do what I told you. After all, I've been through these types of situations before."

This person's office is has pictures of various teams that he has participated in, family pictures, and mementoes of every office party ever attended. The placement of the seat is designed for easy, casual conversation.

This person's office is rather stark and bare. The seat probably has a high back and is arranged opposite you and slightly above the visitor's.

This person's office is somewhat stark but has company-oriented mementoes and plaques and awards placed throughout. It seems to be utilitarian.

This person's office is stuffed to the gills with papers that are so scattered and messy as to be unbelievable. The person's organizational system is to remember approximately on which side of the office something is located.

"I wonder where all of the competent people went to?" he asks. "The only way to get something done right is to do it yourself."

"I know that management and the union are seemingly on opposite sides of the fence. Let's get everybody together to see how we can resolve the situation for our mutual benefit."

Answers to Exercise 19-1: Four Personality Types

"We all know just how important it is to do exactly what is expected of you—no more and no less. A company ought to get what it pays for and it doesn't pay us to make up new company policies."
> Bureaucrat: shows a need to perform exactly what is expected and not to modify policies.

"A department is run efficiently if all of the people are working in accord with one another. This virtually insures that the company is getting optimal performance."
> Socialite: shows an emphasis on interpersonal relationships as the primary determinant of effectiveness.

"The company requires that you pay attention to both the needs of the individual and the objectives of the department. Neither is always right."
> Executive: shows a realization that there are two sides to the issue.

"There can be one leader on a project and one leader only. When I want your opinion I'll ask for it. Till then, just do what I told you. After all, I've been through these type of situations before."
> Dictator: shows a need for individualized command.

This person's office is has pictures of various teams that he has participated in, family pictures, and mementoes of every office party ever attended. The placement of the seat is designed for easy, casual conversation.

Socialite: shows an emphasis on group activities.

This person's office is rather stark and bare. The seat probably has a high back and is arranged opposite you and slightly above the visitor's.

Dictator: shows control implications in the seating arrangement.

This person's office is somewhat stark but has company-oriented mementoes and plaques and awards placed throughout. It seems to be utilitarian.

Probably an Executive, although it is too vague to tell. Remember that people do not always fall into a rigid category.

This person's office is stuffed to the gills with papers that are so scattered and messy as to be unbelievable. The person's organizational system is to remember approximately on which side of the office something is located.

Again, the information is too vague to categorize this person.

"I wonder where all of the competent people went to," he says. "The only way to get something done right is to do it yourself."

Dictator: shows insistence that he is the only competent person.

"I know that management and the union are seemingly on opposite sides of the fence. Let's get everybody together to see how we can resolve the situation for our mutual benefit."

Executive: shows a realization that there are two sides that deserve attention.

Personal Leadership and
Nonverbal Rapport

Perhaps one of the most important yet least understood and taught aspects of management is the concept of leadership. Today's graduate business schools teach their students how to manage finances and materials and tend to handle personnel as just another kind of material. Yet, any company's employees are its greatest asset. This is especially true in areas of creativity, where no amount of automation can take the place of the innovative individual.

Many managers are chosen from the ranks of successful business school graduates, but being successful in business school does not necessarily translate into being a good leader. Being a good leader requires the ability to communicate with your employees in such a way that they will desire to follow you and your company's policies. This is particularly important when you want to avoid using the carrot and the stick approach to encourage both obedience and loyalty.

As a manager, you are, by definition, an authority figure for the vast majority of people with whom you come into contact on a professional level. Because of this, some may feel intimidated or nervous. Those responses, or even the common situation in which people "mind their P's and Q's" in your presence, indicate that they are feeling at least mildly defensive and are NOT being totally open with you. Defensiveness is of particular importance when working with creative people, because it can affect their level of creativity. Wouldn't it be useful to have the skills that allow others consistently to feel very comfortable in your presence?

The secret is to communicate two things: a genuine interest in and concern for your employees and the ability to understand how they feel about things and what motivates them. Simply put, if you want someone to follow your lead, you must first establish what Robert Dilts refers to as a meaningful *rapport* with them. Let's explore that idea for a moment.

> "Who is the most fascinating person in the world? I am! At least to me. And the second most fascinating person is someone who is just like me. The more that they are like me, the more comfortable I am with them. Now, I don't mean someone who mimics me; that can be insulting if taken too far. But someone who thinks like me, who *speaks my language,* who sees things the way I do (even if he doesn't agree with me). That's someone I'm comfortable with, someone I'll listen to."
> [Quote attributed to anyone's unconscious mind.]

Have you ever met someone that you seemed to agree with entirely, but with whom you couldn't get comfortable? On the other hand, have you ever met someone with whom you seemed to have nothing in common, but were very comfortable with? We all have. The difference is that we had something called *rapport* with one and not with the other. That may have something to do with your selection of new employees. We are far more likely to hire someone with whom we identify than someone with whom we don't.

What is rapport? Rapport might be defined as the ability to step into someone else's skin and to experience things the way that they do, from their point of view. As such, it is very much like empathy and helps us to communicate our understanding and acceptance of the other person. Yet, the ability to develop rapport with another person goes far beyond the words that we use when we speak. In fact, some psychologists estimate that as much as 90 percent of communication occurs on an unconscious level and has little or nothing to do with what is being discussed. That is why it is possible to develop deep levels of rapport with someone with whom you disagree.

Have you noticed that some of us seem to just establish rapport naturally, while others have great difficulty? Frustrating, isn't it? Why is one person very popular, successful, and listened to very carefully, while another, who may be much more intelligent, is ignored and has difficulty developing relationships? One reason may be their level of interest in people, their *warmth* (see *Psychological Profiling* in Chapter 13).

If the second most fascinating person in the world is someone who is just like us, surely tied for second is someone who communicates a genuine interest in us. Whenever we really focus our attention on someone and try to understand what they are saying, we almost automatically begin to build rapport. How to develop, enhance, and maintain rapport on the unconscious level is the subject of the next few chapters.

Pacing

Essential to the development of unconscious rapport is a process called *pacing*. We pace another person when we are in physical, mental, and emotional alignment with him. Basically, it is a way of becoming similar to another person.

Since we respond to people on three primary levels (i.e., physical, mental, and emotional), people to whom we can relate on multiple levels often become our friends, or at least our employees. Those with whom we don't relate never get close to us and rarely get hired. One way to increase the chances of making someone a client or a friend, is to become as much like that person as possible. The same is true for getting them to follow your leadership.

We have already pointed out that you unconsciously use many techniques in building rapport whenever you genuinely pay attention to someone in whom you are interested. Unfortunately, things we do unconsciously we too often do inconsistently. As you learn to utilize these communication skills consciously, you will develop the ability to establish rapport consistently with whomever you wish, whenever you wish, and to deepen any rapport you have already established.

You should recognize that pacing is made up of a number of different aspects, no one of which is sufficient to accomplish your task by itself. *It is the combined effect of all of the methods of pacing that will virtually guarantee your ability to establish rapport with anyone you wish.* What we are saying is that no single pacing method will automatically enable you to establish rapport with another person. However, *the cumulative effect of these basic techniques will assist you in creating "chemistry" with virtually anyone that you wish.*

Positive Motivation

How wonderful it would be if we knew what made employees or customers tick. How much easier it would be to meet their needs. In fact, one of the most important puzzles that any manager is called upon to solve is how to motivate his personnel.

While money and recognition have traditionally been the most popular motivators among executives, they are rarely the most effective with employees. In addition, if you are dealing with salaried employees, using money as a reward may not be an available option for you. Fortunately, each of us is motivated by a combination of key themes that drive our behavior and are very easily ascertained once you know where to look. Some of these are fully explained in Section VI, "Leading and Motivating Creative Personnel." In addition, the sales applications of these themes are explained in detail in our sales book, *Consultative Selling Techniques for Financial Professionals.*

Once you understand the motivational themes that control our lives, people will become much easier to both understand and manage. Then, when motivational problems occur, you will be able to deal more effectively with the problem at hand. This is the mark of a true leader.

Physical Rapport

Have you ever been in a restaurant and without even hearing what's being said been able to tell who the friends and lovers were? Or those who were angry? How did you know? Unconsciously, we can tell who is in rapport and who is not. In this chapter we begin to explore the rapport-building process.

As we said before, whenever we are very interested in someone (or even just what they have to say), we tend to open ourselves, psychologically, to their influence. In doing so, we also tend to follow their lead and unconsciously seek deeper levels of rapport. Matching body postures is just one of the ways that we do this.

Matching Body Posture—Mirroring

We like those who are most like ourselves—literally and figuratively. Matching body posture is one of the easiest and most effective ways of unconsciously influencing someone.

You can see that matching is just what it seems to be. When you wish to establish rapport with someone, match, almost as a mirror image, their posture, breathing, and gestures. This doesn't mean that you have to be exact, and it certainly doesn't mean mimicking them by moving as they move (that would be noticeable and insulting). What it does mean is that if someone were watching you and the other person, they would notice many similarities in your posture and gestures.

When you first meet someone, observe how he sits and then sit the same way. If you allow him to sit first, it becomes easy to sit the same way. If you are already seated, simply readjust your posture after he sits. For example: Have you ever gone to a party and looked at three people sitting together on a couch? Interesting isn't it? They almost always sit the same way. And, if one of them changes, they all change. That's matching on an unconscious basis.

When someone with whom you are speaking adjusts, or changes, her posture, wait a few moments and then *casually* adjust your own posture to match hers. As long as you wait a moment first, your shift will rarely be noticeable. Remember, we are social beings and it is natural for us to establish rapport. As you sit, stand, or gesture like your employee, you communicate a shared means of expression to her on an unconscious basis. The way we sit, stand, and gesture are all means of communicating, and anyone who does them like we do is communicating like us in some way. Thus, they are already "speaking our language" at one level.

Mirroring may feel awkward at first. Sometimes it may even feel as though there are too many things to pay attention to at once. That's natural. What is ironic is that you already do this very well, at least part of the time, without thinking about it at all. With a little practice, you'll be able to do it whenever you wish without ever having to think about it.

Test it for yourself. During a conversation with a friend or family member, begin by matching them. Notice how the conversation progresses. Then, after a few minutes, change your posture and mismatch them as completely as possible, and notice what happens to the conversation. After just a few minutes, match them again and notice again what happens to the conversation. What differences did you notice? In yourself? In them? Fascinating, isn't it?

Now think about the implications of this concept when communicating with your staff or superiors. To a remarkable extent, people's receptivity to our ideas or wishes is dependent upon the level of rapport we share at that moment. The greater the level of rapport, the more open they are to our ideas. At the same time, the greater the level of rapport, the freer they will feel to share their ideas with us.

Initially, some people feel awkward following this procedure. However, after doing it a few times, it becomes automatic. You will soon find that your interactions with people are more comfortable and easygoing when you employ these techniques.

You may notice that the other person will sometimes shift his body posture so that you are no longer matched. Merely wait a few moments, and then *casually* change your position until you are again somewhat matched. The key is to do it casually and to be as subtle as possible.

Sometimes simple matching isn't enough. Occasionally, you will run into someone who is so restless, or fidgety, that it seems that they just can't sit still. Trying to continuously match them would not only be difficult, but would also make you uncomfortable. One technique for dealing with this is called "cross-matching."

Cross-Matching

When you are with someone who often shifts his body position, matching him move for move almost has to result in his becoming aware that you are mimicking him and could hurt the very rapport that you are trying to establish. To avoid this, while continuing to "match," we utilize a technique known as cross-matching, in which you match some part of your body to another part of your listener's body. For example:

- If the person with whom you are speaking is sitting with his legs crossed, cross your arms but keep your feet flat on the floor.
- If their arms are crossed, cross your wrists, your legs, or your ankles.
- An individual who leans back in his chair might be cross-matched by just leaning to the side and slightly back.
- If he puts his hand on his chin you can cross match him by putting your hand near your head. As long as your hand is in a *similar* position, you're fine.
- If you are interviewing someone who is sitting with their legs spread apart, you can cross-match him by having your arms open.

The real key to matching is adjusting your body so that you *resemble* the posture of the person with whom you are speaking. Now, what about that restless or fidgety individual?

➥ If he likes to slowly bounce or move his legs to some internal rhythm, tap your fingers at the same rate that he moves his legs. There is very little chance that he will become conscious of what you are doing. Yet, unconsciously, you are maintaining your rapport.

An alternative to tapping you fingers could be a slight, almost unnoticeable, movement of your head (like nodding your head slightly to their rhythm). Again, there is very little possibility that he will ever notice this minute movement. Yet, *his unconscious is aware,* and this awareness will correlate the rhythm of the two individual movements and will maintain or deepen your rapport.

Something this subtle might be difficult for a third person to observe. However, as long as you do this, you will increase the rapport that you need to develop effective communication and leadership.

Matching body posture to obtain rapport is a nice idea. But, how do you know that you've achieved your purpose? The next subsection will give you a procedure to "test for rapport."

Leading to Test for Rapport

Just how do you test to determine if you really have established rapport? One way to do this is through a process called "leading." To test via leading, follow these simple steps:

➥ Once you have matched a person's body posture for several minutes, change your posture slightly and wait a few moments (typically between 2 to 40 seconds) and notice if she readjusts her body posture to match yours. That is, once you change, does she follow your lead by repositioning herself?

➥ If she does, then you have established rapport on the unconscious level. If not, go back to matching her for a while, and then test again.

Note: It is important to realize that often over a half a minute will pass before she will follow your lead by changing her posture. Don't expect her to follow your lead immediately. You should also realize that it often takes several minutes of matching before you can successfully lead.

While verifying rapport is very useful, leading has several other important applications:

➨ You can lead an employee or customer to move from one posture to another. When they do this, the physiological change will often bring about a corresponding psychological change. For example: be aware of your own emotional changes as you conduct the following experiment.

A) Notice exactly how you are currently sitting or standing and the feelings that you associate with that body position.

B) Now change your posture to one that is either more relaxed or less relaxed and again notice any changes in your feelings.

C) Now, sit absolutely straight, and then allow yourself to sink into the chair. Again, notice your feelings.

In which position could you most easily carry on a casual conversation? In which would it be the most difficult?

Do you associate specific emotional states with certain body postures? Most people do. If people associate certain emotional or psychological states with corresponding physical states, then consider the ramifications of this thought: *You can influence your mental or emotional state just by changing your posture!*

Try it out. Take a moment and stand in the way that you stand when you are really proud of something you've accomplished. Be sure that if someone were watching you they would be able to tell that you were really proud of something. If appropriate for you, stand tall, throw your shoulders back and your chest out, and smile.

Notice how easy it becomes to suddenly remember the many times when you have felt proud of something you've done. Notice how those feelings return and how proud you begin to feel. Take a moment and relive one of those moments fully. Experience it now as if it were happening again. Remarkable, isn't it? How might this help you when making a presentation to your staff or superiors?

Now, change your posture and let your shoulders slump. Just slouch and let your chest sink. Lower your head and your gaze. What happens? Note how the intensity of the feeling changes. Now, return to your original "proud" position again. These positions, or postures, are good examples of kinesthetic "anchors" (See Chapter 6). These anchors allow you to modify your internal state by changing your body posture.

Leadership and Rapport

You have just demonstrated to yourself that you can change the way that you think and feel simply by changing the way you sit, stand, or even breath. Wouldn't it be useful to be able to lead your employees the same way? Now you can!

When you are speaking to an employee who is in a "negative" state (e.g., discouraged, angry, or any state that would keep them from listening openly and positively to what you are saying), you can *lead* them into a more positive state by following these simple steps:

- ➡ Establish rapport by matching your body to theirs.

- ➡ Gradually shift your body into a posture that will lead them into a different mental state as their own "anchors" take effect.

Remember that they may have different anchors from your own. So, if the first state that you lead them to is not an improvement, continue to lead them through different postures until you obtain the response that you desire. Here are some examples:

- ➡ You may wish to lead an anxious individual into a relaxed posture and state from a stiff or rigid posture and state. This will make it easier for him to work more effectively.

- ➡ Try leading an individual who is too relaxed into a posture and state normally associated with being excited and enthusiastic (e.g., sitting up straight, smiling, leaning slightly forward, and maintaining good eye contact).

- ➡ Lead an irritable employee or customer into a relaxed posture and state.

- ➡ Lead an indecisive person into a dynamic, decisive posture and state (e.g., the "proud" pose you experienced, above).

- ➡ Become aware of the postures, gestures, breathing, etc. of your staff when they are enthusiastic about a new idea or concept. The next time they seem discouraged about the progress of any project, lead them into their enthusiastic and creative posture.

As you combine leading their posture with leading their breathing and their rate of speech, you will be able to achieve even deeper levels of rapport and even greater influence with your staff.

Matching Breathing

Matching your rate of breathing to that of someone whom you are interviewing is one of the most powerful techniques for enhancing rapport. This is a simple technique whose impact occurs below the level of conscious awareness and, if combined with the previous techniques, can significantly increase your level of rapport. To match breathing, simply breath at the same rate as your client.

- If you are conversing, time your breathing to match the inhalations and exhalations of her speech rate, or time your sentences to match her breathing. This technique can be especially effective when speaking on the telephone, since it is one of the few things you can match over the phone.

- Watch the rise and fall of the person's chest or shoulders, since this correlates with their breathing. Note: When dealing with female employees and customers, focus on the shoulders or you may communicate the wrong message.

- Remember that there will be times when you do *not* wish to match someone's breathing (e.g., if they suffer from asthma or emphysema). When this occurs, use a cross-matching technique such as moving your head, finger, or foot at the same pace as their breathing.

Summary

The amount of productive innovation you develop in your department will depend a great deal upon how comfortable people are about coming to you with problems. Do they feel it is dangerous or safe to confess that they are running into road blocks in a project? You communicate an atmosphere of trust and acceptance or distrust and rejection all on a nonverbal level, just by the way you hold your body.

Hence, we're sure that you can see how matching and leading add an entirely new dimension to the concept of leadership. But when you think about it, isn't that what charisma consists of? Now, if matching someone's breathing, along with matching their posture, can significantly enhance the depth of your rapport, just imagine what you can accomplish if you really do "speak their language."

How Speed Affects Your Communication

One of the first steps in learning to "speak someone's language" is to match the speed and energy of their speech. Have you ever spoken with a person who talked so quickly that *you* felt rushed? How about a person who spoke so slowly that you wanted to try to speed them up? How did you feel as you conversed with them: comfortable or uncomfortable? How did you feel if that person was a superior, or an employee? At some level, most of us feel at least some form of discomfort when this happens. Even when we can't put our finger on just what is bothering us, it's obvious to us that something is wrong.

Think about it. If you feel uncomfortable when your boss or employee is too fast or too slow for you, she probably feels the same way. In the same way, if she's too slow for you, you're probably too fast for her. Now both of you are experiencing that slightly uncomfortable feeling. Even though you may not be consciously aware of it, such differences contribute to what we call "bad vibes."

Think about the traditional door-to-door saleswoman. She is almost always portrayed as speaking too quickly. It could be that she's just so excited about what she's selling that she gets carried away. Or, she may be afraid that if she doesn't get her message out fast her customer will slam the door before she finishes. Or, maybe she's just nervous. In any case, her rapid speech pattern can be self-defeating unless her customer speaks as quickly. The same is true for almost any kind of presentation.

Think about the last time you attended a meeting and the presenter spoke so rapidly that you became uncomfortable. While she was giving you fast-paced information, you may have needed time to think. However, to give you that time to think, she had to slow down. Did she? After all, it's not easy to listen to her *and* process what she's saying at the same time. If she didn't slow down, one of three things probably happened:

➡ You processed the information that you caught but didn't hear everything that she said.

➡ You listened to her but didn't get a chance to think about what she said.

➡ You tried to do both and ended up confused.

When you think about it, frustration is an almost inevitable result of any of those possibilities. After all, asking someone to just absorb information and make a decision without thinking about it doesn't show much respect for your listener and will frequently make her feel "pushed." At the same time, speaking too slowly can leave her bored and just as frustrated. Therefore:

Think about what effect your rate of speed might have on your employees during a meeting when you are presenting a new research project or marketing campaign. If you speak too quickly or too slowly for your staff you may lose most of them. Result: less interest and enthusiasm for the project or campaign. Remember, whenever you think, you need time to do it. If you get the time you need you can make a decision and act upon it. If you don't, you are likely to feel pressured and frustrated or confused. Show your employees the same thoughtful respect that you would like to be shown.

Of course, some people are very fast thinkers, even if they don't speak quickly. How can you tell when your listener is following you? Note her expression, the relevance of her questions, and the changes in her voice quality, speed, tone, or other things which might be indicators for her. Remember, if you speak slower than your listener, speed up. If you speak faster than she does, slow down.

Leading

In the last chapter we showed how you could test for rapport through leading. Once you have established rapport with someone, simply modify your posture slightly and see if she follows your lead. If she does, you have established rapport.

You can also test for rapport by modifying your speech. Once you have matched someone's rate, you can incrementally change your rate, making it either faster or slower, and see if she follows your lead. If she does, you have established rapport. She usually will, without even consciously becoming aware that she is doing so. Think of some of the ways this might help you:

- Increasing the effectiveness of any presentation.

- Building rapport during an employment interview.

- Making a proposal to your boss.

- Trying to calm down an employee or customer (initially, match her rate of speech and then lead her into a calmer state by gradually slowing your own rate of speech).

- Generate interest or excitement by speeding up your speech and increasing your energy. Remember the concept of anchors and body positioning. It also applies to speech.

Summary

Whether you match posture or speech, your behavior sends an important message to your listener. If you want to lead her around to your way of thinking, you'll become more effective the more levels on which you match.

Positive Speech—
Positive Attitude

So much of our ability to be innovative depends upon our attitude. When we feel confident and positive, we know that we can solve any problem and our creative juices flow. Unfortunately, when we feel discouraged and negative, it sometimes seems as though someone has shut off our creative ability. The way we think affects how creative we are. The way people speak to us and we speak to ourselves affects how we think. Most managers we interviewed considered a positive attitude one of the most important traits to look for when hiring creative staff or other managers.

How many times has someone told you, "Don't worry?" What did you do? You worried! After all, "What am I supposed to not worry about?" The problem is that to not do something, we have to think about doing it first, and then add DON'T. Doesn't help much, does it. Try this: DON'T THINK ABOUT A GREEN GIRAFFE! How did it work? If you're like most of us, you thought about a green giraffe, even if only for a microsecond, before moving on to something else.

Interesting isn't it? When you are on a diet, what are you supposed to NOT think about? Food, right? But what is almost every waking thought filled with? Food! The harder we try to push the thought out of our heads, the more attention we must focus on the thought (food) to do it. No wonder so many of us have difficulty "losing weight." The point is that in order to NOT think of something, you HAVE TO think about it first. That's because our language mediates the way we think. Remember, we communicate with ourselves, and communication is the purpose of language.

Here's another thought; what do you do when you lose something? You look for it until you find it. For many of us, the same thing happens when we lose weight. We seem to search until we have not only found every pound that we've lost, but also a few more that we weren't even looking for.

Considering the previous comments, have you thought about the effect of negative statements on your employees?

"Don't worry about the project."

The employee has to think about potential problems in the project in order to NOT WORRY about them. The probability that he will become concerned about problems with the project increases. After all, why did you bring it up unless you thought that there might be a potential problem? Makes sense, doesn't it? How about a few others like:

"Don't be late!"

"Don't forget about tomorrow's meeting with marketing."

"Don't make a decision until you've heard what our research department has to say."

This may explain a lot of misunderstandings and "surprises" that occur with employees and customers who forget something important or bring up concerns about future projects. All that they are doing is exactly what we directed them to do unconsciously. We literally set ourselves up to obtain the very results that we wished to avoid.

Think about what might happen differently if we speak in positive terms. We might say:

"Be on time."

"Remember tomorrow's meeting with marketing."

"You can depend upon the research department."

Our words are very powerful because they can direct the thoughts and memories of our listeners (especially when we're the listener). These thoughts and memories then influence their attitudes, behaviors and beliefs. If we accept that our unconscious mind cannot deal in negatives (try to think of nothing), *or* that our minds have to briefly focus upon the unwanted concept in order to make sense of a negative statement, then we get the following communications formula: The Original Statement (OS) Minus the Negation (N) Equals the Unconscious Message Received (UMR).

$$OS - N = UMR$$

This means that a negative statement becomes unconsciously transformed into the opposite of what we intended, whether we are talking to ourselves (thinking) or to someone else. For Example:

Do not feel bad. – Not = Do feel bad.

Do not forget. – Not = Do forget.

I do not want to be late. – Not = I do want to be late.

Do not worry about the next delivery. – Not = Do worry about the next delivery.

Summary

It's obvious how easily we can unwittingly program ourselves and others to fail to obtain our objectives. A positive attitude is absolutely essential if you are to maintain faith in the projects you supervise or engender that same faith in your creative staff. Little kills innovation quicker than a negative attitude. Since our speech is a reflection of how we think, speaking in positives is much more effective.

Speaking the Language of Thoughts

We've mentioned the concept of "speaking someone's language" several times. So far, we've shown how the nonverbal component of communication, that is, everything that we do (how we sit, stand, and breathe, and even how fast we speak), affects our ability to convey the idea that we are just like them. Now let's examine language itself and the ways even the words people use tell us something about the way they think.

Have you ever heard someone say, "It LOOKS good to me" or "It SOUNDS good to me" or "It FEELS good to me." Phrases like these, as well as others like them, provide important information about how people think or process information. By learning to recognize and use the clues that people give you about how they think, you can communicate so that they will perceive you as being "just like them."

Before continuing, let's review for a moment. In Chapters 7 and 8, we discussed the concept that each of us processes and assigns meaning to data based upon sensory interpretation. Most of us have the tendency think in terms (use vocabulary) that are consistent with our sensory preferences. Some of us think by *seeing* images in our mind, others by

171

discussing a concept with ourselves to *hear* how it sounds, while still others need to determine how something *feels*. Regardless of how we process information (visually, auditorily, or kinesthetically/with feelings), we tend to verbalize our thoughts using words and phrases that most closely match how we think.

Although we are born with five senses, as we mature we begin to rely on one or two more than the others. Hence, we develop a tendency to remember that sensory aspect of an experience more completely than the others. For example, if we tend to rely on our sight, we are more likely to remember the visual aspects of an experience. As a result, when we relate it to someone else, we will tend to use visual terms to describe it. The same would be true when relying upon the other senses. For example:

➡ "I think that my favorite memory of spring is of the *beautiful colors* that *appear* as the trees and flowers come into bloom. You can *see* it everywhere, even as you *watch* the birds return for the summer, their *colors* enhanced as they prepare to mate." (visual)

➡ "I think that my favorite memory of spring is of the *sound* of children playing in the parks after a silent winter. You can *hear* spring everywhere, even as you *listen* for the first *song* of the robin building its nest, and the *buzz* of the honey bee moving from flower to flower." (auditory)

➡ "I think that my favorite memory of spring is of the first *sensation* of *warmth* returning in the spring sun after a *cold* winter. You can *smell* the flowers and the trees and *feel* the rebirth of the world around you." (kinesthetic)

Of course, some experiences will dominate a specific sense regardless of which one we tend to rely on. For example: a cold shower would dominate the kinesthetic sense, while a symphony would compel the auditory, and a rainbow, the visual. Because of that, even a person who relies primarily on his sight will sometimes use auditory and kinesthetic terms.

Remember, once we begin to rely on one sense over the others, the data received through that sense tends to dominate our thought processes. As a result, we may even begin to "specialize" in that sensory mode in the way that we think.

Since we understand the familiar more quickly than the unfamiliar, we also "understand" words and phrases that most closely correspond to those that we use in our thinking process. In short, something as simple as our choice of words can make the difference between whether or not we are understood by others. For example: if your listener uses words and phrases that are primarily visual (sight-oriented), and you use phrases that are primarily auditory (sound-oriented), you may actually confuse them. We call these sensory-oriented words "predicates."

In the same way, if you want to communicate clearly with someone who uses a particular sensory orientation in his thinking, you will be most successful if you use sensory-oriented words that match the way that he processes the information. Try it! You'll be amazed at the improvement in understanding that occurs when you match predicates, compared to the difficulty created when they are mismatched.

To illustrate this point, read the following scripts of a discussion between a product engineer and his manager. After you finish them, determine which individual you think has the best chance of continuing the presentation.

Reading I

#1:   I just came across a report on that new process we've been examining that looks interesting. If you have a moment, I'd like to show it to you.

Manager: Sounds interesting. I'd like to hear some more.

#1:   Well, I just saw something that shows that this process is very cost effective.

Manager: What do you mean? I've heard that the process is really expensive.

#1:   Yet, this technical financial report clearly shows that it has really improved, which is why you . . .

(Manager interrupts.)

Manager: My gut reaction is that it hasn't changed at all.

#1:   What have you seen to make you think that way. I perceive the change as very positive.

Manager: Well, I've been hearing just the opposite.

#1:   Look, I want to show you a few things which should give
           you a better picture.

What was your gut feeling as you read this dialogue? Were you
comfortable, or did you feel that, somehow, the engineer and his manager just weren't on the same wavelength? Go back and read it again,
then go on to Reading II.

Reading II

#2:   I just came across a report on that new process we've been
           examining that looks interesting. If you have a moment,
           I'd like to show it to you.

Manager: Sounds interesting. I'd like to hear some more.

#2:   Well, I just heard something that states that this process
           is very cost effective.

Manager: What do you mean? I've heard that the process is really
           quite expensive.

#2:   Yet, this technical report clearly states that it has really
           improved, which is why you . . .

(Manager interrupts.)

Manager: My gut reaction is that it hasn't changed at all.

#2:   What have you heard to make you think that way? I feel
           the change is very positive.

Manager: Well, I've been hearing just the opposite.

#2:   Listen, I want to tell you a few things which should give
           you a better feeling.

Which engineer do you think has the better chance to continue the
conversation? Most people think that engineer 2 has the better chance.
They usually comment that engineer 1 was more confrontive and aggressive, while engineer 2 is usually labeled as being more supportive,
understanding, and responsive.
    Let's look at the two conversations again and compare them word
for word.

#1:   I just came across a report on that new process

#2:   I just came across a report on that new process

#1:   we've been examining that looks interesting. If

#2:   we've been examining that looks interesting. If

#1:   you have a moment, I'd like to show it to you.

#2:   you have a moment, I'd like to show it to you.

Manager: *Sounds* interesting. I'd like to hear some more.

#1:   Well, I just *saw* something that *shows* that

#2:   Well, I just *heard* something that *states* that

#1:   this process is very cost effective.

#2:   this process is very cost effective.

Manager: What do you mean? I've *heard* that it's really very expen-
            sive.

#1:   Yet, this technical report clearly *shows* that

#2:   Yet, this technical report clearly *states* that

#1:   it has really improved, which is why you . . .

#2:   it has really improved, which is why you . . .

(Manager interrupts.)

Manager: My *gut reaction* is that it hasn't changed at all.

#1:   What have you *seen* to make you *think* that way?

#2:   What have you *heard* to make you *think* that way?

#1:	I *perceive* the change as very positive.
#2:	I *feel* the change is very positive.

Manager:	Well, I've been *hearing* just the opposite.

#1:	*Look,* I want to *show* you a few things which
#2:	*Listen,* I want to *tell* you a few things which

#1:	should give you a better *picture.*
#2:	should give you a better *feeling.*

If you're like most people, after a second reading you're amazed that the mere change of sensory-oriented words (mismatched by engineer 1 and matched by engineer 2) makes all of the difference. The change in response occurs outside of conscious awareness. You can see for yourself the difference that matching someone's sensory-oriented words can make in virtually any situation.

For example: Someone from marketing approaches you to discuss a proposal for a new product that one of your company's customers needs, and says, "I've been *looking over* this proposal and I'm sure that you'll agree that it *shows* excellent potential. Let's take a minute and I'll put you in the *picture."* You might respond in any one of several ways; such as:

A) "It certainly *looks* good to me. Have you *shown* it to anyone else in the department, yet?"

or

B) "It certainly *sounds* good to me. Have you *discussed* it with anyone else in the department, yet?"

or

C) "It certainly *feels* good to me. Have you shared your *grasp* of it with anyone else in the department, yet?"

All three responses *mean* essentially the same thing, don't they? But note the difference. Which response most closely matches the way the proposal was presented? The first response. The other two responses mismatch the speaker and may actually result in a misunderstanding or in confusing him. You might say that the last two responses might convince the speaker that you just can't *see* what he's getting at.

If you've ever tried to learn a foreign language you can probably recall how you had to mentally translate into English when someone spoke in that language. Pretty frustrating, wasn't it? Whenever someone speaks to us using sensory-oriented words that are different from our own (e.g., if we're speaking in visual terms and they say something in auditory or kinesthetic terms), we have to unconsciously translate what they are saying into our terms. This takes a moment and can confuse us. They're not "speaking our language." At this point, we can either attempt to shift gears and speak in their terms, or allow ourselves to become frustrated and annoyed. Which option we choose will depend upon how important it is to make that person comfortable. For example:

➡ Have you ever explained something very "clearly" to an employee only to have him respond with confusion? Did his understanding improve the second or third time that you "explained?" If not, it may not be that he is being stupid. Rather, it is possible that the two of you were "speaking" different languages and that he just wasn't "grasping" what you were "saying." Notice the predicates placed in quotes in the previous sentences. If you were using one set of predicates (perhaps visual), while he was using another set (such as auditory), your visual concepts may have caused his confusion.

Before we can ask an employee to be innovative, we have to communicate clearly the parameters of the problem we need him to solve. Unfortunately, if we mismatch his language, we also mismatch the way he will try to conceptualize the very ideas we wish him to explore. (See chapter note on page 183.)

Leadership consists of selling your ideas to your employees. Effective management consists of selling your ideas to your employees, your customers, and your superiors. Matching predicates allows even more effective communication and can strengthen your ability to lead your employees. Literally and figuratively, matching predicates allows you to speak the same language. Hence, if you want to lead someone, speaking their language will greatly increase your effectiveness. Listen for the predicate system an individual uses before giving directions or answering a question. Then match it. You'll probably get a much more satisfying response.

Unspecified Predicates

Since mismatching someone's predicates can lead to confusion and misunderstanding, how do you open a conversation before you know their sensory preference? Just as there are predicates that match a particular sensory orientation, there are others that are neutral and that can be used with any orientation. We call these words "unspecified," and they can be very useful when opening a conversation with someone new. For example:

> ➡ "Mr. Jones, our department *anticipates* significant growth over the next year that we think will be very exciting. As you *contemplate* this, I hope you'll *consider* joining us."

For your convenience, we have provided a brief listing of sensory-oriented, or predicate, words and phrases below.

Sensory-Oriented Words [Predicates]

Visual	Auditory	Kinesthetic	Unspecified
Aim	Announce	Active	Accept
Angle	Articulate	Affective	Activate
Appear	Audible	Bearable	Admonish
Aspect	Boisterous	Callous	Advise
Clarity	Communicate	Charge	Allow
Clear	Converse	Concrete	Anticipate
Cognizant	Discuss	Dull	Assume
Conspicuous	Dissonant	Emotional	Believe
Examine	Divulge	Feel	Cogitate
Focus	Earful	Firm	Communicate
Foresee	Earshot	Flow	Comprehend
Glance	Enunciate	Foundation	Conceive
Hindsight	Inquire	Grasp	Conceptualize
Horizon	Interview	Grip	Consider
Illusion	Hear	Handle	Contemplate
Illustrate	Listen	Hanging	Create
Image	Loud	Hassle	Decide

Visual	Auditory	Kinesthetic	Unspecified
Imagine	Mention	Heated	Deliberate
Inspect	Noise	Hold	Depend
Looks	Oral	Hot	Determine
Notice	Proclaim	Hunch	Develop
Obscure	Pronounce	Hustle	Direct
Observe	Remark	Intuition	Discover
Obvious	Report	Lukewarm	Evaluate
Outlook	Resonate	Motion	Help
Perception	Ring	Moves	Imagine
Perspective	Roar	Muddled	Indicate
Picture	Rumor	Numb	Influence
Pinpoint	Say	Panicky	Judge
Regard	Scream	Pressure	Know
Scope	Screech	Rush	Manage
Scrutinize	Silence	Sensitive	Mediate
Scene	Shrill	Set	Motivate
See	Speak	Shallow	Permit
Show	Speech	Shift	Plan
Sight	Sound	Soft	Ponder
Sketchy	Squeal	Softly	Prepare
Survey	State	Solid	Prove
Vague	Tell	Stir	Reckon
View	Tone	Stress	Repeat
Vision	Tune	Structured	Resolve
Vista	Vocal	Touch	Think
Watch	Volume	Warm	Understand

Sensory-Oriented [Predicate] Phrases

Visual	Auditory	Kinesthetic
An eyeful	Blabber mouth	All washed up
Appears to be	Clear as a bell	Boils down to
Bird's eye view	Clearly expressed	Chip off the old block
Catch a glimpse of	Call on	Come to grips with
Clear-cut	Describe in detail	Cool/Calm/Collected
Dim view	Earful	Firm foundation
Eye to eye	Express yourself	Floating on thin air
Flashed on	Give an account of	Get a handle on

Visual	Auditory	Kinesthetic
Get a perspective on	Give me your ear	Get a load of this
Get a scope on	Heard voices	Get the drift of
Hazy idea	Hidden message	Get your goat
In light of	Hold your tongue	Hand-in-hand
In person	Idle talk	Hang in there
In view of	Idle tongue	Heated argument
Looks like	Inquire into	Hold it
Make a scene	Keynote speaker	Hold on
Mental image/picture	Loud and clear	Hot-head
Mind's eye	Power of speech	Keep your shirt on
Naked eye	Purrs like a kitten	Lay cards on the table
Paint a picture	Outspoken	Light-headed
Photographic memory	Rap session	Moment of panic
Plainly see	Rings a bell	Not following you
Pretty as a picture	State your purpose	Pull some strings
See to it	Tattletale	Sharp as a tack
Short-sighted	To tell the truth	Slipped my mind
Showing off	Tongue-tied	Smooth operator
Sight for sore eyes	Tuned in/out	So-so
Staring off in space	Unheard of	Start from scratch
Take a peek	Utterly	Stiff upper lip
Tunnel vision	Voiced an opinion	Stuffed shirt
Up front	Within hearing range	Topsy-turvy
Well-defined	Word for Word	Underhanded

Being able to "speak their language" by matching predicates is valuable in virtually every situation in which it is important for us to relate to another person. Do you have an employee that has previously been difficult to communicate with? You know, someone who doesn't:

See what you're *showing* him.

Hear what you're *saying.*

Grasp your *meaning.*

Try matching their predicates and see what a difference it makes, not only in your communication, but also in your relationship.

Summary

Charisma is the level of rapport that others feel with you, and your ability to speak their language is critical to that rapport. In addition, matching predicates can radically increase the chances of their understanding and accepting something that you are trying to tell them.

Mastery Exercise 23-1

Read each of the following, and decide which sensory mode is being used. Underline the key words.

"Let's take a look at all sides of the proposal and decide which avenue is most attractive."

"What we have here is a failure to communicate. Everyone's always just talking about what they want, but they never seem to get it down on paper. Talk is cheap, but let me have some time to study the figures. Then I'll know whether or not I'm interested."

"Did you ever get the sense that they don't know exactly what's coming down? They move their mouths, but seem to be missing the entire idea."

"I think that we should consider the proposal very carefully. There are numerous points that need to be pondered."

Exercise 23-2:

Choose the best response for each of the following statements.

"After I read your report, I'll want to speak with a few people on the project to get their input. Based upon their comments, I'll know where we need to go next."

A: "Let me illustrate what we're doing with a few charts that you should find interesting. Then I'd like to show you around the project to help you get a better picture of what we're doing."

B: "I'm sure that you'll get a good feeling once you read over the report. There are a lot of excellent things that people are saying about the project."

C: "After you get a sense of what is going on I'll show you a few things that will make you feel even better."

D: "Once you've read the report, I'll call together a few of the staff to discuss the project and answer any questions you may have before deciding on our next move."

Answers to Exercise 23-1

"Let's take a LOOK at all sides of the proposal and decide which avenue is most ATTRACTIVE."
Obviously, visual.

"What we have here is a failure to COMMUNICATE. Everyone's always just TALKING about what they want, but they never seem to GET IT DOWN ON PAPER. TALK is cheap, but let me have some time to STUDY THE FIGURES. Then I'll know whether or not I'm interested."
This person has both an Auditory and Visual orientation. It is interesting that the need to see it is a dominant theme.

"Did you ever get the SENSE that they don't know exactly what's COMING DOWN? They MOVE THEIR MOUTHS, but seem to be MISSING the entire idea."
Kinesthetic.

"I THINK that we should CONSIDER the proposal very carefully. There are numerous points that need to be PONDERED."
Unspecified.

Answers to Exercise 23-2

"After I look over the literature, I want to speak with a few people who already own the product. Based upon how satisfied they are, I'll know whether the literature is telling the truth."

A: "Let me show you some information which you should find interesting. Then I'll relate some comments from satisfied customers which should help."

B: "I'm sure that you'll get a good feeling once you read over the literature. There are a lot of excellent things that people are saying."

C: "After you get a sense of what is going on I'll show you a few things that will make you feel even better."

D: "I can see that once you read some of the literature that you'll be able to make a decision based on a positive gut reaction."

Chapter Note: Over the past ten years the authors have conducted the following exercise with over 20,000 people. Each person is asked to listen while three houses are described. One house is described entirely in visual terms, the second entirely in auditory terms, and the third entirely in kinesthetic/feeling terms. Afterwards, they are asked which house they preferred. Approximately one third of the group prefers each house. However, when questioned further, over one half of the group *actively disliked* at least one of the houses. They were then told that they had actually chosen between three descriptions of *the same house*. When you think about it, the implications for making a presentation are staggering!

Speaking the Private Language of the Innovator

Have you ever felt that you and one of your staff were speaking two different languages? Although the words were all English, you felt certain they no longer meant what you thought they meant. Frustrating, isn't it? Yet this happens to all of us sometimes. Maybe that's why we all chuckle when we see this sign on someone's desk.

> **I know you think you understand what you thought I said. But I'm not sure you realize that what you heard is not what I meant.**

Here is just such a conversation between a job applicant and an interviewer:

Interviewer: We're looking for a person who is absolutely honest and can be trusted around important data. I'm sure that you're familiar with industrial espionage.

Applicant:	That's me. I've always been known for my absolute honesty. You can ask any of my previous employers. There have been many times when confidential matters were discussed. I can assure you that I am not only the soul of discretion, I am constantly alert to the possibilities of information leakage.
Interviewer:	You do look honest. However, the position that I'm trying to fill requires a person who can work alone and who is a self-starter. There are times when little or no direction beyond the barest outline can be offered, so the ideal candidate would also have to take the initiative to creatively solve any unusual problems that may occur.
Applicant:	I also appreciate those qualities in others because I've always prided myself on having them and, unfortunately, find that relatively few people have them. I've spent the majority of time in positions where working alone was normal. If it were not for a high degree of self-motivation and creativity as well as a personal desire for excellence, some of my tasks would not have been completed otherwise. I can assure you that I am a self-starter and highly motivated to succeed.

As for the ability to take the initiative, let me respond by letting you know that I once received a company commendation for handling an unexpected problem in an expeditious manner. I know how to follow the rules, and I also know when to make exceptions. |
| Interviewer: | Well, enough for now. Please send us a completed resume. You are certainly a strong candidate for this position. |
| Applicant: | Thank you very much. It will be in the mail tomorrow. I am definitely interested in being associated with this corporation. |

Interviewer to Vice President of Research and Development:
I think I've found our candidate for manager of new product development.

Applicant to Spouse:
Honey, I think I got the job as head of security!

"I know that you think you understand what you thought I said. But I'm not to sure that you realize that what you heard is not what I meant." If this interview weren't so common it would be funny. However, situations of this sort occur all of the time.

There are times when precise communication is imperative, when a miscommunication can be detrimental. At these times, it becomes important to insure that the message was transmitted clearly and concisely. To avoid misunderstandings, it is useful to have a set of specific tools that insure precise communication. These techniques, associated with effective questioning, are very important to any individual, but they are particularly important to you, a manager of creative people.

The ability to communicate effectively presupposes that we have a relatively good understanding of what the other person is trying to say. Yet many studies on communication suggest that approximately ninety percent of all communication problems occur because we "assume" that the other person knows what we are talking about.

Some of the common assumptions in everyday language may come back to haunt us. That's the bad news. The good news is that this chapter will provide a number of very effective tools to deal with this common problem. You'll be able to employ these techniques with your employees, superiors, customers, friends, and family. The techniques are universal in their application and are derived from state-of-the-art cognitive psychology. These techniques are not something that you would normally use in day-to-day conversations. Their purpose is to both impart and receive specific and exact information when it is necessary to clarify what is being said. It is important to know both *how* and *what* to clarify.

There are certain language patterns that are so pervasive that, when one occurs, we fail to hear it because it is so common. Becoming aware of them is first step to more effective communication. One of the most common errors is to make the assumption that the words we use mean the same thing to our listener as they do to us, and vice versa. We opened the chapter with an example of such an assumption and the danger inherent in it. Here is another example that has significant applications to virtually all businesses:

"Service" is one of the most overused words in business. When buying a piece of equipment for your department, you might say, "I want good service." The salesperson, of course, replies,

"I'll give you great service." "Good service" to you may mean having a repairman out within thirty minutes of your call. However, the salesperson may think that twenty-four hours is exemplary, and the customer service department may be happy, given their volume, with a one-week turnaround. Each person could sincerely do their absolute best and be thoroughly proud of how well they had done, while you might end up being completely dissatisfied. Unless the salesperson knows exactly what you want, he probably won't provide it. Unless the salesperson knows what the customer service department can deliver, neither he nor you can win. Little things like this can ruin a relationship.

"Service" is one of those vague words that has a different meaning for each person who utters it. Other words that are equally vague are: comfortable, satisfaction, safety, and risk.

The words "creative" or "innovative" also mean different things to different people. What do these words mean to each member of your department? Their work and performance is based on their (unconscious) definitions of these words. Do they match yours? Can they be redefined? Later in the chapter, we'll discuss such "fuzzy," undefined words.

The typical response to the comment, "I feel satisfied," is, "I know what you mean." That's impossible! The other person can only have a vague idea of what is meant because the word "satisfied" represents an internal state. It is interesting to realize that many people automatically assume that you have the same meaning, or connotation, for words that they do.

It's important to understand the difference between a word's denotations (dictionary definitions) and its connotations (the emotional meanings we each assign to it). For example: the word, "family," has the same denotation for everyone. The dictionary defines a "family" as "a social unit consisting of parents and the children that they rear," or "a group of people related by ancestry or marriage." However, the *emotional meaning* of the word "family" may vary widely, including:

➡ A warm, nurturing environment in which one was raised.

➡ A place where an alcoholic father physically or sexually abused one.

➡ A place that had no father (or no mother).

➡ An idealized concept in the mind of one who was raised without a family.

Obviously, anyone using the word "family" in an effort to communicate something might find himself obtaining a very unexpected response, depending upon the experiences of the listener. Hence, skills that help you ensure that you correctly hear and understand what someone is saying can be very important. This chapter started with a description of an interviewer and an applicant both using the same words with entirely different meanings and interpretations. Although it was quite exaggerated, situations of this sort do occur.

The basic problem results from the fact that people naturally delete, distort or even overgeneralize information. Although rather immaterial most of the time, on occasion, failure to get complete and accurate information can result in serious problems.

You'll probably find that you already employ many of the techniques listed here. Many of them are based on natural language patterns that are only called into play in relatively rare instances. In many ways, the questioning techniques that you are about to learn are really a sophisticated way of saying "Huh?" These techniques will help you:

➡ Resolve organizational problems more quickly.

➡ Deal with interpersonal conflict.

➡ Understand and deal with the personal problems of employees.

➡ Clear up confusion (muddied thinking).

➡ Deal with distraught employees or customers (when combined with other techniques not yet introduced).

➡ Clarify legal issues.

➡ Conduct effective interviews.

People often delete, distort, or overgeneralize information in their head. This is true of everyone and occurs on an unconscious level. Rather than go through lengthy psychological proofs, lets just say that it is a common problem that you will face on a regular basis. For instance, if an employee told you: "They said that I had better get it resolved to their satisfaction soon." Your response might be, "Huh?" After your initial reaction you would still have to determine:

- Who are "they"?
- What is "it" that needs to be resolved?
- What needs to happen for them to be "satisfied"?
- The meaning of the implied threat behind, "better get it resolved."
- What does "soon" mean? An hour? A week?

In this example your employee deleted information needed for you to understand what was really going on. He needs to provide you with more explicit information about the meaning of some of the key words.

We know, intuitively, that "satisfying" one person is not necessarily the same as "satisfying" another. One person may merely desire an apology, another may need specific operational actions to be taken, while still others may require some combination of both, plus other things. Given the specific example, we also know that finding out the specific criteria needed to satisfy this customer would be important. After all, what a customer wants may or may not be possible (or even reasonable). However, until the issue is addressed, we have an angry customer on our hands who has implied an undesirable next step. The nature of that next step has yet to be determined.

When taking the same concept and applying it to coaching, counseling, and performance issues, we find that similar situations arise when employees say that they have "motivation" or need more job "satisfaction." Each person using the word means something different by it. As we explore motivational issues in Section VI, we will discuss the need to refine our understanding of what motivates our employees. Surprising as it may seem, most people have little idea of what actually motivates them.

One Cause of Burnout

Have you ever seen people burn themselves out? Work so hard that they seemingly can't see straight? Work so hard that they become both inefficient and ineffective? Those people are "driven" by some internal motivation that is getting in their way. And wouldn't it be great if we were able to install some of that internal drive in other employees who just sit around doing nothing.

"I *have to* get this done by tomorrow." "If this doesn't get done there will be trouble." "We need to do this." These are statements that represent a psychological imperative that is driving their behavior or thoughts. It has created a need that *must,* or *ought to,* or *should* be fulfilled. The consequences of not performing the action are intimidating. But, are they really?

So, What? What's the Problem?

Often, people give something a significantly higher priority than it actually deserves. They "have to" do something, even if it's to the detriment of something else. They "must," for instance, work on the XYZ project, even though the phone is ringing and a dozen other problems are not being addressed. At these times, such an individual becomes very narrow-minded and very focused. Sometimes this is good, but sometimes it isn't.

The situation just described would drive most department managers crazy wondering what is wrong with this individual's priorities. We might ask her what she is doing and why. Then, depending upon the answer (there may be contingencies that we are unaware of), we might ask her the equivalent of, "what would happen if you didn't do that right now?" Usually, nothing. This kind of discussion often enables the individual to mentally discover that failure to work on the XYZ project *at that moment* will have few, if any, consequences. Of course, afterwards, we may then wish to help her reprioritize her duties.

Consider some of your employees who spend all of their time "organizing" and "getting ready" to begin work on a project. Other individuals spend substantial amounts of time on low-priority internal housekeeping chores. While these things need to get done, it is apparent that some people use such activities to procrastinate. At those times, it may be necessary to confront them and bring their lack of prioritizing to the forefront. However, you will find that many of these people honestly believe that they are doing what is required. They simply may not have the same understanding of what is required that you do. You can handle them by asking questions that will lead them through the logical consequences of doing or not doing certain things. Of course, some managers prefer to just yell or tell. Fortunately, we already know that motivation through intimidation is counterproductive in the long run. It usually results in resentments and other behaviors that become equally defeating.

If an employee comes to you with a problem, or if you are involved in any sort of difficulty, you'll often find that a good part of the problem is muddied thinking. "They can't see the forest because of the trees" is a common situation. The fact is, objectivity is difficult for anyone when they are too close to a problem. However, this lack of objectivity is then reflected in people's communication and often leads to misunderstandings and destructive feelings. The result: people get into arguments and get off track.

When a person has a problem, we must assume that it is real, at least to them. Almost by definition, if someone goes for help, their problem is real to them. Have you ever gone to your friend, spouse, or boss and inquired, "What did you do that for?" Once they gave you the answer, you may not have agreed, but you were probably at least satisfied. However, before they gave you their answer, important information was missing: the rationale for their behavior. The missing, or "deleted," information was necessary for you to feel comfortable, and it can remain in your mind like an unresolved question. The same is true for others as well. They also have issues, conflicts, problems, confusions, frustrations, etc., that result from missing information or muddied thinking.

Each questioning category that follows is presented so that you can easily recognize it and use it with others. You can also teach it to your employees to reduce or avoid normal, day-to-day miscommunications and conflicts. The smooth functioning of your office or department is dependent upon people doing their jobs in active cooperation with each other. Office conflicts may be very common, but they are easy to avoid if you have the right tools available. A few of those tools are presented in the following subsections.

What to Do About Vague/Fuzzy/Undefined, Yet Seemingly Meaningful Words

Some examples of these words and the confusion that they can cause was introduced in the beginning of the chapter. As a rule of thumb, whenever you are expected to do something, that is, perform some action to satisfy another person, you need to clarify exactly what they expect. A manager saying, "I want you to do a good job," is an example of a statement that would need clarification.

If you told your employees, "Our job is to provide new product ideas in a timely manner, and to maintain a courteous relationship with our customers," the vast majority of your personnel would nod their heads in total agreement, without having any specific understanding of what you mean by the words: "new," "timely," and even "courteous." Language has certain conventions which are theoretically understood. Yet, one person may think that a word like "service" means providing what is asked for, while another person may understand it as anticipating the customer's needs. "New" can mean anything from totally new, never seen or even thought of before, to small or large modifications of existing product lines. Within certain specific parameters "timely" can mean anything from five minutes to five weeks. What is the response time that you require, in what context, and with what exceptions? Any misunderstanding or different interpretation could cause a problem for someone. Finally, try to define "courteous."

Words that are subject to individual interpretation will often be interpreted in as many ways as there are individuals doing the interpreting. (This should be added to the collection of Murphy's Law sayings.)

Overcoming Mind Reading and Assumptions about Other Peoples' Thoughts, Actions, Beliefs, and Feelings

At the beginning of the chapter we discussed the word "assumption" and its attendant dangers. Here are three more examples of assumptions that people sometimes make.

"The other people don't want me to work with them."

"My boss/co-worker/friend/whoever is mad at me."

"I thought that is what you would have wanted."

Any of the statements above requires some verification before it is accepted as fact. The most common question you should ask to get that verification is either, "How do/did you know?" or, "Have you asked that person?" We need the hard, objective evidence that will support the assertion.

A very common problem associated with "mind reading" is hurt feelings. Unfortunately, due to a variety of reasons, some people are very easily insulted and easily get their egos bruised. At the same time, most of the hurts that people experience in life are the result of something that occurs in their own minds. What they've chosen to feel hurt about was not intended to hurt them.

We often give people the following advice: Since people very rarely insult someone intentionally, when you feel that you have been insulted, either:

- Ignore it.
- Pretend that you heard a compliment.
- Ask them what they meant.

If you ignore it, chances are it will go away. If they actually meant it as an insult, they will try again. At the second occurrence, question them as to their intention. If you pretend that you heard it as a compliment, it will drive them crazy. If they meant it as a neutral statement, then they will not correct you. If they meant it as an insult, they will try again. In both cases, assume that the statement was neutral in intent.

If you must question them, allow for the possibility that a miscommunication has occurred by saying something like, "I heard that last statement as potentially insulting. Was it your intention to insult me?" Or, "Is there something that I don't know? Your statement sounded like an insult." Again, the chances are that nothing was meant by it and now the individual will probably apologize and clarify what was actually meant. If, however, they indicate that it was an insult, then you can find out why and work to resolve any conflict that may exist. Of course, you should remember that they too may have misheard or misinterpreted something you said.

Often, it is not *what* was said, but *how* it was said. The inadvertent use of a poor tonality or inflection can turn a regular statement into an insulting one. We'll provide some examples of this in a subsequent exercise.

As a manager, as a professional communicator, you have it within your ability to control potentially explosive situations. The odds are that whomever you are communicating with has neither the knowledge nor the ability to do it. We have found that 99 percent of all such issues are immediately and easily resolved by clarifying and resolving potential misunderstandings before they escalate beyond repair.

All too often, people spend days or weeks fretting about some real or imagined put-down. In our opinion, life is too short to waste that much time, effort, and energy on such trivia. It's easier said than done, but the effort you spend in educating your employees about this approach can pay substantial dividends in improved employee relations.

Overgeneralizations

"*Every* time that I call, they give me a hard time." "*Nobody* at the office *ever* lifts a hand to help me." These exaggerations seem true to that person at the moment. When people are frustrated, it *does* seem like absolutely nothing is going right or will ever go right. All they can do is focus on the problem at hand. In addition, because of their very narrow focus and the feelings associated with the problem, they do not, and perhaps cannot, remember what normally happens.

If someone is giving you such a complaint, the easiest way to break the thought is by searching for the exception to their mental rule. For example: "Do you mean that *every* single time, without exception, they give you a difficult time?" or, "Not one single person in the entire office ever helped you out or gave you a hand?" If the person can come up with *even one* exception, the discussion will take on an entirely different tone. Yet, until you bring it to his attention with your question, he may actually be unable to see that he is involved in the exception rather than the rule. Of course, it could be that, for whatever reason, this individual's co-workers do not help him. If this is the situation, then you have a different problem. Normally though, because of your question, their hard-line statement no longer has its previous power over his feelings. More importantly, one or more of these questions will also usually lead the individual into a mental statement more conducive to logical discussion. (Note: another technique, called "Fogging," is specifically designed to neutralize anger very quickly and is presented in a separate chapter.)

Unraveling Beliefs that People Use to Rule Their Lives:

Throughout our lives, we hear short statements that provide some truth or rule of thumb to live by. These adages serve the valid purpose of teaching children and providing a clear, concise statement that makes a particular point. "A penny saved is a penny earned," addresses thrift. However, "Never talk to strangers," and, "Don't speak unless spoken to," are sayings that would be decidedly disadvantageous to salespeople. Once one of these "statements of authority" is accepted by us as a child, it can take on the power of a major belief that controls our behavior and feelings into adulthood.

Without involving ourselves with the therapeutic questions associated with beliefs instilled in childhood, we will assume that you have already hired people who are not mentally programmed with the "statements of authority"/beliefs above. Rather, let's concentrate on rules that are equivalent to adages that do affect many offices. These are the unstated rules of the office that govern procedures and, often, office behavior. Sort of the this-is-the-way-that-it's-done attitude. New ways are not searched for because the old ways are so entrenched. You can know when this is the situation when you hear definitive statements like, "This *is* how it is done!" or, "They say that. . . ." Who is "they"? you might ask.

We know of one situation when an entire project might have been destroyed because a clerk refused to entertain the possibility that there might be an exception to the rule. He basically set his heels in and refused to budge on shipping something overnight instead of regular postage. Sometimes adhering to rules is good, but in this situation it was in direct conflict with the manager's wishes. The clerk's bureaucratic attitude was not appreciated. In trying to determine why the clerk had been so rigid, the manager later found out that another clerk had lost his job for granting a similar request. The only thing that our clerk did not understand was that the clerk who lost his job did something on his own authority and in substantially different circumstances than was currently the case. However, the impact of someone getting fired instilled the equivalent of a phobic response in this one employee.

Whenever you hear someone say, *"They* say . . .," find out who "they" are. Whenever you hear a definitive statement about how something *should* be done, find out who issued the dictate. Usually, no one really knows.

Another way that these imperatives show up is through the use of statements that contain any of the following words or their equivalents:

Should.

Ought to.

Must.

Need to.

You will often hear these words used when people are "burning out," or when they are not performing according to expectations.

When "burning out," most people have too many of these "shoulds" in their lives. They "should" be at the office before eight o'clock, regardless of how late they worked the night before, and they "should" be addressing every project to which they are assigned with equal vigor, and they "should" be increasing their professional skills and another dozen "shoulds" that are competing for equal attention. Such people pull themselves apart with all of the shoulds that they think they "ought to" be able to accomplish simultaneously. Unrealistic expectations? Absolutely! Something that you may have to deal with? Definitely! Because these things are often outside the individual's conscious awareness.

Employees who are not performing to expectations may be "burning out," but they may also be involved in some internal "conflict." For example: we know of many people who want to do a good job and put in the necessary hours to complete projects on schedule. But, they also want to spend time with their families, enjoy themselves, and exercise. Both parts of their lives are demanding attention, causing the "conflict" we discussed.

Throughout our lives we have been taught that we "should" be able to balance all the aspects of our lives. We've also been taught that we have an obligation to our job or career, our family, our religion, our country, and all of the other things that we "ought to" be doing to demonstrate that we are successful and otherwise nice people.

You might have to address this issue during coaching and counseling sessions with employees. You may also have to be the one to raise the issue because it is often outside of your employees' awareness. Once you've suggested to them that they *list all of their "shoulds,"* they can then *prioritize them* (sometimes with your help). Then they can *sort out* which ones really need attention and which ones can be temporarily or permanently postponed or eliminated. After all, a person can only do so much.

One of the questions that you or they need to ask is, "who gave you the rule that you 'should' do such-and-such?" More often than not, they won't be able to give you a viable answer. Yet, for years they may have been running their lives by these unconscious rules.

It is important to realize that you are *not* giving psychiatric counseling. Leave that to a trained professional. You are, however, asking a few key questions that will often help people get out of their own way. These internal imperatives and internal conflicts are often the cause of personal conflict and poor performance.

A final commentary regarding the "shoulds": these beliefs create a whole series of expectations that often determine how we react to the world in general and other people in particular. Virtually every personal conflict is based upon some "should" that the other person has violated. One key question to always ask yourself and teach others to ask is, "What did you/I *expect*?" We only get angry, upset, or distressed when our expectations are *not* met. However, most of us have several expectations that in and of themselves are totally unreasonable. Once brought to light, these expectations become much easier to handle.

Breaking Down "Associations"

"Associations" are very important when working on motivational issues and job satisfaction. To a large degree, they are more fully dealt with in the chapters devoted to motivation because, in the sense that we will employ them in this book, they establish a decided correlation between certain actions and meanings. An often-used example from marriage counseling is, "If he loved me, he would give me flowers." Somehow, for that individual, flowers equal love. Her partner or spouse could do all of the other things that *other people* would equate with love, but she would need flowers. Unless she tells him or he magically figures it out, he's basically caught between a rock and a hard place. She *expects* him to know that to her, flowers equal love.

It is much the same in business. Some people need a public pat on the back, while for others, a private verbal recognition is sufficient. Chances are that these psychological rewards could be powerful persuaders or motivators for a variety of people in your office. The question is: "Who gets motivated by what?" The answer often depends largely on what form of reward the individual associates with personal success. As we will discuss in the various chapters dealing with psychological profiling and personal motivations, if you know what to search for it becomes quite easy to pick and choose your reward system so that it matches the needs of the individual and motivates them toward further accomplishment. Despite your best intentions, however, if you randomly select a reward and it fails to match the individual's association, you will not have motivated them and could be thought of as not caring.

Summary

When scientific or mathematical jargon is employed, it is easy to assume that everyone has the same definitions for the words we use. However, in most of our interpersonal communications, many of the words we use are open to interpretation and have as many emotional meanings as there are listeners. That's why it is imperative for you, the manager, to be certain that you and your employees mean the same thing when you use a word. Otherwise, not only may you be disappointed in the results of a project, you may unwittingly affect the creativity of your staff.

While the techniques we've presented are just a more sophisticated way of saying "Huh?", it is important to start saying, "Huh?" more often than you probably do now. If you do, you'll find that problems become more easily resolved and that you know your people better. You'll become more effective in your job, and your employees will work harder and with more satisfaction (assuming that you apply some of the motivational techniques presented in other chapters).

Leading and Motivating Creative Personnel to Increase Productivity and Employee Retention

As the manager of a department of innovators, your job regularly requires you to be a consummate salesman. Not only do you have to "sell" your projects to higher management for funding, you also have to sell their requirements to your staff. Selling management's requirements to your staff may not sound very important. After all, as manager, all you really need to do is tell your staff what is required and they will go out and invent it. Right? Unfortunately, that's not the way it works.

Innovative people don't have to be prima donnas to need to be sold on a project that they're being asked to develop. Assembly-line workers produce whatever comes down the line. Whether they're excited about their work or bored with it, they can still produce that product at a consistent rate. However, creative people generate a different products, ideas, concepts, or innovations. If they are bored or uninterested in their work, they will not manufacture the same quality product at the same rate that they would if they were excited about a project they're working on.

The purpose of this section is to provide you with the skills necessary to meet the needs, as well as match the internal model, of your innovative staff so that you can keep them motivated and "sell" them on any project that you assign. By doing so, you will not only increase their overall productivity, you will also meet enough of their internal needs to minimize staff turnover. In addition, these same skills can be used when convincing higher management to fund projects in which you are interested.

Meeting Their
Most Basic Needs

Within industry today, many managers still limit their motivational strategies to either the stick (consisting of real or implied threats) or the carrot (offering some form of power, fame, or money). While these are important, they represent only one portion of the complex configuration of needs, beliefs, and attitudes that makes up the motivational system of any individual. In this chapter, we will explore the themes of power, recognition, and compensation, as well as setting limits and their effect upon motivation and productivity. We will investigate the other needs, beliefs, and attitudes that make up the rest of an individual's motivational system in subsequent chapters.

The Challenge of Creation

Most innovative people love their work. The very challenge of creating something new, as well as the sense of accomplishment that arises when they have completed a project, provides a tremendous source of satisfaction. This is a powerful source of motivation and needs to be utilized.

Be sure that all individuals who have been working on any project are there for the finish, regardless of whether they participated in the entire project or only helped with one small portion. They need to share in the sense of closure that comes with a completed piece of work, as well as the feeling of accomplishment for a job well done.

The managers we spoke with accomplished this in various ways:

➡ The director of R & D at one medical chemical company requires his scientists to work regularly with their customers. Not only does this give them a better idea of what the customer needs, it also lets them bask in the customer's appreciation when they deliver a product they created at the customer's request.

➡ Another manager always makes sure that his scientists are working on short-, intermediate-, and long-term projects at the same time. This avoids the problem of a feeling of lack of closure, which sometimes occurs when individuals are limited to long-term projects. By working on all three, the individual regularly experiences the sense of fulfillment that accompanies the completion of a project.

➡ When an individual comes up with a good idea, give him the responsibility and resources to develop it through to completion. Most studies report that creative individuals are very career-oriented. Assigning the responsibility for an innovation is not only motivating, it can also demonstrate whether or not this individual is ready for greater responsibility.

➡ A major chemical company encourages its scientists to spend a certain amount of time each week working on pet projects they feel may make the company money. The only requirement is that the project be related to their field. Money and resources are provided to support this work regardless of failure rates. As a result, they have developed far more innovative products than many of their competitors. Note: Before the expense of any private project becomes overwhelming, the scientist involved has to demonstrate its practicality.

Recognition/Fame

Like the rest of us, the creative individual needs a sense of accomplishment and fulfillment. For most innovators, much of this is provided internally by their own belief systems and a sense of self-motivation and satisfaction. However, recognition for a job well done is also very important. Remember, "There is no limit to the good you can do if you don't care who gets the credit" (General George C. Marshall).

➡ One powerful way to provide regular recognition on an informal basis is through managing by walking around. This serves two purposes: First, it will keep you informed about the progress and problems of every project, thereby avoiding costly surprises. Second, it gives you a chance to provide constant informal recognition and positive feedback to your staff.

As you move from one office or desk to another, spread the good word; that is, tell the others about the good work Joe or Sally is doing. Try to brag a little about someone different each day. The impact on motivation and productivity may surprise you.

➡ A major chemical company's agricultural division requires its scientists to publish or present a paper each year on their work. This accomplishes several things. It serves as one way to demonstrate progress toward established goals. It also enables the individual presenting the paper to receive the approbation of his or her peers. Finally, because the director of R & D attends the presentations of the papers, it provides him with a good opportunity to praise them as well.

➡ The R & D department of a major toy company regularly holds both informal and formal "show and tell" sessions. Like a requirement for publication, these sessions provide each designer with regular feedback and praise from both peers and superiors, and also remind them of their accountability for their goals.

➡ If you are the director of your department, be sure that you see everyone regularly to let them know how much you appreciate them. One director we spoke to, with operations all over the country, says he makes it a point to spend a day with every single scientist each year. Once he has completed his business with his employee, he takes the employee and his or her family out for the rest of the day and brags about them to their family. He also meets at least monthly with his regional managers and at least bimonthly with his supervisors. Note: He has one of the lowest personnel turnovers in the industry.

➡ To an extent, the assignment of office or lab space can be an issue of both power (prestige) and recognition. However, for creative people, privacy raises another consideration: distraction. Distractions can be a significant drain on creative productivity. As a result, although creative people need an informal atmosphere in which they can feel free to chat with each other about a concept or problem, they also need protection from the minute-to-minute distractions that fill any department or office. Most need private, or at least semiprivate work areas.

Compensation

While creative people may obtain greater internal rewards from their work than others, their need for material compensation is no different. Unfortunately, because their work ideas are often hard to measure in terms of immediate ROI, they are often left without the raises and bonuses found in other departments.

The sense of appreciation for services rendered that material compensation provides is as important as the actual level of income received. Creative people need to feel that they, and their work, are valued as much as that of their peers. As the manager, your job is to fight for their compensation and fringe benefits as you would fight for your own.

➡ When an individual develops something innovative, many companies now reward her with a portion of the profit it makes for the firm. This can be a powerful motivator in the long term.

➡ When raises are based upon a companywide percentage formula, the development of specific, measurable production goals becomes even more important (see Chapters 15 and 33).

➡ Find creative ways to demonstrate your appreciation for innovative work, even if it means spending some of your own money. Sending a secretary and her husband out to dinner doesn't cost much but can mean as much as a raise in salary by what it communicates. If the department has discretionary funds, think of ways you can show your recognition for a job well done. You are limited primarily by your own imagination.

Chapter 25

The Stick

The problem with "the stick" stems from the difficult nature of measuring creative output (see Chapters 33 and 34 for more on measuring innovative productivity). It is easy to terminate someone for infractions of rules and procedures, but EEO and Labor Department rules make it more difficult for productivity. Before considering termination, be sure to use the techniques for counseling provided in Section VII.

An important aspect of the stick for creative staff is the need for flexible limits. While most jobs have hours from eight to five, creative jobs often have periods in which even sixty- and seventy-hour work weeks become common. At those times, flexibility with report-in time and comp time off becomes critical. If not, you risk not only burning out your most important asset, you also risk their not completing a task on time because they now refuse to work overtime. Cooperation is a two-way street. Finally, of course, since long hours are a source of stress for the individual's family, lack of flexibility and appreciation on your part could result in their resisting your efforts to increase productivity when you need to meet a deadline.

Summary

Although power, recognition, compensation, and limits represent only about 30 to 40 percent of what motivates an individual to work, they are important. Your own creative efforts to meet the needs of your staff in these areas can pay off in vastly increased productivity and job satisfaction on their part.

Primary Motivational Programs

This chapter deals with some of the key unconscious mental programs that drive behavior. It provides information that you will be able to employ immediately in a variety of situations with both your innovative and your support staff. For example, you'll be able to use these techniques in coaching and counseling sessions and product development meetings. They can also be used to select and recruit personnel and to assign them to creative teams with a greater degree of accuracy than has previously been possible. Overall, the applications are enormous and the techniques work with virtually everyone.

Over the years many studies have been done to determine what motivates people. Unfortunately, various research conclusions have used words and labels that often contradict each other. A very brief overview of some of the landmark studies will establish the background for the highly pragmatic approach that we will be teaching.

In his research, Abraham Maslow demonstrated that each of us has a variety of needs, and that those needs can be placed in a hierarchy of importance. That is, until the most basic needs have been met, it is impossible to really seek fulfillment of our higher needs. For example:We need food, clothing, and shelter in order to survive. Once these needs are met, other needs such as entertainment and luxuries can be addressed. Eventually, as a person goes up the economic ladder, the purchase of gadgets, gizmoes, and toys may dominate his thoughts. At this point, all of the key needs have been easily met and it is *assumed* that they will continue to be met. Of course, a major disaster may seriously challenge this very common assumption.

Consider the feelings that most people had immediately after the Stock Market Crash of 1987. People who had invested heavily in the stock market were frightened that day. Their very foundations were shaken, and long-held beliefs about the financial security of their futures were undermined. As a result, people changed the way they invested their money, they became very cautious and began to invest in financial instruments that were considered "safe" (such as bank certificates of deposit and blue chip bonds and stocks).

Because many individual's savings were destroyed overnight, their confidence in the future was shaken. People who had been purchasing all of the toys of the "Yuppie" generation had suffered a substantial "erosion of capital" and went into a survival mode, with change to "safe" investments being the theme of the day. Without belaboring the point, the investment game changed on that day. In one form or another, everyone reading this book was mentally affected. Your subsequent response was partially determined by what you saw, heard, and felt over the days that followed. It was also determined by your background and the way you usually approach the world in your normal day-to-day affairs. The key point is that the dividing line between cool, calm, and collected and very frightened is often extremely thin. This is true of everyone, without exception. Hence, someone's reaction to a threat to their financial security may be substantially different than you would have predicted.

This accounts for part of the confusion that some managers feel about using financial compensation as a primary motivator for creative people. Whenever our security is threatened, money becomes an extremely powerful motivator. However, for many people (especially the creative), once sufficient finances have been accumulated to provide a certain level of "security," additional money ceases to be an effective source of motivation. At this point, other, more basic motivations take over.

Crisis situations not withstanding, most people habitually employ, and are motivated by, certain common patterns called *primary programs*. In the next few pages, we'll describe three of those programs discovered by Harvard psychologist, David McClelland: the Need for Power, the Need for Affiliation, and the Need for Achievement. Each of us has all three of these needs at one time or another, but will concentrate on one. Just which one predominates and how it is modified by other motivational needs will determine some of our most important drives.

In the following chapter you will be introduced to additional programs. As you read this material, it will be easy to think of someone you know who employs each pattern. Remember, no single pattern is good or bad in and of itself. Rather than using it to label people, think of it as useful information for helping them be their most productive.

Later you will combine some of these patterns to make a whole that is far greater than the sum of its parts. The theory of these first major patterns has enjoyed a degree of popularity over the years because its concept makes so much sense.

Need for Power

Do you know someone who always seems to want to take charge of the situation and likes to direct and control others (either directly or from behind the scenes)? Interestingly, there are many reasons why someone may want or need to take charge. The people who take charge because it makes them feel good or powerful or in control are individuals who demonstrate a *Need for Power.* If they say "Jump," they want someone else to say "How high?"

You see them everywhere, in all walks of life. If the person is in management, she likes to make her employees do as they're told. These managers are usually very forceful and react negatively to questions or any type of delay (which are often viewed as a personal affront). In a word, the typical "Dictator." The same is true for the creative individual who is motivated by a need for power. In a bureaucracy, this person is the clerk who takes great pleasure in enforcing each and every one of the rules. Our "Bureaucrat" may be this type of person if control of others is a primary motivation.

Power-oriented innovators are often something of prima donnas who want to have complete control over their research as well as all of the credit for anything that is accomplished. As a result, they respond very favorably if you publicly ask their opinion about things—whether it be some strategy that the department or team should employ to solve a problem, or a recommendation regarding the selection of a new project. However, individuals who have an extreme need for power would then use the opportunity as a public forum for "dictating from on high." If appropriate, delegate some responsibility to them (such as being team leader on a project), and let both them and others know that there may be more to come. This can create a good deal of personal loyalty to you from such individuals. Of course, be sure to monitor them so that they do not abuse the authority.

There are other things that you can do to motivate and persuade a predominantly power-oriented person. These will become obvious as other primary motivational programs are explored in the next chapter. A summary of pure power-oriented motivations and ways to deal with them is presented below.

Power-Oriented Motivations

➡ Control of others and various situations. They want to be the boss. "Do it my way," and, "Follow my directions," are key patterns.

➡ Position of real or implied authority.

➡ Position and status.

➡ Ability to influence, supervise, or control other people.

Words and Phrases Used by Power-Motivated People

➡ "Me," "Myself," "I."

➡ Control.

➡ Power.

➡ Authority.

➡ "Do it my way."

➡ "*I'm* the boss."

➡ "That's *my* decision to make."

How to Recognize a Power-Motivated Person

➡ They try to stand apart from the crowd.

➡ Their desk and office tend to be rather stark.

➡ They often lean toward people with whom they are speaking, often making their listener want to step back.

➡ When they speak about something, they are rarely tentative. They tend to use absolutes, implying that there couldn't possibly be any serious opinion that differs from theirs.

Methods for Dealing with a Power-Motivated Person

➡ Acknowledge their achievements, status, position, and authority.

➡ Provide symbols of authority such as a preferred location.

➡ Obtain their opinion (preferably publicly).

➡ Acknowledge their contributions.

➡ Delegate authority to them, but always be certain to supervise the use of that authority.

➡ Show them how doing what you want will also get them what they desire.

In essence, the way to deal with power-oriented people is to give them as much power as they can handle without disrupting the department or your authority. If they are completely motivated by power, it may not be appropriate to place them in charge of others because their very orientation will tend to discourage creativity in others. However, let them know that they win when they support you. Finally, remember that very few people are completely power motivated.

Need for Affiliation

The person whose primary motivation is *affiliation* is substantially different from the power-oriented individual. For him, the goal is association with other people. The need to be part of a group and to be accepted by others is of paramount importance on the unconscious level. You can easily identify these people because they tend to have pictures of groups and group activities surrounding them. They like to be around others and feel demotivated and perhaps even depressed when they have to work alone.

In fact, "alone" is not a word that they are comfortable with in virtually any environment. This is not to say that they cannot work alone or that they are never alone. However, if you were to offer this person a private office, you would not get the same favorable reception as you might from someone who is power-, or achievement-oriented. If you were to remove them from the mainstream of the office to work on an independent project, you might have a disgruntled employee who would spend significantly more time around the coffee machine, in the lounge, or visiting other people at their work area. Hence, this person works best when assigned to a team.

Essentially, affiliation-oriented personnel have a need for regular personal contact. They judge their worth by the consensus of opinion. The "group" is always right. The team is important. The "group" can be members of the same profession, church, social organization, family, or so on. Their most often used pronouns are "we" and "us." Working in association with others dominates their thinking. They are very similar to the "Socialite" introduced earlier. People who are very socially or group oriented have the following characteristics:

Affiliation Motivations

➡ Being a member of the team.

➡ Needs to be liked.

➡ Needs acceptance and interpersonal relationships.

➡ Wants to work with people.

➡ Minimizes conflicts.

Words and Phrases Used by the Affiliated Person

➡ "We," "Us," "Let's," "All," and "Others."

➡ "Let's get together."

➡ "Let's do something for . . . "

➡ Group participation.

How to Recognize an Affiliation-Oriented Person

➡ Pictures of groups to which they belong.

➡ Dress like their contemporaries.

➡ Go to the popular restaurants, activities, etc.

➡ Always involved in group activities.

Actions to Take with an Affiliation-Motivated Person

➡ Reward contributions to the group, e.g., social function.

➡ Thank them for helping others.

➧ Smooth over potential conflicts.

➧ Talk in terms of group effort and what others are doing.

In essence, the way to deal with someone who is highly affiliation-oriented is to present them with concepts in terms of the needs of the group. Present ideas by defining them in terms of other people. Get them involved with the process. Throw them a party. Be warm and friendly.

Need for Achievement

Achievement-oriented people place a high premium on the accomplishment of their goals. They are task-oriented as long as the task has measurable results and they can feel a sense of pride of accomplishment. They respond well to plaques, awards, and other types of certificates that can be prominently displayed on their walls and desks.

They can be left alone to do a job. While they usually work well with others, their primary motivation is to get the job done, not the social interaction derived from group activities. They will take control and occasionally take power, but to get the job done rather than for the personal aggrandizement sought by the power-oriented individual.

In summary, these individuals want and need a sense of accomplishment. They obtain this sense of accomplishment from challenging or competitive situations. Realistic and achievable goals are set within a framework of achieving personal excellence. Achievement-oriented people share the following characteristics:

Achievement Motivations

➧ Set long-range, accomplishable objectives.

➧ Plan for contingencies.

➧ Compete against a motivating standard.

➧ Satisfaction from completing the job or task.

➧ Satisfaction also from working on the task.

Words and Phrases Used by Achievers

➧ Innovative ideas.

➧ "Let's plan ahead."

➧ "Let's get the job done."

➧ Feeling of accomplishment.

How to Recognize an Achievement-Oriented Person

➥ Awards/Plaques/Certificates.

➥ Participation in group social activities only after the work has been done.

➥ Task orientation.

➥ Asks specific questions about objectives, deadlines, and details.

➥ Remains focused on the task.

➥ Rarely involved in power struggles or in socialization.

Actions to Take with an Achievement-Motivated Person

➥ Recognize their achievement with words or awards (e.g., give titles).

➥ Encourage initiative.

➥ Encourage independent thinking.

➥ Allow participation in goal-setting activities.

➥ Keep projects interesting and challenging.

In essence, you work with an achievement-oriented individual by providing challenges that are meaningful to them. This individual is highly motivated by the successful completion of one task and is always looking forward to the next project. Note: Achievement-oriented people may not respond well to long-term projects that do not provide a sense of closure and accomplishment as each phase is completed. Be certain that you define the milestones that you and they will use to determine progress on a project before they begin. Once finished, they respond well to recognition that a job was well done.

Summary

The Needs for Power, Affiliation, and Achievement are themes that drive behavior. They are pervasive, but not quite as black and white as we have presented. Most of us have all three needs to some extent, with one consistently predominating within a given context. For example, a person who is power-oriented at work may have a strong affiliation orientation at home. A person who is predominantly affiliation-oriented may also have a strong desire to achieve a particular goal. For the duration of his work towards that goal, his behaviors will appear to be more achievement-oriented.

Situations and people change. Yet, when combined with key motivations and other primary programs, this information will enable the aware observer to understand more completely the individual involved.

Motivations Ruling Our Behaviors

Psychologists have found that each of us has various unconscious motivations, or criteria, that we use to make decisions. These criteria, such as "quality," "image" and "convenience" become motivational themes that often form the basis of our decisions. To a large extent they determine what we like or dislike, what we are attracted to or repelled by. These criteria or motivational themes are quite consistent for most of us, most of the time.

This is one of the concepts behind "benefit selling," the technique we presented in our book, *Consultative Selling Techniques for Financial Professionals*. By being able to identify others' motivational themes, a sales professional can make presentations to the "individual" customer instead of the "generic" customer. The presentation becomes personally meaningful because the sales professional gives information targeted at the customers' unconscious motivational themes. This substantially deepens the rapport already established between them and further allows the customer to feel comfortable with his competency. These same concepts can also be applied when selling an idea or concept to your staff or superiors, or just motivating them to be as productive and "successful" as possible.

For a few people, the motivation to success is the "stick" of fear—fear of failure, fear of being fired, etc. For others, it is the "carrot" of success—a higher standard of living, wealth, the admiration of peers, security, etc. However, each of us is different, and motivational techniques that are limited to fear, financial rewards, or fame miss a large number of innovators and other employees who could become stars in their own right if only the correct "button" were pushed.

It has been truly said that people work for one of three reasons:

➡ Out of fear

➡ Out of duty

➡ Out of love

Of the three, the individual that works out of love is obviously the best. It is he who looks forward to coming to work because it's exciting and fulfilling, rather than going to work because it's the right thing to do or because there are bills to pay. As managers, it is our job to help our employees develop a love for their work that will help insure their "success" as well as their becoming more self-motivated. What constitutes success is determined by each individual for himself. Some people would consider having a billion dollars success, while others consider themselves successful every day they complete a given amount of a project towards some goal.

Why are some people self-starters and self-motivated? It is because they have a clear understanding that performing certain actions will lead them, step by step, towards definite, clearly defined goals. They have a mental image of where they want to be and also a way of measuring the incremental steps made toward that goal. Finally, they feel some type of personal satisfaction for the steps made. Rather than eventually becoming "successful," these highly motivated individuals are always in the process of "succeeding." Success is a daily activity rather than something to be eventually attained.

Here is a brief exercise which should demonstrate something of significance about you and, by extension, about most of the people you know. For each of the six questions on the next page, please circle the words that are applicable to your situation.

What do you want in a car that you might purchase?

1) Reputation
2) Available options
3) Style/Looks
4) Location of dealer
5) Service from dealer
6) Bargain
7) Dealer integrity
8) Dependability
9) Warranty
10) Performance

What would you like about a company that you either work for or would consider working for?

1) Reputation
2) Career alternatives
3) Appearances
4) Location of office
5) Service orientation
6) Money
7) Company integrity
8) Reliability
9) Contract offered
10) Company track record

What would you consider important qualities in a business associate?

1) Reputation
2) Different interests
3) Cleanliness/Looks
4) Can meet with easily
5) Helpful
6) Worth the effort
7) Honesty
8) Reliability
9) Fulfills promises
10) Consistent performance

Why do you frequent certain restaurants?

1) Reputation
2) Good selection
3) Atmosphere/Ambiance
4) Location
5) Good service
6) Prices reasonable
7) Integrity
8) Consistent quality
9) Satisfaction assured
10) Gets better and better

What do you pride yourself on as a manager; or what would you choose as the attributes of a person to emulate?

1) Good reputation
2) Seeks new challenges
3) Provides good image
4) Ease of accessibility
5) Offers assistance
6) Paid for work rendered
7) Trustworthy
8) Reliable
9) Fulfills verbal word
10) Constantly improving self

What are some of the qualities you would want in a friend or spouse?

1)	Confidence in person	2)	Wide range of interests
3)	Attractive	4)	Is there when needed
5)	Helpful	6)	They're worth the effort
7)	Trustworthy	8)	Dependable
9)	Keeps promises	10)	Self-improvement conscious

The numbers listed below will allow you to indicate how often you chose to a particular response. If you chose the answers associated with number 1 on five of the six questions, you would write the number 5 in the appropriate place. Please do this for each of the ten numbers.

1)	_____	2)	_____
3)	_____	4)	_____
5)	_____	6)	_____
7)	_____	8)	_____
9)	_____	10)	_____

Most people used a few numbers rather frequently. The words associated with each number were synonyms of each other (e.g., all the number 3s mean basically the same thing). Any words or equivalents used on three or more occasions can be considered a personal "key criteria" or "motivation" for you when making a decision.

We've presented variations of this exercise to over six thousand people and found that the vast majority of people have at least two or three major criteria that affect a variety of decisions. The point we're making is that if you learn someone's basic themes you can package your presentation much more powerfully.

Think of how this can make your project presentations to your staff or superiors more effective. Instead of presenting a variety of features, benefits, and advantages and "hoping" that your customers can figure out what it means to them, you could now do something substantially better. You can elicit the individual's *unconscious* decision-making motivations and then feed them back to him in a way that completely matches their thinking pattern. This will allow you to tailor-make a presentation that is highly meaningful to your target audience.

When combined with knowing a person's psychological profile (Dictator, Bureaucrat, Socialite, Executive), their mode of thinking (Visual, Auditory, Kinesthetic), and their meta-programs (Power, Affiliation, Achievement, etc.), you have the ability to become extraordinarily per suasive. It will be as if your listener had written your presentation for himself.

As a manager you have the opportunity for extraordinary persuasiveness when you motivate, coach, teach, and lead your professional and support personnel. Remember, this information can easily be elicited in casual conversation in the office or over lunch. You may even desire to make notes to remind yourself which frames of reference will be most useful with a particular person in your department. Then, when you discuss a project with her, your effectiveness will be substantially enhanced.

You may be wondering just what you need to listen for. Below is a brief list of personal motivations and their equivalencies (synonyms). If you hear some of these words used in a variety of contexts, you can be sure that they will be highly persuasive when you use them to further empower your people.

1) Advertising	Reputation	Familiarity	Awareness
2) Alternatives	Variety	Selection	Product line
3) Appearance	Looks	Atmosphere	Ambiance
4) Courtesy	Consideration	Service	Respect
5) Credit	Cash Flow	Bargain	Discount
6) Dependable	Reliability	Reputation	Confidence
7) Habit	Tradition	Familiar	Sentimental
8) Image	Style	Status	Prestige
9) Integrity	Honesty	Trustworthy	Honor/Trust
10) Professional	Competent	Expert	Authority
11) Quality	Value	Craftsmanship	Reliable
12) Relationship	Loyalty	Friendliness	Affiliation
13) Safety	Security	Guarantee	Warranty

Although people tend to use consistent themes to make decisions, they rarely describe these themes using the same words all the time. For example, someone may go to a particular gas station because of the "large product line"; a particular clothing store because of the "good selection"; a restaurant because of the "variety" of dishes on the menu; and may select "diversity" of interests in friends. In each case, the theme of "available alternatives" was dominant.

In discussing a project assignment with such a person, you could motivate him by emphasizing the variety of approaches he could take in working on it, the many possible uses the project could have, etc., by using synonyms that indicated choice. Then allow him to make the decision on which three approaches he wants to try and when this week he will initiate one of the ideas. Of course, you've noted that they *had* to choose three items and they *would* do it this week. You feel good *and,* most importantly, they feel good.

It's generally easy to discover key motivations if you ask a few astute questions over a period of time. Simply ask your employees questions that might normally come up in a social or business situation or meeting, such as what they like about a given product or restaurant, and note the criteria that they consistently raised. For example, in the conversation below, look for potential decision-making criteria from the employee (Emp.). The important probes from the manager (Mgr.) are italicized.

Mgr.:	Bill, I notice that you own a Jaguar. I'm thinking about buying one myself, but I haven't quite made up my mind. *What do you like about yours?*
Emp.:	Well, I think that it's a well-made car, and it's lots of fun to drive.
Mgr.:	*Anything else?*
Emp.:	Sure. It's a sharp-looking car. Not like some of the boxes they're selling today. And my friends like it.
Mgr.:	They certainly look great. Where do you get it serviced? I mean, I'd guess you must want a factory-trained mechanic to work on it.
Emp.:	That's for sure. I don't take any chances with it. I take it to the dealer where I bought it, in Smithtown.
Mgr.:	That's a little out of your way, isn't it? *What made you choose that dealer?*
Emp.:	Frankly, I didn't like the quality of the service that I was getting at the dealer here in town. The dealer in Smithtown always has the car when he says he will and does a quality job. For that, I don't mind the inconvenience of paying a little more and having the extra drive. Besides, he always gives me a loaner while the car's in the shop.

Did you notice the information that the employee provided? We'll provide it again, this time italicizing possible criteria.

Mgr.:	Bill, I notice that you own a Jaguar. I'm thinking about buying one myself, but I haven't quite made up my mind. What do you like about yours?
Emp.:	Well, I think that it's a *well-made* car, and it's lots of *fun* to drive.
Mgr.:	Anything else?
Emp.:	Sure. It's a *sharp-looking* car. Not like some of the boxes they're selling today. And my *friends like it.*
Mgr.:	They certainly look great. Where do you get it serviced? I mean, I'd guess you must want a factory-trained mechanic to work on it.
Emp.:	That's for sure. I *don't take any chances* with it. I take it to the dealer where I bought it, in Smithtown.
Mgr.:	That's a little out of your way, isn't it? What made you choose that dealer?
Emp.:	Frankly, I didn't like the *quality* of the service that I was getting at the dealer here in town. The dealer in Smithtown always has the *car ready when he says* he will and does a *quality* job. For that, I don't mind the inconvenience of paying a little more and having the extra drive. Besides, he always *gives me a loaner* while the car's in the shop.

Let's examine the criteria that the employee mentioned and suggest possible correlations.

well made = quality or reliability
fun = enjoyment
sharp-looking = appearance or status
friends like it = opinions of others
don't want to take any chances = security
quality (mentioned twice again)
gives me a loaner = services
car ready when he says = reliability

Two or three other questions (e.g., about favorite restaurants, etc.) can easily confirm these criteria or provide additional criteria. You can also ask questions about products (yours or a competitor's) that the employee is knowledgable about, or what he likes about his job or the firm. These can be particularly useful because they are more closely related to what you are trying to accomplish. However, because they are job related, he may be more likely to try to provide answers he thinks you want to hear.

In addition, while your employee is answering these questions, you are also finding out about his psychological profile, his thinking preferences, and his motivational criteria. Your future discussions will be more productive and will be structured to meet the employee's multi-level needs.

This takes practice. One way to practice eliciting someone's criteria is to occasionally ask your friends or associates, "What do you like about ___?" It doesn't matter what you ask about. Just be curious. After asking this a few times about different things, you will probably notice that you are beginning to receive similar responses from people. Remember that you will probably be getting this information over several conversations.

Summary

Everyone has multiple decision-making and motivational criteria. The ability to elicit these criteria will greatly enhance your ability to motivate virtually anyone. There are numerous ways and opportunities for you to elicit and use this information. One idea is to psychologically profile the most productive innovators in your office and determine if they share similar themes in terms of motivation or work ethic. If they do, then look for similar motivational themes when interviewing potential new hires. In addition, our project meetings will take on added power if you specifically meet the needs of the entire group.

Our next chapter will further explore ways to elicit an individual's psychological needs and thinking patterns. Before proceeding, take a moment to review the mastery exercises, below.

Mastery Exercise 27-1

Read the next three paragraphs and decide which themes have the greatest frequency.

A: "I chose to work for this company because it has an excellent reputation for quality. Everything they do indicates that. The fact that it offers me so many career paths is also important to someone like me who is upwardly mobile. It's also a very well-known company."

B: "There's a great restaurant down the street that I'm sure you'll enjoy. It has a large menu which always gets rave reviews from the relatively few of us who know about it."

C: "I like people who have a lot of different interests because it makes them interesting to talk to. But, more than anything, I must know that I can turn my back on them without fear."

Answers to Exercise 27-1

Read the next three paragraphs and decide which themes have the greatest frequency.

A: "I chose to work for this company because it has an excellent *reputation for quality*. Everything they do indicates that. The fact that it offers me *many career paths* is also important to someone like me who is *upwardly mobile*. It's also the most *well-known* company of its kind in the world."

B: "There's a great restaurant *down the street* that I'm sure you'll enjoy. It has a *large menu* which always gets *rave reviews* from the relatively *few of us who know about it*."

C: "I like people who have *a lot of different interests* because it makes them interesting to talk to. But, more than anything, I must know that I can *turn my back on them* without fear."

This person has variety (multiple career paths, large menu, many interests) as a key motivation. Additionally the issue of "trust" is evident (good reputation, rave reviews, turn my back). Although "down the street" may indicate a location issue, it is only evident once.

Motivational Programs

Extremes in Thinking

Individuals who think in terms of black and white, good and bad, right and wrong, etc., tend to think and respond in extremes. They appear to be very definite and opinionated. They see the world through their own "rose-colored glasses" and, as far as they are concerned, everyone should think and believe exactly the same way they do. These individuals have made up the ranks of the world's zealots since history began.

It is very difficult to argue with someone like this about one of their beliefs. They are right and they know it and are willing to tell anyone and everyone who will listen. Confronting them in front of a group is usually a disaster because they just dig in their heels and stay put. This can easily lead to an escalation of the argument where either you back down or are forced to take punitive action. Obviously, neither solution is desirable. At the same time, such people can be very frustrating for other members of a creative team to work with.

You must deal with people who think this way one-on-one. When you need to convince them that there is something beyond the level of their own experience, merely search for the exception that negates the extreme statement. Usually, if you find even one exception, they have to admit that, just possibly, they do not have all of the answers. For example, during one project team meeting a design engineer informed the team manager that he had no intention of wasting his time using a new piece of testing equipment because it was worthless. The manager employed the procedure that we had suggested and made the following statement: "You sound very certain. What *specifically* did you read in the operating manual or professional journals to allow you to come to that conclusion?" The engineer got flustered and had to admit that he associated this particular testing equipment with another one by a different company that had performed poorly in the past. The blustering engineer became significantly more cautious in future team meetings.

It would have been better if the manager had confronted the engineer on an individualized basis. However, the engineer had, in effect, challenged the manager in front of the entire team. The manager was careful with his tonality so that his question sounded curious, rather than sarcastic or confrontational. More than one member of the team got the message.

Past—Present—Future

One's orientation to time is an important key to how some people think, respond, and are motivated. We all know people who constantly refer to the "good old days"; while others constantly refer to "how things will be." Whether the person is oriented to the past, to the future, or those who are popularly called the "now generation" (present-orientation), knowledge about people's orientations can be very important to the process of managing and motivating them.

Past-Orientation: People with a strong orientation to the past tend to live on their past accomplishments, in "the good old days." Many people seem to live their lives in the past and use the past as their primary basis of reference.

"They don't build cars like they used to," and a series of other past-oriented phrases would let the astute manager know that the key to dealing with such an individual would be to emphasize "the continuance of the creative quality we have always had" and the "enhancements to the basic designs that have served us so well over the years." The phrases used by the manager indicate a past reference, which would then match the individual's past time orientation. This is particularly useful to remember when you have to convince a past-oriented superior to support your innovations.

The way to demotivate such an individual is by emphasizing the modern, state-of-the-art, tradition-breaking aspects of the product or service. These references, of course, would appeal to people with the "present" or "future" time orientation.

Because innovation means future thinking for most people, few past-oriented individuals enter fields where creativity is required. However, they are often very good at finding new uses for existing technology or products. Generally speaking, *a past orientation is fine as long as there is also a good grounding in the present.*

Present-Orientation: People with a strong orientation to the present are involved in what is happening at the moment. They occasionally review past memories and plan for the future, but they live in the present. *"Now is the time to get things done."* When working on projects, they tend to become very involved with whatever aspect they are currently working on. Unfortunately, because they tend to ignore both the past and the future, they are often very poor planners and may not learn from past mistakes. *They need to learn from the past and set future goals.*

Future-Orientation: People with a strong future orientation make up a large portion of innovators. They are constantly thinking about ways to make things better for tomorrow and develop new concepts to implement their ideas. However, in the extreme, they are sometimes more concerned with the way things will eventually be than they are with working right now. They can tend to live in a fantasy world in which things will always work themselves out. They are always talking about the things they are about to do. "Things will be better/different, tomorrow" is typical of the way they deal with problems. Unfortunately, many of them never get anything done.

Future-oriented people are often people who talk about the next big deal that will save them. Unfortunately, most of these great deals never happen, and the individual continues to live in a fantasy world where some magical happening will occur.

A future orientation is fine as long as there is also a good grounding in the present. Remember, innovation means future thinking.

When dealing with such a person, emphasize the benefits they *will* receive for a particular project. They will modify their behavior as long as they have a goal to look forward to.

People—Places—Things—Activities

"People-oriented" individuals are usually talking about others. *Relationships are very important* to them. This pattern is synonymous with the Socialite and the Affiliator presented previously.

You could motivate such a person by making references to group activities, how everybody would obtain benefits, or how everyone would appreciate what he or she is about to do. "You'll be able to proudly tell all of your friends," would be another approach to persuade this person.

"Place-oriented" people are generally talking about all the places they have been. "Last year we went to Europe and spent some time in Paris. Oh, what a wonderful city. Have you ever been there?" Motivating this person with a vacation trip or a dinner at an exclusive restaurant would work much better than a plaque or a round of applause from the group.

"Thing-oriented" people are exemplified by those people who accumulate things for the sake of ownership. "He who dies with the most toys wins," is a popular saying. Creative people are often also thing-oriented, but for a different reason. Being creative themselves, they are often fascinated with the latest developments and gadgets in a wide variety of fields. It is interesting to note how many people can be motivated by being able to select from a high-tech catalogue or some other type of catalogue. You often know this person by the number of gadgets they own.

"Activities-oriented" people often talk about the things they have done and the interesting activities they have taken part in. "Place-oriented" individuals associate places with their self-worth and frequently wish to travel. However, before labeling someone as place-oriented, remember that the key question is "WHY." If they like to travel to visit the various places, then the person is place-oriented; however, if the person intends to ski the Alps, hike in the Black Forest, and do a series of other activities, you know that he is activities-oriented. This person goes to a resort because of the things that can be done.

Global versus Linear

Global thinkers often see the big picture and are generally not interested in the details of a situation. Present a concept and they grasp the meaning and are often mentally exploring other potentials and ramifications while their contemporaries are still trying to understand the basic ideas. While global thinking is great for some things, it can be disadvantageous for certain types of jobs that require a more step-by-step orientation.

Linear thinkers take things one step at a time. They tend to be great at procedures and relatively poor at "what if" scenarios. Yet, it is usually good to have a least one person who can do linear thinking on your team because they will make sure that the logical sequence is taken into consideration and few, if any, things are left to chance.

Chunking

Chunking refers to the detail required in presenting information or ideas. Information chunk size can often be correlated to global or linear thinking. However, the correlations are not precise. If an individual needs a tremendous amount of detail in order to understand what is necessary, provide it. Mentally make note of it and, the next time you give instructions, you'll be able to provide it in the most advantageous way for that individual.

Of course, you must take into account the person's relative familiarity with the task that they are about to undertake. Even a global thinker, who prefers the big picture, will need additional details if the task is new.

The trick is to be able to explain something using both extremes—details and global. If you can do that you can then explain anything in the middle.

Emotional versus Logical

"I *feel* that this is the right way." "I just know that . . ." These people often have an intuitive method of coming to a conclusion. They often "react" very quickly and with a great deal of emotionalism. While gender stereotypes are no longer appropriate, psychologists used to refer to this as the feminine side of an individual's personality.

In contrast, the male side of the personality, epitomized by the ancient Greek philosophers, would be represented in the logic-oriented person. For them, things need to be logical. Often they deal exclusively in their head instead of their heart. They are frequently considered cold and aloof and certainly detached. They rarely get very excited, nor do they easily get depressed.

The emotional individual would be influenced by you "sharing your feelings" with him. They respond more readily to the rah-rah of many motivational speakers. Of course, they could have the opposite response and be turned off by such speeches. Either way, they will have an emotional response.

The logical person responds to appeals to the intellect. Try to motivate him with an emotional appeal and you'll find he has a decided lack of interest and even possibly mild disgust that someone would do something so illogical.

I/We

"I think that the way to do it is my way. . . . I remember when I told a client what I thought and, of course, I was right. . . . I thought to tell you something that I discovered." You probably know someone who represents this extreme "I" orientation. These people are not going to motivated by team spirit. "This is what's in it for you," must be clearly, distinctly and exquisitely stated. A power or achievement orientation may increase the persuasiveness of your comments. Affiliation is a very remote possibility.

"We-oriented" individuals are similar to the affiliation-oriented person discussed in Chapter 27. "Let's get the gang together and all pull towards the common objective for our mutual benefit." The regular use of "we," "us," "let's," etc. is not a guarantee that affiliation is the approach. You'd want to consider other behaviors to verify your suppositions.

Internal versus External Motivation

How a person is motivated is a key to working with them. Some people are internally motivated; that is, they motivate themselves and maintain their own pace. They know they are good by an internal check. A person who is externally motivated needs reinforcement from others. Sometimes a pat on the back. For another, it's an award, and for still others, it's money.

An internally motivated person enjoys contests with himself by beating his own personal best. An externally motivated person would be more responsive to outside feedback.

A person's motivational needs are one of the key hiring characteristics to consider during the initial interviews. It's easy to observe individual's in their day-to-day activities and make note who is internally versus externally motivated. It is substantially more difficult to do this during the hiring interview. Not too many people would respond "No" to the following question: "Are you a self-starter?" Unless the person has come from a different planet, they are going to indicate that they've always been and always will be a self-starter who requires little or no supervision.

Toward versus Away as a Goal-Setting Strategy

People tend to look either ahead or behind. Some people move through life seeking positive goals, while others take the same journey to avoid unpleasantness. While their actions may be identical, their motivation patterns are not. What motivates one, leaves the other cold.

For example, an individual says, "I don't want a job with a lot of rules and regulations." or "I'm not interested in being constantly supervised." These two statements are indications that he is moving away rather than towards something (i.e., away from rules and regulations and from supervision). He seemingly knows what he *doesn't* want, but does he necessarily know what he *does* want? Remember, just because he doesn't want a lot of rules and regulations doesn't mean that he is not a good job candidate. After all, his opposite number may speak of *wanting* the independence to make his own decisions and exhibiting a willingness to accept responsibility for the outcomes. Both of these individuals may represent the ideal candidate. The difference is in the way you appeal to them.

When trying to motivate the "away-oriented" person, you might say something like, "I know you'll enjoy this new project. You won't have the budget problems we faced last time and there won't be anywhere near as many restrictions." However, to the "towards-oriented" person, you might sell the same project by saying something like, "I know that you'll enjoy this new project. The budget is larger and you'll have a free hand in choosing the direction you want to go." The project is the same, and each will probably perform excellently, but neither will respond to the other's motivational pattern.

Win/Lose

Similar to good/bad and all/none thinking, this pattern identifies almost everything in terms of "Did I win or lose?" Some people get into the habit of being a "loser," while others allow losing attitudes to affect their lives to a significant degree. Consider what is called "The Murphy's Law Syndrome"—a person consistently thinks, "if anything can go wrong it will go wrong." When something goes wrong they blithely say, "Murphy's Law," as if that excuses everything. Certainly this is a fine and even healthy reaction occasionally. Sometimes this attitude allows us "not to sweat the small stuff" and to contextualize problems as something basically trivial. It's also good to plan for contingencies by taking into account all of the things that can go wrong. This attitude is great for strategic and tactical planning, but has no real place in everyday affairs because people with this outlook are mentally throwing their fates to the wind by putting their success in the hands of fate.

In an innovator, most of us want someone who makes her own success, who doesn't wait for opportunities to occur but makes her own opportunities. When a problem occurs we want this person to either fix it or deal with it, but then go forward from there without dwelling on what could have been.

There are many other characteristics of the perfect innovator, but one additional one that comes to mind when considering this section is that they want to win and want others to win. It would be ideal if they would also regularly assist others in winning, but if they merely allowed others to win without sabotaging, that would be good too. It's interesting to note that the *stars* of your department and of any industry usually have this "win-win" trait. They have already made it. It is okay for other people to shine also.

Compare them to the members of the dreaded "coffee klatch," who knock, berate, sabotage, bend, fold, and otherwise mutilate those who are not members of their little group. This is the type of affiliation that can be detrimental to your office and your career.

Summary

There are many, many different patterns that people commonly employ. Very few are intrinsically good or bad. Almost all of them can be either advantageous or disadvantageous depending upon the context. The trick is to pay attention to these patterns in your day-to-day dealings with people.

As you learn to first recognize and then respond to these patterns in ways that make sense to the other person, your overall effectiveness is enhanced. It demonstrates that you have a series of individuals in your employ rather than generic nonentities. It also means that you will be able to motivate people to achieve more of their potential, which is a "win-win" situation. It also allows you to recognize when problems with a particular person are occurring and provides the tools, along with other techniques presented in this book, to resolve more quickly and easily those problems.

The patterns that have been presented thus far are but a few of the standard responses that allow you to predict behavior. We have presented the ones that are easily observable and that will give you the greatest personal leverage. It is important to combine this information with characteristics presented in other chapters. Extending the concept a bit further, we can psychologically profile current "ideal" employees to determine which criteria contribute most significantly to their success.

As an experiment, please think of an "ideal" innovator and respond to the following questions so that you can get a feel for the potential ramifications of having this information. Is this person:

➡ Oriented to the past, present, or future?

➡ Self-motivated (i.e., able to maintain a good work pace without reliance on external sources)?

➡ Interested in power, affiliation, or achievement?

➡ A global or linear thinker?

➡ Moving towards a goal or moving away from something?

➡ Pro-active or reactive?

➡ Want to continue doing the job in the same way as usual or does he always try to do different things?

The answers to these questions are important because they determine how successful this person will become. By eliciting the motivational themes and programs of a few of your star performers, you can develop both a clearer picture of the mental and behavioral characteristics necessary for success and a better guideline to use when hiring others.

A potential difficulty you face is that most people will "consciously" indicate that they are pro-active, or global thinkers, or whatever most closely matches their self-image or their ideal. You cannot just ask people what they are. However, you can determine it through multiple observations of behavior, in addition to asking certain astute questions and decide whether a new candidate will fit the same mold as the star producers.

Stress and Motivation in Creativity

Introduction

In the last few chapters, we've discussed important ways that you can effectively motivate your creative employees to give their very best while enjoying what they do. In this chapter, we will explore "stress overload," one of the great "de-motivators," which, if ignored, can cost you lost production, high personnel turnover, and an increase in costly errors.

How does stress affect our level of motivation and that of our staff? Is it possible to overstress our employees in our efforts to motivate them? We've all seen individuals who lose their enthusiasm and seem to give up, become frequently ill, or develop family problems or a drinking habit. We've also seen individuals who are so hard charging that when the "burnout" comes, we're hardly surprised. The fact is that stress and motivation (or lack of motivation) frequently go hand in hand. But what is stress, and where does it come from?

"Everyday in every way . . . (things are getting more and more stressful)." At least that's what most of us seem to think. According to pollster Louis Harris's new book, *Inside America,* 89 percent of *all* adult Americans (roughly 158 million people) report experiencing high levels of stress. Almost 60 percent say that they feel "great stress" at least once or twice a week and nearly one third (over 30 percent) feel that they are living with high stress every day. Depending upon the industry and the demands placed upon them by their superiors, creative individuals are often very susceptible to stress.

In 1967, Dr. Robert Eliot, the well-known cardiologist, was called to Cape Canaveral to help the U.S. Government determine why young aerospace engineers (some as young as twenty-nine) were dropping dead at an alarming rate. Dr. Eliot found that these young creative engineers were dying from stress caused by the government's policy of firing 15 percent of the project work force after each successful rocket launch. He reports,

> "From 1965 to 1973, the work force at the Cape was cut in half, from 65,000 to 32,000. One month these highly trained young professionals were putting in sixteen-hour days in, highly paid jobs. The next month they were out of work. Worse, they had no transferable skills. I found them repairing TV sets, sacking groceries, and working as ticket-takers at Disney World." (Eliot and Breo, *Is It Worth Dying For?,* p.15.)

Stress has been shown to be a major contributor to physical and mental illness (insurance companies and medical authorities indicate that over 75 percent of *all* time lost from work can be attributed to stress), family breakup, drug and alcohol abuse, and suicide. Many psychiatric authorities feel that stress is the major cause behind most mental illnesses. Among high-stress jobs (police, fire fighters, aerospace engineers, insurance salesmen, executives, psychotherapists, etc.), stress may easily be the single greatest cause of physical and mental problems, especially divorce, suicide, and burnout.

These are grim statistics, and, considering the nature of the responsibilities of today's manager, it might be useful to explore the nature of stress and how to combat it. After all, stress may cost you not only the efficiency and effectiveness of your employees, it may also affect you! At the same time, anxiety over stress can be overdone. After all, its also possible to have too little stress!

What Is Stress?

Probably the simplest way to define stress is the amount of challenge you experience. Physiologically, stress can be defined as anything that moves your body out of a state of "homeostasis" (balance). If you think about it, this can include eating, playing tennis, over even being affectionate with your family (none of which are usually life threatening).

Overall, most authorities agree that stress overload results from feelings of losing control over events that affect our physical and emotional well being and our sense of self-worth. Once this is added to a gradual loss of hope that things will improve, we become overstressed and begin to risk "burnout." Let's look at a graph of how our level of stress, or challenge, affects both our efficiency and our enjoyment of life.

As you can see, too little stress, or challenge, can lead to boredom and loss of energy and enthusiasm. We need a certain amount of challenge to keep our enthusiasm. However, too much challenge can lead to stress overload, which can further lead to burnout, loss of production, family problems, and even a breakdown in our immune system with a subsequent loss of health.

As a department or team manager, you have far greater control over many of the factors that affect your well being than most people. However, while you have more control than your staff, there are still many events that affect you that you cannot control. Examples might include such elements as the state of the economy, foreign competition, requirements from the home office, and new government regulations. All of these factors influence the potential productivity of your department, but you can't control them. In addition, while you have only limited control over your staff's productivity, you are held accountable for it.

To avoid or overcome this sense of being helpless and out of control, it is important to develop personal values that reflect what is meaningful and important to you. Too much stress suppresses the immune system, which can leave you vulnerable to illness. In addition to potential physical ailments, you may also develop a loss of identity and self-esteem.

Do you have any employees who have performed well in the past but who seem to be losing their innovative ability now? Someone who may even appear to have "given up?" How about an individual who has become virtually obsessed with work and "trying to get ahead?" For many of us, stress overload can lead to feelings of anxiety, depression, and even a sense of being driven. Often, in our attempts to regain our sense of control, many of us cross the line from productive to self-destructive behaviors. What is most ironic is that stress overload is a self-inflicted wound.

Today, we are constantly surrounded by reminders of what we have to own, look like and accomplish to be considered "successful." If we accept the concept of "success" presented by media advertising, it is easy for us to develop feelings of inadequacy over failure to obtain the lifestyle presented. This can lead to a sense of being trapped and the development of feelings of hopelessness and helplessness in trying to get what "you really want" out of life. According to Dr. Robert Eliot, a far more important question to ask is, *"Am I winning?"* Also, ask yourself whose standards you're using to determine your level of success. Then look at those standards and decide whether anyone could meet them. Too many of us demand the impossible of ourselves and others. If you are impatient with anything short of perfection, you may be setting yourself up for "failure," frustration, and those feelings of hopelessness.

To avoid this trap, study Section VII, on coaching and counseling, where we suggest that you explore your (and your employee's) goals and your plans for achieving them. If you are feeling stressed, look at what you're trying to accomplish and ask yourself three questions which we find quite helpful:

➡ "Do I know *how to* achieve this goal?" In other words, do I have the technical knowledge to solve this problem?

➡ "Do I have a *chance to* achieve this goal?" That is, is the goal reachable? Do I have the resources necessary to achieve it?

➡ "Do I really *want to* achieve this goal?" Is this really my goal or one which has been imposed upon me by someone else? If the goal has been imposed, can I really make it mine? If so, do it!

Once you've answered these questions satisfactorily, there are three others that need to be explored to clarify the source of stress:

➡ "Is this goal *real?*" Is it really achievable? To a degree, this is an extension of *chance to.*

➡ "Can I *win* the goal using my current strategy?" Often, we choose excellent goals but fail to achieve them because we have selected an ineffective strategy to achieve it. Evaluate your problem-solving strategies for their effectiveness before committing significant resources.

➡ "Will achieving my goal be *worth* the cost and effort required?" There are many financially successful people who would gladly trade their success to regain the good health or the family they lost in attaining it.

Hot Reactors

With all of this talk of the effects of stress, you may be wondering, "How does all of this affect me?" Dr. Robert Eliot (the author of, *Is It Worth Dying For?*), has made a series of discoveries regarding the way our responses to situations affect our physical and mental health.

One of his discoveries indicates that some people respond to simple challenges (e.g., completing a billing form or figuring a commission) in the same way that they would to a life-threatening situation. He refers to these individuals as *"hot reactors."* In addition, his research has indicated that nearly one-fifth of all people who feel that they are under stress are "hot reactors," and, in some professions (e.g., top insurance salesmen), the number reaches as high as forty percent (during a recent study involving a major brokerage firm, Dr. Eliot found that as many as 80 percent of the top producers were hot reactors).

If you are a hot reactor you may experience the physical reactions of an "alarm" response, such as adrenaline production, to simple challenges as often as forty or more times a day without even being aware of it. In some cases, your blood pressure may even double. In any case, subjecting your body to this kind of reaction on a constant basis will eventually cause it to break down.

In addition, if you feel overly challenged or threatened over a period of time, your body goes into the "resistance mode" , adding the hormone cortisol to your system. This hormone raises your blood pressure and keeps it up. Then, when alarm occurs again, your body's system begins its alert from higher levels of blood pressure, blood thickness, stomach acidity, etc. This addition of more adrenaline to a system already flush with cortisol can literally lead the heart muscles to tear themselves apart—one of the common findings in sudden death (80 percent).

The worst quality of a hot reactor is that he or she is not as easily spotted as a "Type A" personality. Recent research by the American Medical Association indicates that there are just as many "Type B" hot reactors as there are "Type A's."

Each year, more than 1.2 million people suffer from heart attacks. Over half of those heart attacks are caused by too much stress and, in nearly one third of the attacks, the first symptom is *death!* That means that over 1200 people die from stress related heart attacks *every day!* How many people do you know who have died of a heart attack?

In addition, remember that stress overload attacks more than just the heart. Few people seem to realize that too much stress is probably the single greatest cause of impotence in men and frigidity in women. Failure to recognize this problem and discuss it openly and with understanding has hurt many marriages when one or both partners began to fear that they were losing their sexuality. Needless to say, an employee who is worrying about divorce or family problems is not giving his full attention to his work and will not be very creative.

The Million Dollar Round Table

In 1985, Dr. Robert Eliot conducted a study with the members of the Million Dollar Round Table (the insurance industry's highest producers). He found that 39 percent were hot reactors, and another 25 percent were undiagnosed hypertensives. That is, two out of three of the top producers in the insurance industry were in imminent cardiac danger. He also found that 80 percent felt that their lives were not fulfilling and they were not happy. Interestingly, these kinds of numbers are not unique to the insurance industry. In fact, recent studies have indicated that things are even worse for stock brokers. How healthy are your top employees?

These are grim numbers for anyone who wants to be successful, especially in sales. However, there is a happy ending. Dr. Eliot and his group worked with the members of the study to help them learn how to deal with and reduce stress in their lives, and the results were phenomenal. Six months later, all of the participants were healthy. *None* were hot reactors and *none* were hypertensive. All reported that life had taken on new meaning and that life was good. In addition, the average work week for these individuals had dropped from seventy hours per week to just forty to fifty hours per week. And, best of all, each had significantly increased their production during the same period.

1986 was a fantastic year for the insurance industry. On the average, members of the Million Dollar Round Table increased their production by 11 percent over the previous year. When Dr. Eliot did a follow-up of his test group in January 1987, he found that everyone was still healthy and happy. In addition, the smallest increase in production for a member of the group was *40 percent* (note: he was undergoing a divorce), while the average increase was in excess of *100 percent* over the previous year.

Why discuss insurance sales professionals in a book about managing the needs of creative people? Dr. Eliot's study clearly demonstrated that people under stress risk their health, their productivity, and their enjoyment of their work. It also proved that stress could be treated relatively inexpensively and that doing so not only reduced health risks and loss of productivity, it *significantly increased productivity!*

Summary

What all of this boils down to is that you can have it all. Success doesn't have to mean ulcers, heart attacks and an early grave. In fact, it can mean just the opposite. You can succeed and enjoy yourself while you do it! All you have to do is learn how to handle stress in your life. Something else worth thinking about is that people who feel stressed often leave their jobs in order to reduce it. Happy employees don't leave!

How to Manage
and Reduce Stress

Stress Isn't All Bad

As we mentioned before, stress, or challenge, isn't *all* bad. Effective time management (or event management) is an important tool in coping with stress. Review your life for a moment and try to determine whether you have too much stress, or not enough. If you have too many challenges (which seems to be the most common complaint among department and team managers and their personnel), begin to learn to say, "NO," to additional responsibilities. To do this, you may even need to cut back on some of your current work load or social obligations.

However, if you don't have enough challenge in your life, begin to say, "YES," to additional challenges and responsibilities. Look for additional projects to develop, or publish an article on some of your work. You may find yourself not only with more to do, but also more energy to do it with. Note: We realize that as a manager, you probably don't have this particular problem.

In any case, make a list of your current activities. When you have completed it, determine which activities you are involved in because you really have to do them, which you're involved in because you really want to do them, and which you're involved in for any other reason. Then make a notation next to each for "have to," "want to," and "neither." When you are done, start eliminating the activities that you've marked as "neither" on your list.

Make a Plan

Hyrum Smith, the great time management expert, points out that no one can manage time. What we *can* do is manage the events that impinge upon us in time. To do this, write down those events and factors that have the most impact on you. Those that you can control (e.g., the number of meetings you schedule), and those that you cannot control (e.g., the economy). Once you have determined which is which, develop and follow a plan to *take control of the things that you can control,* and to lessen the impact on you of the things that you can't control.

Attainable Goals

The importance of establishing attainable goals for ourselves cannot be overemphasized. Without goals, our behavior becomes directionless and without meaning, and if the goals are not attainable, they quickly become a source of frustration and stress. Below is a summary of the conditions necessary to establish a well-formed goal:

➡ State your goal in positive language: write down what you want rather than what you don't want.

➡ The goal must be within your control. If you are sixty years old, a goal of winning the decathlon in the Olympics is probably not in your control.

➡ The goal should preserve your "ecology." That is, be sure that attaining the goal will not cost more than it's worth. Remember REAL, WIN, WORTH. We know of many a millionaire who lost his family in gaining his "success" who would gladly trade his millions to have them back again.

➡ Be very specific both in describing your goal, and in how you will know when you have achieved it. From your description, someone else should be able to recognize when you have reached your goal.

→ However you view your current state, there are probably many positive aspects about it. Your goal must maintain these positive aspects or you may find yourself unconsciously defeating your efforts to obtain it.

Once you have established your intermediate and long-term goals, break them down into daily increments. Each day set yourself a goal that you can attain and then reward yourself for attaining it. The nature of the reward is up to you (a few holes of golf, watching a ball game, reading a novel, a treat, etc.), but see that you earn and give yourself a little reward every day. You'll be surprised what it does for your attitude.

Point of View

One interesting result of studies in stress management is that far more important than the actual events in your life is the way you interpret those events and the meaning that you assign them. In his book, *Man's Search for Meaning,* Dr. Viktor Frankl speaks of his years in a Nazi extermination camp. While there, he would frequently try to determine which prisoners might survive and which would be unable to cope. At first he made his determinations based upon the youth and physical strength of the prisoners, but too frequently, young, healthy prisoners would come into the barracks and announce that they had given up. The next day they were found dead in their bunks. When they lost the will to live, they died!

Others (many in their forties and fifties), who were not in top physical condition, survived. Despite all of the odds against them, they were still alive when the camp was liberated, four years later. Frankl determined that there was a single great factor that separated those who gave up and died and those who held on until they were liberated. That factor was the "meaning" that they assigned to their lives and to the events that occurred.

Dr. Frankl says that if life has meaning, then all suffering has meaning and can be born, no matter how great. If life is meaningless, then all suffering is meaningless and is unbearable, no matter how small. Remember, it is not the event that causes stress, it is the meaning that we assign to the event.

When something doesn't go our way, do we interpret it as a failure, proof that we are unworthy? Or do we look for what we can learn from the experience? As you explore the motivational criteria of your employees, you will also discover the way that they assign meaning to events, especially "failure." One of the great blessings of "failing," is that it makes us more willing to try something different.

What's Your Point of View?

Ask yourself what is the meaning of your life? If you are not sure, think about it. How would you like to be remembered after you are gone? Do you just want to be remembered for being a world-famous innovator or a successful executive, or are there other, more important things? What are your motivational criteria and beliefs?

Thoughts versus Feelings

Perhaps Solomon said it best over four thousand years ago, "As a man thinketh, so is he." What you think about and how you think about it (the meaning that you assign to events), determines how you feel and the impact that the event will have on your health. Review the exercises we shared in Chapters 11 and 12 on becoming more creative. Then try this simple exercise:

> Relax and get as comfortable as you can, take a deep breath, hold it for a slow count of three and let it out. Now think back and remember the happiest moment of your life (perhaps the day you got married or proposed, your third birthday party, or possibly the first time the doctor handed you your new child to hold). Try to really get into the memory, and rather than seeing yourself doing something, feel yourself doing it. Reexperience everything as if you were actually there and reliving it all again. Do this for about one minute and then return.
>
> How do you feel? Pretty good? Now do the same thing, but this time relive a moment of minor irritation such as a traffic delay, getting "bawled out" for something, or missing an important putt in a golf game. Again, make it real and hold it for about one minute, and then return.
>
> How do you feel now? Not as good? Finally, return to the happiest moment of your life. Again, relive it as it was then and

make it real. Modify the submodalites involved to enhance the positive feelings associated with the memory. Do this for one moment and then return.

Notice how good you feel. What happened? Did you notice how what you thought about determined how you felt?

Now, take a 3x5 card and on one side of it write down ten qualities that you possess that others might find admirable or attractive (e.g., your concern for others, your professionalism, etc.).

On the other side, write down five of the happiest moments of your life and five successes in your life (achievements that made you feel that you could do anything, overcome any obstacle, such as a new innovation you thought of, a new marketing angle, a piece of research where your input made the critical difference, or even "acing" a course in school).

Carry the card with you and the next time that you feel discouraged, take the card out and read your good qualities. Remind yourself that you are a good, competent person. Then turn it over, relax, and relive each of the ten moments you've written there for one minute apiece. Before you complete number five, you will find that you have completely regained your confidence and positive outlook. *Take control of how you feel!*

Humor

Developing a good sense of humor and the ability to laugh at ourselves and the situations in which we find ourselves is one of the easiest and most effective ways to regain control of the impact that circumstances have on our feelings. It also lets us see ourselves and our circumstances from a different point of view (humorous instead of ego- or life-threatening. In their book, *Frogs Into Princes*, Richard Bandler and John Grinder point out that since we often say to ourselves, "Someday I'll probably look back on all this and laugh," *why wait?!* Laugh now instead of letting circumstances overwhelm you. Set the example in the office. If you can laugh at problems, it will be easier for your employees to do so, and you will easily reduce the levels of stress within the branch. Note: Of course we are not suggesting that you develop a flippant attitude towards problems. We are suggesting putting them into perspective and not letting them cost more than they are worth.

Helping Your Family Help You

Your family can either be a lifesaving support, or an additional threat. Today nearly twenty-six percent of all sudden cardiac deaths occur on Monday mornings. Twenty-five percent occur on Saturday mornings. These are the times when we switch from one source of stress to another. There are several steps that you can easily take that will not only help you to cope with stress in your own life, but will also help you avoid becoming a source of stress for your family and employees. You may wish to encourage your employees to take some of these steps and support them in their efforts to do so.

Keep Your Balance

Anyone can lift and carry two-to-three times more weight if it is well balanced than if it is unbalanced. This is also true of psychic burdens such as stress.

To really cope with the complexities of today's world we must develop and maintain a sense of inner balance between our mental, physical, emotional, career, social, and spiritual selves. If any one of these areas is overemphasized at the expense of others, it can leave us without the resources to fully cope when circumstances put us under pressure. We all want our creative employees to become so excited about their work that they want to work late into the evening several nights a week. However, it's important to take into account the costs to families and the potential backlash from that source if we overdo it.

Prepare for Change

In the competitive arena of innovation, change is more than inevitable, it is constant. To deal with change we must learn to expect it and prepare for it and its impact upon our lives and the lives of our families.

If you are new to management, the odds are high that your family and loved ones are not prepared for the changes that will occur in their lives as a result of your change in career. After all, your level of responsibility increased significantly with your promotion. Be certain that you discuss your job with them regularly and, especially, that you discuss not only your own goals for your career, but also *their* goals for your career. After all, you are asking them to support your work. Encourage your employees to do the same.

Just one of the changes that families may have to deal with is that of the work hours. Depending upon the industry, few creative shops work a strict nine to five shift. Today's innovators are often called to work late for weeks at a time to complete a project on deadline or to prepare for a major client or management presentation. If your family and loved ones are not already familiar with such a pattern this can be a severe disruption. If you have already told them and they appear to be understanding and supportive, don't be lulled into a false sense of security. Until they have experienced the change they won't really know what kind of an impact it will have on them.

Once a pattern has become established (e.g., your "being home" every night), it is natural to unconsciously expect that pattern to continue. We develop further patterns of meeting our needs around that pattern, and when one person changes, it affects many. Imagine the typical family of five as pictured in Figure 30-1.

Each letter represents a family member, and the lines connecting the letters represent relationships among the members and between each member and their outside commitments (e.g., work, friends, church, etc.). Notice what happens in Figure 30-2 when one member {F} changes (e.g., begins a new job, becomes an adolescent, etc.). The relationships stretch, adding tension (and stress) to *all* of the relationships in the family.

There are only three ways to reduce those tensions.

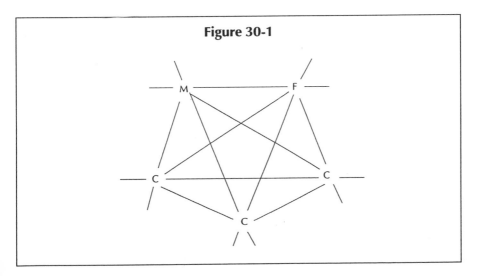

Figure 30-1

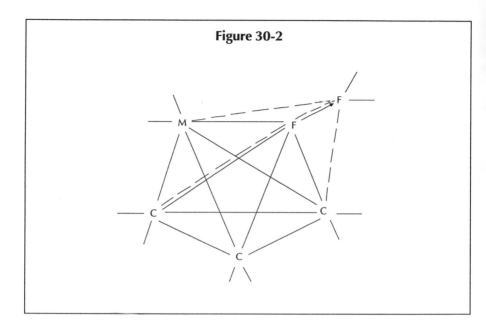

Figure 30-2

→ *First,* best, and hardest, is for the family to work together to adjust to the change (see Figure 30-3).

Your family's ability to do this effectively can radically affect their ability to cope with stresses in their lives. If this does not

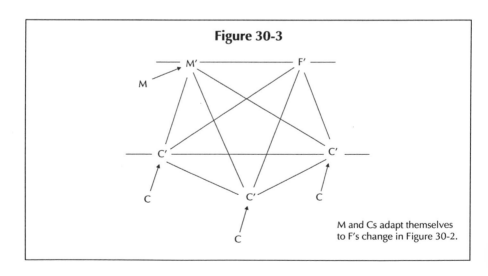

Figure 30-3

M and Cs adapt themselves to F's change in Figure 30-2.

occur, you may find that the tension you bring home from work shows up in your child's poor grades or behavior in school.

→ *Second,* the family can exert so much pressure on the person who has changed, that they change back (e.g., quit their job), as in Figure 30-4. A lot of new creative people end up leaving their jobs because of this.

This occurs because, like your body, your family is a system and no system can tolerate tension for very long. As a result, it always moves to reduce that tension. This is one reason why so many alcoholics have difficulty staying sober; once their families have adjusted to the individual as an alcoholic, they resist the further adjustment needed to cope with him sober. They will subtly pressure him to drink again.

→ The *third,* and most tragic way to adjust occurs when the family system cannot cope with the tension any longer (see Figure 30-5) and "cuts" the relationships to the stress-producing individual.

This is seen in divorce, suicide, murder, running away, alcohol and drug abuse, and mental illness.

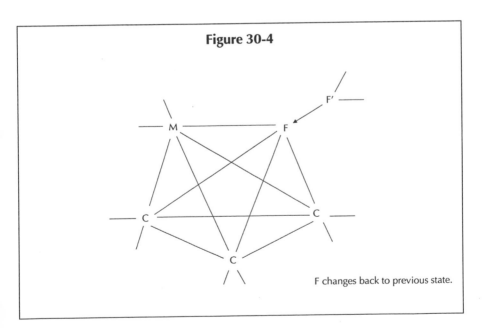

Figure 30-4

F changes back to previous state.

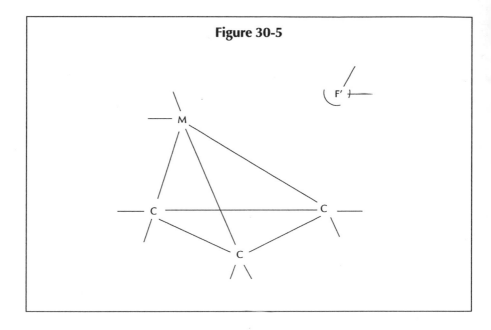

Figure 30-5

Keep Courting

What else can you do to avoid having your family see your job as a rival for your time and attention? Court your spouse *and* your children. For so many couples the courtship ends as soon as they have said, "I do." Everyone needs to feel courted, needed, and loved. One way to do this is to make sure that the time that you do spend with your loved ones is *"quality time."* That is, time in which your main objective is to meet their needs. This isn't easy and requires periods when they have your total and undivided attention.

If you are going to work two to three nights per week, have your spouse bring the children to work at six and go out to eat as a family (e.g., MacDonald's) instead of remaining in the office. Help the children to see your late nights as potentially fun instead of empty. When dinner is over, take one of the children back to the office and let them use the desk next to yours to do their homework. Managers who have encouraged their employees to do this report very positive results in the form of increased family loyalty to the firm and more work at night to increase production. Note: We realize that the ability to do this will depend largely upon the nature of your work.

When the evening is over, stop for some ice cream together on the way home. By having the children take turns, you can have a special experience with a different child each week.

If you regularly work late, once a week try to have your spouse join you alone for dinner. After dinner, have her or him join you and do whatever work they've brought home from the office on the desk next to yours. If they haven't any work, let them help you in your tasks in some way. At the very least they can keep you company by watching television in the meeting room while you work. On the way home, stop for a milk shake or something.

Call your spouse and go out on a *date* once a week. The nature of the date will be far less important than being able to look forward to it.

Family Council

Hold a family council each week to discuss each family member's progress toward *their* goals. Find out their needs and discuss their responsibilities, their goals, and any help they need from other members of the family.

Mail a note home to your spouse and each of the children each week (or slip it in their lunch or pocket) telling them that you are thinking of them. Bring home a surprise that you know they like to let them know they're special. It doesn't take a lot of money to say, "I love you," but it can be very important.

Loving Memories

Last of all, have you ever experienced a time when you were having difficulty with a family member such that you dreaded going home because you knew that there would be a "fight?" One way to alleviate this fear is before leaving work, take a moment to relax at your desk, close your eyes for a moment, and remember a loving moment shared with that family member. If the problem is with your spouse, remember and relive how you felt the day you got engaged. If the problem is with a child, remember and relive how you felt the first time the doctor handed him or her to you as an infant. You'll be surprised at how unimportant "problems" and misunderstandings become, and as you change so will they.

Family and friends can either increase your level of stress (25 percent of all heart attacks occur Saturday mornings), or they can reduce it. Which effect they have is up to you. Take the time to strengthen your support groups.

Positive Mental Attitude

In computer terminology, "GIGO" means, "garbage in—garbage out". Your brain is the most sophisticated computer known, yet this rule still applies to it. Each day, little discouragements, news items, business changes, and rejections of project proposals by higher management fill your brain with negative information. All around you there are people and circumstances telling you that you can't win and there's no point in trying. Even if you don't listen to them with your conscious mind, your unconscious does and after awhile even the most optimistic of people can become discouraged. When this occurs, pull out the 3x5 card we discussed earlier and bring your spirits back up. But to avoid letting that happen in the first place, program your mind to think positively.

"PMA" Books

Your local bookstore has hundreds of excellent books on maintaining a positive mental attitude (see attached list for several ideas). Most say the same thing in different ways (just as most bad news falls into several categories stated in slightly different ways), but all are good. Each carries the message that *you are a winner, and you can accomplish anything that you set your mind to!*

Read a chapter each morning before you go to work to program yourself for success, and encourage your employees to do the same. If you have a rough morning, read another chapter during lunch. Finally, read a chapter before going to bed (reading this aloud with your spouse can be excellent for a marriage). Psychologists have found that the last thing you think about before sleep programs the unconscious for the remainder of the night. If you go to bed worried and upset you will spend the night that way and awaken suffering from the Wrong-side-of-the-bed Syndrome. That's when you wake up grouchy and no matter how many things go well that day it was just luck (if you even notice at all). Why not program yourself to wake up with the Right-side-of-the-bed Syndrome? Then spend the rest of the day feeling good, despite any unimportant setbacks. Consider building a lending library of PMA books in the office. *Negative attitudes hurt creativity!*

"PMA" Tapes

Another aid in maintaining a positive mental attitude is audio tapes with the same messages as PMA books. You can listen to them while commuting, or getting dressed in the morning. The important thing is to take control over what gets programmed into your mind. Many department managers we know have a substantial collection of such tapes in the office for loaning to employees.

Work Environment

A few department and team managers encourage their employees to eat at their desks during lunch. This may have unfortunate results in terms of health and overall production. The unconscious mind tends to label areas as work areas, play areas, eating areas, etc. In addition, co-workers and management are rarely impressed with materials that are sticky or have coffee rings.

Eating away from your desk becomes particularly important at lunch. Trying to eat while dealing with the stress of calls from customers or other managers is a very effective way to give yourself heartburn, if not gastritis, an ulcer, or worse. When you eat, leave the office behind and go somewhere where you won't even think about work. Recharge your batteries. Read a novel or positive mental attitude book. Go window shopping or take a brisk walk. Studies have shown that doing so can radically increase your effectiveness after lunch, while failing to do so can leave you ineffective and exhausted by the end of the day. Remember, always eat away from your desk.

Watch out for the office crank. Almost every office seems to have one individual who thinks that the world will end tomorrow. Be pleasant about it, but let him know that you're not interested in his talking about negative things.

Mickey Mouse

Do you have someone at the office or elsewhere who upsets you even when you just think about him? Take a moment to mentally see him now. While you think of him, imagine him with ears like Mickey Mouse and a beak and voice like Donald Duck. Does he still upset you? Change other things about him until thinking about him doesn't bother you. With a little practice, every time you see him you'll see Mickey Mouse and hear Donald Duck.

The important thing to remember is that you are in control of your life and your health. Take control.

Change Your Stress

When you have worked all day at a desk, it is often difficult to come home and just sit down and relax. If this occurs, first change the nature of your stress. If you've been working on mental problems, do something physical (like playing tennis or taking a twenty-minute walk). Afterwards you will find that you will be able to relax more easily (note: the physical stress should be something you *enjoy* doing), if for no other reason than you will have burned off some of the stress chemicals stored up in your body during the day.

Eat Right

There are many excellent books on diet and stress. Or, you may wish to consult with your physician about a diet. In any case, a safe rule of thumb is to always eat intelligently and avoid extremes. Avoid the use of tobacco and alcohol since both exacerbate stress.

Be sure to get plenty of fiber, and concentrate on complex carbohydrates such as vegetables. Finally, eat because you are hungry, not because you are tired, working, or watching television.

Exercise

Exercise is also a matter of moderation and intelligence. Handled properly, it can not only burn off stress chemicals, it can also raise your metabolic set point and burn off excess weight.

Before beginning an exercise program be sure to check with your doctor to determine what is appropriate for you. After that, find something that you enjoy doing and do it three to five times per week, working your way up gradually to thirty minutes at a time.

In school, the coaches used to tell us, "No pain, no gain." This is not true. When your body hurts, it is trying to tell you something important and you should listen to it. If you are exercising and it hurts, stop! Cool down gradually and call it a day. Continuing could lead to injury.

Summary

It is possible to have either too little or too much stress, or challenge, in our lives. Too little can leave us dull and bored while too much can leave us feeling hopeless and helpless, exhausted and even ill. Both are demotivating. By actively taking charge of our lives and the meanings we assign to the events in our lives, we can control the level of challenge we face each day and use it to help us to maintain maximum efficiency and enthusiasm.

Coaching and Counseling the Creative Employee

The creative individual can be your most productive employee. However, it is still occasionally necessary to counsel one. This section will deal with how to handle prima donnas, angry employees and customers, and just how to counsel with those who are not performing according to standards without making them defensive and hurting their productivity.

The Art of
Calming Angry People

Whether employees, customers, or other managers, all of us have dealt with angry or upset people many times. Regardless of the cause of their emotional state, it was probably very difficult to deal with effectively. How do you calm down an angry and upset person so that they will "listen to reason," and work with you to solve whatever problem is bothering them? The purpose of this chapter is to provide a series of steps that can be used when dealing with these individuals.

Of course, the first thing to remember is that you cannot control the situation unless you are in control of yourself. Unfortunately, this is often easier said than done, because almost everyone becomes a little defensive when approached by someone who is angry or aggressive. That's because we tend to take personally feelings that are directed at us. However, as a department or team manager, you are a professional, one who always does your best for your employees, your superiors, and your customers. As a result, regardless of the underlying problem, *you* have no need to take others' anger personally or to become defensive. By remaining in control of yourself, you will easily be able to gain control of the situation by following the steps outlined below.

Establish Rapport

Regardless of the relationship or the nature of the interaction in which you are involved, *always* establish rapport before taking any other action. Of course, this does not mean that you should respond symmetrically, by getting angry in return. (Note: Remember, symmetrical interactions are those in which both parties respond in the same way; both friendly, both hostile, etc.) That response will only result in a round of escalating anger that may lead to a breakdown in the relationship. (See Chapter 14.)

In the case of an angry individual, establishing rapport consists of matching their energy level and their speed and intensity of speech. Once you have matched them and established rapport, begin to lead them into a calmer state using the "leading" technique (presented in Chapter 14) or using the highly specialized questioning process about to be introduced.

Speak Their Language

Remember, most arguments and hurt feelings are the result of simple misunderstandings. These misunderstandings happen occasionally when two people speak to each other using two different predicate (sensory-oriented) systems. Make sure that you match their system. If they are visual, use visual terms with them. If they are auditory, use auditory terms, and so on. (See Chapter 23.)

Questioning

Misunderstandings and angry or hurt feelings also occur because of unmet expectations. Most of us simply assume that everyone else assigns the same meanings to words and actions that we do. This may be because the circle of family and friends with whom we grew up did. However, we rarely work with the same people into adulthood. As a result, the people we meet now often have different meanings for words and different expectations of behavior from ours.

When you become involved with an angry or hurt individual, it is important to discover both the exact cause of their current state and the specific circumstances necessary to alleviate it. Without this information, it is not only difficult to keep them calm in their present circumstances, it will be impossible to avoid a repetition.

In Chapter 24, we discussed a program of questioning that enables you to elicit the specific information that you desire by focusing on vague expectations, deletions, etc. Once you've established rapport, begin to question them, using the model questioning program, even before they have become completely calm. We'll discuss clarifying techniques in more detail after the next subsection.

Break the Pattern

Angry disagreements almost always follow a recognizable pattern of symmetrical (similar responses) or complimentary (opposite responses) interaction. One individual, in a Dictator style, approaches the other in a hostile, aggressive manner. At that point, the recipient of all that hostility and aggression responds either complimentarily (submits and tries to withdraw), or symmetrically (responds with anger and aggression of his own). If you have ever watched such a situation develop, you already know that neither response works because both lead to a trap.

If you respond to all angry aggression by giving in, you will establish a habitual complimentary pattern of relating that can be very hard to break. At that point, both you and the other person know that all he need do is become angry or aggressive and you will submit to his desires. This is an unhealthy win-lose situation that is very much how the classic "school yard bully" accomplishes his ends. Once he has established his dominant position, it is almost never challenged. This is bad enough when dealing with childhood bullies, but it is intolerable when dealing with employees, peers, or superiors.

On the other hand, if you always respond symmetrically, with counter-hostility and -aggression, you establish a power struggle in which you must continue until one of you submits, creating another win-lose situation. It is important to recognize that NO ONE EVER WINS A POWER STRUGGLE, or any other win-lose situation. If you, the manager, win, you risk losing a good employee, a customer or a future law suit, depending upon the nature of the struggle. In every case, you lose the relationship. If that relationship is important to you, you may find out too late that your victory cost more than it was worth.

Use your rapport, communications, and questioning skills to maintain a flexible, parallel style of relating that disarms your opponent without increasing either your hostility or theirs. As you demonstrate your genuine interest in them and their concerns, it will become increasingly difficult for them to maintain their anger.

Entering the Realm of the Dictator

As we mentioned above, regardless of an individual's normal mode of relating, when they become hostile and aggressive they are entering the realm of the Dictator. Remember the needs of the Dictator when dealing with them:

➤ The need to be "special." Regardless of how thoughtful we may normally be of others, when we are angry or hurt our only interest becomes the meeting of *our* own needs. Put other agendas aside and be certain that you give them your undivided attention.

➤ The need to be "better" than others. Another variant of being "special," this need is manifest in hostile language, sarcasm, and "putting down" others. When we are angry or hurt, we become defensive and may manifest that defensiveness by verbally striking out at others. Avoid placating or responding hostilely. These responses will only result in your falling into the traps discussed previously. Use the "CLAPping" technique discussed in the next subheading.

➤ The covert need for security. Most people are actually a little threatened by their own hostility and aggressiveness and secretly wish that someone would take control of the situation before it escalates beyond repair. By remaining in control of the situation and your own feelings, you fulfill that need.

➤ As mentioned above, most people tend to become angry when their "reasonable" expectations aren't met. As a result, their "trust" has been broken. As you establish rapport and demonstrate a sincere desire to understand their needs and requirements, you will also help to reestablish that trust. By using the specialized questioning techniques of Chapter 24, in combination with "CLAPping," described below, you will be able to determine specifically what criteria need to be fulfilled to complete that process.

Why So Hot?

As you question angry individuals regarding the causes of their anger and the nature of the remedy that they require, you will also obtain information regarding their motivational criteria. That is, what specific factors make them angry, and what specific factors will remove that anger. We've already mentioned this several times and it may appear that we are only repeating ourselves. However, the concept of what causes anger and what is necessary to remove it must be looked at from several perspectives.

When we try to sell effectively an idea to someone, we examine every aspect of the way he thinks, feels, and makes decisions so that we can match him completely. Hence, we look at:

- His psychological profile and emotional needs.

- His sensory orientation; i.e., does he think in terms that are predominantly visual, auditory, or kinesthetic?

- His motivational criteria for decision-making or buying.

When you begin to work with an angry individual, it is just as important to obtain the same information about him if you are to "sell" him successfully on the concept of calming down and working with you. Hence, the apparent redundancy of criteria type questions.

Examples of questions that you might ask an angry individual are provided below. However, use the "CLAPping" technique first, to show your understanding of the individual and his anger. Also, remember that validating someone's anger, or even their right to be angry, is not the same as agreeing with them about the cause.

- "Well, I can see you're upset. Tell me what will provide what you need."

- "It's obvious you really mean that. In your opinion, how should it have been done differently?"

- "If I understand you correctly, you feel that you've been treated unfairly. Is that right?" [response] "I think I understand. What specific things will improve the situation?"

Each of these questions is designed to help you to maintain control of the situation while eliciting the criteria necessary to eliminate the other's anger.

CLAPping

To overcome an individual's anger and aggression, or even his resistance to a desired action, there are four easy steps which should be followed before even attempting to respond to the individual's position. After these four steps have been followed, you can respond to the individual's concern and, if appropriate, return to your own agenda. The four steps are:

1) C (clarify).
2) L (legitimize).
3) A (acknowledge).
4) P (probe).

Clarify

Before attempting to overcome someone's anger or negative attitude it is important to be sure that you are dealing with the real source of his concern. It is easy to begin to respond to what we think he wants without checking first to see if we are on track. Doing this can complicate your efforts to deal with his resistance by trying to deal with something other than the real problem. This might happen in either of two ways:

➡ First, sometimes an individual will act angry or aggressive because he doesn't understand something being done that affects him. Often this is merely the result of a breakdown in communication. He may even have difficulty in explaining exactly what is upsetting him.

In such cases, it is important for you patiently to help him explore the cause of his discomfort until he can identify it and discuss it. Attempting to overcome the anger and resistance without doing so first will inevitably result in resentment on his part. Remember to match his intensity and rate of speech. The questions will lead the individual from an emotionally charged state to an intellectual state.

→ Second, sometimes the cause of the anger first shared by the individual is not the real reason for his anger (e.g., he may say that he is upset with his supervisor for only calling when he has a complaint, when in reality he may be too embarrassed to admit that he's really angry because he feels that his supervisor doesn't take him seriously). For this reason, it is very important to persist in your efforts to *clarify* and not to quit until *all* of the causes of the individual's anger and resistance have been uncovered and dealt with. For example, here is a discussion between a manager and an employee, with you as the manager:

Example of the Clarifying Sequence

Employee: I'm getting really frustrated with this new medical insurance. Every time we need to see the doctor, we have to drive halfway across the county to find one that's associated with this group, and it seems like they don't know what they're doing. Even then, we rarely see the same doctor twice. They just have you see whoever's handy.

You: [PROBING] Are there any other areas of concern for you?

Employee: Not really. I'm just tired of the inconvenience only to end up feeling like the doctors are idiots. At least my old doctor knew my family and actually seemed competent and interested.

You: [CLARIFYING] So, your primary concern is that you feel like this new program is forcing you to use a medical group that doesn't really care about your family and doesn't seem very competent. And, to make it worse, you have to drive some distance to see them when you need them. Is that right?

Employee: Yeah. Basically.

You: Are there any other areas of concern for you? Anything else that is bothering you about the medical coverage?

Employee: No. That's it.

In a word, you are asking, "Are there any other areas of concern for you, Mr. Employee?" However, you will still wish to further clarify the specifics of what he *wants* to make him more comfortable. Use the questioning techniques from Chapter 24 here.

Once you have *clarified* the nature and cause of his anger and resistance, you must communicate to him that you both *acknowledge* and understand his concern, and that you also accept it as *legitimate* (an individual's feelings and concerns are *always* legitimate, even when they are unfounded). *Remember:* failure to legitimize someone's anger or concern is the same as telling him that you don't consider it (or him) to be very important.

Legitimize and Acknowledge

When someone is angry with us, it is frequently because he has concerns, or *anxieties* that we haven't relieved. Unfortunately, before we can respond to his feelings, we must successfully communicate to him that we understand those feelings and that it is all right for him to be angry or anxious (i.e., that we are not threatened by his feelings). We'll continue our previous example:

You: [ACKNOWLEDGE and LEGITIMIZE] I can certainly understand why you might feel angry if you really believe that the doctors in your group don't know what they're doing and don't care about your family. I think anyone would be upset if they *had* felt that way. [Continue to CLARIFY] So they've *never* given you good medical service? [PROBE] Not even once?

Note: this does not mean that you agree with him, only that you acknowledge and understand his concern and legitimize it. It is here that many people try to *tell* an individual that they understand without first demonstrating their understanding. In so doing, they appear defensive and will certainly cause the client to become defensive. Always remember that as a professional, you will *never* need to be defensive because you will *always* do the best possible job for your customers, employees, and superiors. Hence, if one is upset, it won't be because of your performance. Please also note the use of the past tense "*had*" in the sentence, "I think anyone would be upset if they *had* felt that way." By using the past tense, you subtly imply that the problem existed in the past but does not exist *now*.

Employee:	Well, maybe not never. But almost never. But once you get there you still have to wait for nearly an hour sometimes because they always seem to overbook.
You:	[CLARIFY] It sounds as though you feel that its not fair to have to drive half way across the county to then wait forever for poor medical service. [PROBE] Is that basically correct?
Employee:	That's right.
You:	[Further CLARIFY] It must have been very frustrating, Bob. If we could resolve those two problems, would everything else be all right? [PROBE] Or are there other concerns?
Employee:	No. That's it.

Probe

Having communicated your understanding and acceptance of the individual's concern, you must *probe* to determine if you have been accurate in your assessment. You've noted that we probed after every clarifying, legitimizing, and acknowledging remark in the examples above. Even if you have been incorrect, you will have gained in two areas:

➡ First, you will have demonstrated your interest to him.

➡ Second, you will know that you are on the wrong track and will be able to go back and try again until you are correct. This prevents wasting time and risking your relationship with the individual by becoming frustrated over trying to solve the wrong problem. The worst that can happen is that he will appreciate your efforts to understand him and he will try again.

However, if you are correct in your assessment of the problem, you not only improve your level of rapport with him, you also lower his resistance and now know that you and he are on the right track in terms of meeting his needs. Even if the nature of the problem is such that your agenda is not completed, you do complete the conversation having improved your relationship with him for your next meeting.

Paraphrasing

Perhaps the easiest way to "CLAP" is through the use of *paraphrasing*. When the someone becomes angry or brings up a concern, paraphrase that concern back to him in your own words and probe to see if you are correct. In so doing, you simultaneously *clarify* the nature of his concern, *acknowledge* and *legitimize* it, demonstrate your understanding or at least your desire to understand, and verify the correctness of your understanding. For example:

Employee: I submitted my last travel and entertainment voucher over three months ago and I still haven't been reimbursed. I'm getting really tired of this!

You: Let me make sure I've got this right, Mrs. Jones. You turned in your T & E voucher before Christmas and you still haven't gotten paid. Is that right?

Once you have demonstrated your understanding to the individual, it is safe to tell him that you understand and to respond to his concern.

Responding

Having successfully determined the cause of the individual's anger or the nature of his complaint, you must now respond to it. It should be remembered that overly long answers tend to be given by individuals who are nervous and unsure of themselves, so use the *"KISS"* principle— "keep it short and sweet." If you appear nervous or defensive to him, he may interpret that as evasiveness or weakness and become even angrier. This can quickly undermine the rapport you have just built through "CLAPping."

Remember the case of the little boy who asked his mother where he came from. His mother became acutely embarrassed and provided a detailed answer that included a complete description of how babies are conceived and born. The boy looked increasingly confused throughout the discussion and his mother became increasingly uncomfortable as her "lecture" progressed. Finally, when it was over and she "probed" to see if he were satisfied, he said, "Gee, Mom, that's wild! Johnny comes from Chicago."

You can always expand an answer, but it is very hard to take back information that may end up confusing your listener or increasing his discomfort.

Also, when someone is angry or negative, you be positive. Turn potential frustrations into successes by "reframing" what he has said into something else you can use. For example:

Employee: I don't know about this, John. Bill Jackson, over in engineering, says that he doesn't think that this new wing strut will take the stress load.

You: It sounds like you're worried that he might be right. Is that it?

Employee: Yeah.

You: I can understand that. I can't tell you what a pleasure it is to have someone like you take the effort to double check this kind of thing with another department. Bob, you know that our field people report that they've tested the new wing strut in the wind tunnel and it has held over twice the load that we had expected. Would you like me to send you the report? Then you and Bill could go over it and reassure yourselves. If you're still not satisfied, come back and we'll see what we can do verify any data you're still concerned about. Would that be okay?

Employee: Sure.

You: Good. I'll do that today. Then, after you've had a chance to look over the test reports, we'll chat again. If you're still uncomfortable with the wing strut, we'll look for alternatives. How does that sound?

Probe Again

Once you have dealt with the individual's objections, it is important to probe again to determine, first, if he has *understood* and *accepted* your response and, second, if he has any further questions or concerns. Once this has been accomplished, you may return to your agenda if you feel that it is still appropriate.

Summary

As a professional who always does your best for your employees, your superiors, and your customers, you need never become defensive in the face of someone's anger. Use the techniques discussed in Chapters 10 and 11 on creating a state of excellence to practice these effective ways of dealing with angry people, and then anchor this new state to situations in which you commonly face anger in others.

Counseling Creative Employees

For many people, the quintessential innovator is temperamental, inconsistently productive and even (to some) of limited value. Most of the time, this has more to do with the hiring practices and management style of the employer than it does with the nature of creative employees. However, regardless of how productive an innovator is, she will need regular feedback regarding the quality and quantity of her work if she is to continue to be productive.

Support staff also need frequent feedback to maintain their optimum productivity. It is a rare employee who consistently rates "Far Exceeded Expectations" on his or her performance review. It is rarer, still, for any company to have more than 20 percent of their employees rated so favorably. This is true for both line and staff positions, for laborers to members of upper management. What happened to the other 80 percent?

Numerous studies on employee performance have concluded that most employees can retain their job by performing at 20 to 30 percent of their capabilities. They further concluded that people can consistently perform at 80 to 90 percent of capacity if motivated to do so. The gray area between 30 and 80 precent can be positively affected.

Most courses on, and approaches to, this concern have dealt with managers appropriately motivating their subordinates (of course this assumes that managers are already self-motivated and "have their act together!"). However, have you, or anyone you know, ever had a day in which everything went absolutely right? You know, where you were great, motivated, "on," "hot?" Has anyone you know ever had a day where they just didn't get things done right? Again, you know, not perform up to expectations, or had enough motivation or desire to get going? Most of us have these days. However, for most of us, they pass rather quickly and we return to our normal productive state. For others, the poor days can stretch into weeks or months (longer term symptomatic behavior is characterized by different terms: "burn out," depression, demotivation, attitudinal problem, etc.).

Besides liking one mental state and disliking the other, what are the thinking differences between the good state or the other? The answer isn't in the conscious awareness. If it were, we would always have good days. Yet, by definition, there is a difference.

In most organizations, the majority of the people perform at the lower end of the productivity spectrum. Within these organizations there are usually also a few "key personnel" who are not quite maximizing their contributions to the firm. How much productivity, how many ideas, how much money is lost because of these "partial contributors?" The amount is incalculable. Yet, what organization can afford to allow this to occur? In this chapter we will discuss why substandard performance occurs, how to deal with it and twelve good rules of thumb for providing feedback to employees and peers.

Why Substandard Performance?

When you think about it, failure to perform according to expectations can only be the result of any combination of the following three factors: first, does the individual really want to perform; second, does he know how to; and, third, does he have the chance to?

Want To

An individual usually has a conscious choice in deciding whether she wants to do a particular thing. Yet, we all know of the situation where a person *wants* to do what is expected, but something stops her from doing it. Assuming that there are no environmental factors (outside influences actually preventing the action), that something comes from the unconscious mind. This may take the form of some fear, a competing desire, a belief, etc. For whatever reason, a conflict is present.

Therefore, even if a person wants to perform actions to keep her job performance at peak levels, she might not be able to because of the internal conflict. The conflict might take the form of "damned if I do; damned if I don't." "If I work harder I'll accomplish more, but if I do work harder I may be given more responsibilities and fail at those." Logical analysis is great—sometimes. But, logic doesn't seem to work when an emotional conflict is present.

Often, an individual's performance problem is simply a matter of motivation. If we, as managers, know how to motivate someone, she will "want to" perform most tasks satisfactorily. Where lack of motivation is the cause, use the skills that you have already developed in communications, psychological profiling, and motivation to move her in the desired direction. If you uncover a concern that good performance will result in ever-increasing demands, or eventual "failure," deal with it. However, if it appears that a deeper conflict is present, you may wish to consider other options.

How To

Sometimes, the individual in question really wants to do a good job. However, if she is missing certain background information she may not be able to do it even though she would like to. Usually, a book , a training course, observing others, or asking questions will resolve this situation. That's how most people learn.

Unfortunately, sometimes the person is too embarrassed to ask or to search for information that cannot be obtained in a book. (Note: this may be similar to an internal conflict that needs resolution.) Also, standard sources sometimes don't provide the information needed, information such as precisely how to communicate with someone else, or how to become creative.

When you first hired this individual, did you adequately explain your expectations and how she would be evaluated? Was the training she received adequate for the demands of her current task? Often, job descriptions change and expand, and the initial training becomes inadequate for the new requirements.

Finally, you already know that failure to match someone's thinking process (e.g., their sensory orientation) can result in confusion, rather than the desired understanding. When she was oriented and trained, were explanations provided in a "language" that she could relate to and understand? Were adequate checks made of her understanding? If not, the substandard performance of your employee may be your fault, not hers.

Chance To

If environmental factors actually prevent the person from doing the job (e.g., paperwork from another department arriving too late, parts delivered late, covert sabotage, etc.), then those environmental factors must be identified and remedied. If they cannot be remedied, then job responsibilities should be changed to allow for those factors.

Now What?

Once a so-called subaverage performer is identified, there are only a limited number of possible actions. They are:

- ➡ Transfer the individual.
- ➡ Demote her.
- ➡ Modify (redefine) her job responsibilities.
- ➡ Terminate and replace the individual.
- ➡ Provide additional training and hope for the best.
- ➡ Counsel her.

With the exception of the last two alternatives, such actions necessitate the replacement of that person with someone who *you hope* is more qualified. This replacement requires the expenditure of additional time and money until her replacement proves herself and fully assumes her new responsibilities. The last two choices will *potentially* work. However, a certain amount of time must be allowed for the training or counseling to take effect. During the transition period, the subperforming individual is still not making a full contribution. If the replacement works out, great! If not, you're back to the original four choices. Before we examine ways of counseling an employee with mediocre performance, let's briefly discuss each choice more fully.

Transfer the Individual

This is frequently a viable solution because people are often promoted to their level of incompetence (the "Peter Principle"). The most common example seems to be the star research chemist who is promoted to department manager, but who doesn't have the requisite leadership skills to manage well. Or, sometimes, an effective employee or manager is transferred from one department to another and loses her effectiveness. It may not always be possible to return her to her previous position. (Note: this may be construed as a demotion, but will probably retain the employee within the organization.) However, if you do send her back to her old position, she has to be replaced by someone else (by using a modified selection process). Unfortunately, the transition period for the newly appointed manager costs the company money in terms of unrealized productivity. Yet, in this situation, perhaps, it can't be helped.

Modify (Redefine) the Job Responsibilities

There are times when it just isn't practical to either transfer someone or fire her. When this occurs, it is often possible to reach a compromise in which you redefine her job responsibilities to meet her abilities and level of functioning. Needless to say, this is far from an ideal solution and results in virtually validating substandard performance. However, sometimes the individual in question is performing below standard because of stress problems. When this is the case, temporarily modifying (or even reducing) her responsibilities may be all that is required to help her regain control of her work and return to full effectiveness.

Demote

Most people tend to take demotions "personally," usually resulting in their looking for other employment. This results in lower morale and poorer production. In addition, when someone is demoted, not only is there temporary loss of productivity as she assumes her new, lower responsibilities, but she will also require a replacement for her old position. Hence, at least two positions have lost productivity. Note: as a rule-of-thumb, it is safe to assume that the replacement cost of any individual is more than twice her annual salary and, depending upon her level, can easily reach three times her salary.

Terminate

Terminating an employee is far more complicated than just "firing" her. Today, laws protect most people's jobs to the extent that you may be required to counsel them several times regarding their job performance before you can fire them without risk of a law suit. You may also risk a law suit or action by the Office of Economic Opportunity if the individual you terminate is female or a member of a designated minority group.

In addition, depending on the position of the employee, she may require outplacement services, termination pay, etc. Then, her replacement must be found, trained, and given a chance to grow into the new job. As already noted, this can be very expensive.

Train

During the period of time that they are being retrained, employees are not able to maximize their performance. Assuming that the training is effective, then the company may have salvaged a key person. At this point, however, it is important to consider the underlying reasons for the poor performance. If the person was not motivated to do the job, or if she had some sort of family crisis, all the training in the world may not improve her performance.

Coaching and Counseling

When you first recognize that an employee isn't fulfilling her job responsibilities, it is important to call her in and determine the cause. Remember, essentially all performance problems can be reduced to "Want To, How To, Chance To." Regardless of the cause of her substandard performance, you will have to counsel her regarding that performance and your expectations for the future. Always remember that the most important message that you wish your listener to hear is that you *care* about her. If you don't, you will only confirm her worst fears and you may destroy what motivation and self-confidence she has. People often become defensive when they are counseled and you can never guarantee that the person you counsel will do what you wish. However, there are several things that you can do to minimize her defensiveness and increase her motivation to change. Here is a list of twelve rules of thumb for counseling an employee:

Rules of Thumb

1. Be sure to choose an appropriate time and place before you begin to counsel. A good rule of thumb is: *"Praise in public, rebuke in private."* In addition, it is generally unwise to respond to someone when one or both of you is angry or upset. Wait for a calm time.

2. *Always* establish rapport before you begin to counsel. Do this whether they have come to you or you have gone to them. It's the surest way to communicate that "I care" message (see Chapters 22 to 26).

3. After you listen to what someone has said, use paraphrasing to make sure that you understand what they mean and, especially, what they feel. Remember, if you're going to work from their point of view, you need to be sure that you understand what it is. For example:

   You: Don, it sounds as though you're feeling a little frustrated over this new field work policy. Is that right?

4. Always discuss the individual's *behavior* rather than the *individual*. For example:

   You: Sally, it's important to be back from lunch by one o'clock so the others can go. [effective]

   Not: Sally, I understand that you have developed the bad habit of coming back late from lunch. [ineffective]

5. Share your *observations* rather than trying to *read the individual's mind* regarding why she did something. If you don't know what someone is thinking or feeling, don't guess, ask! Mind reading builds barriers. For example:

   You: Bill, you have arrived late three times in the last week. Is everything all right? [effective—opens further communications]

   Not: Bill, it's obvious that you don't care enough about your work to even come in on time. [ineffective—promotes immediate defensiveness]

6. Describe what you feel and what you have experienced rather than making judgements about the other person or her actions. Judgemental statements make people defensive and close lines of communication instead of opening them. For example:

   You: Harry, I'm concerned about the number of problems that seem to be developing on that new project. When can we meet to discuss it? [effective]

   Not: Harry, with your record on this new project, you must be the worst research chemist in the department. I want to see you in my office in five minutes to find out what is holding you up! [ineffective]

7. Don't deal in extremes or generalities. In other words, don't label people and remember that no one is all good or all bad. Avoid words like "always" and "never." Once we label someone, we paint them into a corner that leaves them little room to improve. After all, if you think that they're *always* late, why should they bother to try to improve? You probably won't give them credit for it anyway. For example:

   You: Jane, you were late with your progress reports three times this month. Is there anything I can do to help? [effective]

   Not: Jane, you're *always* late! You *never* have your progress reports in on time! Why can't you get with the program? [ineffective]

8. Avoid giving advice. Whether the advice is good or bad it changes the nature of your relationship. If your advice is bad (or improperly followed) and fails, she may blame you instead of taking responsibility for the outcome herself. If your advice is good and it works, you will have gained a dependent who will be tempted to come to you to solve all of her problems instead of doing it herself.

   Of course, there will be times when it may be necessary for you to go beyond giving advice by giving the employee an order. As a rule, however, aid your employee (especially your creative staff) in *her* exploration of alternatives until she feels comfortable in making a decision for herself. Even if you have a better solution, let her try her own and experience the consequences— either good or bad—unless they are illegal, unethical, or will endanger her health or the project.

9. Before you release your emotions, ask yourself why you are communicating to begin with. Are you trying to help her to be a more effective member of the department, or just to blow off steam? Remember, your emotional release may make you feel better but may also cost you both the relationship and the employee's confidence. What value do you wish your communication to have for her?

10. Only give the person you're counseling as much "feedback" as she can handle. Most of us have many habits or failings that we

could afford to improve, but when someone shares all of them with us at once they can be a little overwhelming.

In most cases, it's best to comment on only one or two behaviors in a given meeting. More than that can be hard to remember *and* be discouraging. Once progress has been made in those areas, praise her for her progress, then go on to the next area for improvement.

11. Determine her psychological profile (Dictator, Bureaucrat, Socialite, or Executive) at the time that you begin counseling her and be prepared to deal with the emotional needs that underlie her profile. For example, an individual who is a "Dictator" needs to be reminded that she is "special" and that you have high expectations of her performance because of her great talents. Motivating her to do her job may be as easy as reminding her that its the kind of job that you would only give to a few individuals. On the other hand, that kind of approach might be very threatening to a "Bureaucrat" or a "Socialite."

12. Finally, remember to "speak her language." If she has a visual orientation, use visual terms. Auditory words may only confuse her.

Setting Goals in Coaching

When you sit down with an employee to discuss her progress or concerns, help her to establish meaningful goals using the steps provided in the chapter on goal setting. In doing so, you will help her organize her thoughts about both her concern and the solution in a way that will improve her chances of following through on it. Remember the requirements for establishing a goal:

➡ The goal must be stated in positives. What does she want? *Not, what doesn't she want?*

➡ The goal must be in her control. If there is something you want her to do, she must be convinced that she wants it as well. Otherwise, it is your goal and it is *not* in your control.

➡ The goal must maintain any positive aspects (positive from her point of view) of her current situation. For example: If a positive aspect of too much time socializing with other employees is the synergy it develops for her creativity, then you must be sure that she gets some form of socializing that will fit within the accepted limits of the department, or risk losing that synergy.

➤ The goal must be "economical;" that is, it must not cost more than it is worth. If an employee sets a goal of regularly working sixty hours a week but damages her health in the process, it's not worth it.

➤ Finally, the goal must be testable. As you work with her to select performance goals, be sure that you both understand how her progress toward achieving those goals will be measured.

Summary

By using the techniques presented in this chapter you can now provide helpful, timely feedback for both your creative and support personnel. Increased productivity (increasing a person's performance from 20 to 30 percent of capacity to nearer 80 to 90 percent of capacity) is the goal of most businesses. Usually, reliance on traditional methods of motivation will produce some of the results. However, traditional methods are limited.

Rather than employing the traditional solutions to continued underachievement (firing, demoting, etc.), now you can salvage employees who have the potential to make significant contributions to your branch. The counseling techniques described in this and other chapters will enable you to more fully realize the potential of your employees, with the expenditure of relatively minor amounts of time. After all, the alternatives are far too costly and really not viable over the long term.

After you have determined whether a performance problem is the result of "Want To, How To, or Chance To," make the necessary decisions about how you will deal with the problem. In most cases, you'll find that simple counseling will do the trick. Then use the twelve rules of thumb for counseling provided, and establish new goals of performance.

Monitoring and Evaluating the Creative Process

How do you measure the productivity of creative people? One of the most important reasons some managers are uncomfortable working on innovative projects or with creative people is because, on the surface, monitoring creative progress and evaluating the results appears to be a very complex job. This is particularly frustrating if the manager is required to justify all expenditures by the return on the investment.

In reality, monitoring and evaluating the productivity of creative people or innovative projects is no more difficult than for any other process, if the right policies and procedures are established and utilized. This section will explore simple techniques for establishing evaluation criteria and then provide case studies showing how two very successful creative departments measure their productivity.

Measuring Creative
Productivity

Much of the apparent difficulty involved in measuring the productivity of creative work or innovative programs derives from a failure to apply managerial common sense. Even excellent managers can have this problem because of a tendency to define "creative" problems as different from "run of the mill" management problems. Once a manager recognizes the similarities between the two processes, he is half way to solving his monitoring problem.

Whether the problem is how to increase market penetration in Buffalo, or how to develop a new insecticide that won't combine with the smog in Los Angeles to create environmental problems, much of the process is the same:

➥ Define the problem and its parameters.

➥ Define the solution and its parameters.

- Explore and define the obstacles that will have to be overcome to solve the problem.

- List the resources that will be needed, or that are currently available, to overcome each obstacle.

- Determine whether solving the problem will be worth the resources and effort required. That is, will introducing a new pesticide hurt sales of existing pesticides and, once the new pesticide is developed, is there a large enough market to justify it at the cost of its production?

- Finally, assign someone to develop a plan (normally the individual or team who developed the idea) and hold him accountable for its successful completion.

More Complicated Than It Looks

Whether these steps are followed at the corporate level for a major innovation or at the departmental level for a recommended change in procedures (such as using the copying machine), they still have to be followed in some form. However, despite the apparent simplicity of such procedures, the difficulty of objectively evaluating performance remains. One reason for this difficulty is the evaluation's apparent reliance upon management by objective (MBO).

Raudsepp and Yeager (1981) point out that one of the greatest weaknesses of MBO evaluation is the fact that the individual manager's bias will have a greater impact upon the evaluation than the individual's performance. Outside of sales or piece work, there are few areas in business in which an individual's performance can be objectively measured (the sales professional produces so many orders per month, or the piece worker produces so many new pieces per hour). Hence, the process usually consists of the manager and employee sitting down and establishing goals together for the coming year. However, those goals are rarely the joint venture they appear, but are instead designed to ensure the employee's compliance with the superior's desires, without taking into account the lack of trust in most manager-employee relationships.

Since evaluation is actually an intrinsic part of any organization's political process, truly objective evaluation is virtually impossible. In addition, it becomes even more difficult when goals are set for a team instead of an individual.

Built-In Measurement

To overcome these weaknesses, Drucker (1986) suggests a three step plan for building the measurement and judgement of creative performance into the controls of the business from the start.

➡ Step one builds into each innovative project feedback about everything from results to expectations. Such feedback provides indications of the quality and reliability of both the innovative plans and the innovative efforts involved in the project.

➡ Step two implements a systematic review of all innovative efforts together. On a company level, this means reviewing all of the major innovative projects of the company. At a departmental level, the same thing can be accomplished less formally. Drucker also points out the importance of carefully reviewing the innovative efforts of the company's major competitors.

➡ Finally, effective management of a company's innovative projects, people, and departments requires judging the company or department's total innovative performance against its innovative objectives, together with its performance and standing in the market and its performance as a business or department.

We have found that there are additional ways to measure performance. A manager, of course, must follow the company's policies and procedures manual regarding the use of specific forms and criteria. Additionally, each manager should endeavor to apply objective standards to each member of his team. This insures that both the manager and the employee are protected in an increasing litigious society.

In Chapter 15 we summarized effective goal setting for individuals. Because well defined goals are so critical to effective performance measurement, we have listed them again here for your convenience.

1. Establish the parameters of the problem to be solved.

2. The goals must be written.

3. Goals must be stated positively.

4. The goals must be within your control.

5. Each goal must be testable.

6. Be sure that the goal is really understood with respect to the outcome, the results of that outcome, obstacles to be overcome, and resources needed to overcome them.

7. A goal should maintain the positive aspects of the current situation.

8. The goal must be worth the effort.

The previously enumerated concerns about performance are often bypassed when this goal-setting procedure is employed. This occurs because the procedure takes into account most of the factors that are the causes of poor performance. In Chapter 32 you learned a series of performance diagnostic questions that focus on whether the employee Wants To, knows How To, or has the Chance To do the job. These questions are critical for effective performance evaluation.

Management By Walking Around

Little is more disastrous than finding out about a problem after it's gone on too long or it's too late to fix it. Preventing problems from getting out of hand requires constant supervision without giving the impression that you don't trust your own people. Establishing this kind of system takes time and a genuine interest in your employees and their day-to-day work.

The successful managers we spoke to all indicated that constant contact with both their subordinate managers and their creative employees was one of the single greatest factors in enabling them to keep on top of all progress and problems within their department.

Each manager (both directors and subordinate managers) indicated that in addition to regular progress meetings (both formal and informal), he spent at least half of his work day moving around the work areas of his people to discuss their projects and "press the flesh." They also reported that management by walking around both helped them maintain the pulse of the department and its projects, and also enabled them to provide timely support. Such support ranged from help solving problems to praise to providing necessary resources. The result: high morale, high productivity, and timely awareness of both progress and problems.

Management by walking around also insures that you become aware of situations before they become problems. You will notice when an employee is having a difficult time performing a particular task and be able to take remedial steps earlier. You may also find that previously defined goals were "easier said than done."

There are times when the performance standard is very difficult to enunciate and to measure. The goal of solving a particular problem or creating something specific may or may not be as easily accomplished as was first thought. Sometimes people fail to perform and can berate themselves for failure. What can be even worse is when they are chastised for failure by their managers.

There are two types of measurements that can be employed: absolute and relative. Absolute performances can be easily measured. Did you invent the widget, or not? Did you publish a paper, or not? Was the job done, or not? Unfortunately, this black and white approach cannot be employed in all situations and often cannot be used to evaluate all aspects of a person's job performance.

At those times when a person's absolute performance did not meet expectations (realistic or unrealistic, possible or impossible), realizing that they probably contributed to the company's bottom line in different ways may be more appropriate. In this case we suggest judging the relative performance by asking such questions as:

- What did you learn from the process that can be used by you or others in the future?
- What strategy did you employ to solve the problem? What alternative approaches might you now use?
- How might this information be utilized in the future?
- What obstacles did you have and how did you overcome them?
- What might other people learn from your efforts?
- Whom did you assist?
- What projects received or will receive positive benefit from your work?
- In the process of seeking "X," did you invent "Y"?

In addition, we often suggest that employees keep a daily record listing the meetings that they attended, who they helped, and a list of their accomplishments. Often, when it comes to the final performance review people fail to remember all of the things they did. Once it is listed, both the employee and the manager have something definitive to work with. A list of accomplishments also provides a useful analysis of how an employee spends his time. If, for example, a person indicates that he spends a large amount of time brainstorming with others, you can either praise him for generating new ideas (especially if this approach *is* part of his personal creative strategy—see Chapter 9), or counsel him that other aspects of the job need additional attention.

Summary

The specific techniques used to measure the productivity of employees working on creative projects will vary slightly depending upon the context. However, whether dealing with an individual, a team, or your entire department, consistently following basic management and leadership principles will solve most measurement problems. Define your situation and solution and establish guidelines for progress.

Get involved with your people and their projects. Supervision that is too distant can leave the people you depend on feeling that you are inaccessible. Management by walking around can provide important insights into the day-to-day development of your projects as well as the creative people working on them.

A Case Study of Productive Creativity

In our interviews of successful managers of creative departments we found several programs that epitomize the style of management that obtains the greatest amount of productivity from innovative people. In each case, the managers at every level followed a few simple procedures that have been proven effective in any creative environment. However, one case that really stands out is Fisher Price Toys.

Case Study: Fisher Price Toys

Fisher Price Toys has been a leader in producing high quality toys for decades. Much of that success has been the result of the work of the company's founder, Herb Fisher, and the system of management and development he established. For the purpose of this case study, we will focus upon Fisher Price's Research and Development Department, the driving force behind their success in developing innovative toys that last for generations.

R & D Organization

The vice president of R & D has six directors who report to him; three are directors of new product development for specific product lines and three are directors of support groups or departments within R & D.

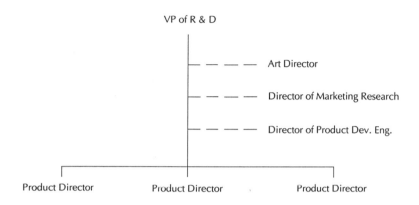

VP of R & D

— — — — Art Director

— — — — Director of Marketing Research

— — — — Director of Product Dev. Eng.

Product Director   Product Director   Product Director

Each director of new product development is responsible for one or more toy lines, such as crib and playpen, dolls, or trucks. The Art, Marketing Research, and Product Development Engineering departments exist within the R & D department for the sole purpose of supporting the product development staff. For example, product development engineering is responsible for making up all drawings, details, and specifications for a new toy, then turning it over to manufacturing engineering.

Measuring Productivity

Within R & D, each director of new product development has several managers working for him, each responsible for six to eight designers who are divided into product areas. Depending upon the size of a project, the manager determines how many designers to assign to it.

To evaluate the progress of each project, as well as to maintain contact with the members of their staff, the director and managers follow a series of formal and informal reporting procedures:

➥ Each director meets informally with each of his managers on almost a daily basis to get progress reports to enable him to keep up to date with the overall picture. In addition, each manager maintains informal daily contact with each of his designers. Management by walking around is the key to providing each designer with support and encouragement and to keeping the manager aware of progress and problems.

➡ Every two to three weeks, each manager and his team provides their director with an informal show-and-tell regarding all the projects that team is working on.

➡ The department meets frequently (sometimes as often as once a month) with their director for a day-long show-and-tell in which everyone participates. These regular meetings keep everyone informed on the department's projects and helps to build inter-team synergy. Several days later, each manager meets with his marketing counterpart to provide them with an informal update on project status and get marketing's input on the project. When desired, these meetings might occur more frequently.

➡ Any time a manager feels that a project is running into problems, he reports to his director during their daily meeting. The director then goes down to meet with the designer or team and the manager at the designer's desk. Each director spends about half of each day managing by walking around.

Informality and flexibility are of prime importance to maintaining a comfortable, creative atmosphere while maintaining accountability. Many informal meetings are needed between individual managers in R & D and their counterparts in marketing and manufacturing engineering. These informal meetings between the "lower" management levels (as opposed to the VPs) of these departments keeps the flow of communication open enough so that when a toy is finally ready to go into production, there are few, if any, surprises for either marketing or manufacturing. This constant communication keeps the cost of manufacturing engineering down and ensures that the toy will still be appropriate for the market when it is manufactured.

VP of R & D

Key personnel from each major department meet formally on a regular basis, sometimes as often as every four to six weeks if there is a need. This meeting is attended by the VP of R & D, the directors of new product development and their managers, and the directors of marketing and their managers.

Each director's group gives a show-and-tell for the vice presidents of R & D and marketing. During the presentation, each designer is invited to briefly explain her project and to "show off." This serves two important purposes:

➥ First, along with the semimonthly meetings with her director, it provides each designer with regular reporting dates where she is held accountable for her projects. This, in turn, enables the vice president of research and development to maintain a solid evaluation of the progress of all the projects within the department.

➥ And second, it gives each designer a chance to obtain praise and support from higher-ups.

Note: The product development engineering department (which is part of R & D) assigns an engineer to each design group to act as a resource for the designers. Close cooperation is maintained throughout the design process to minimize both design engineering problems and turn around time when the designs are given to manufacturing engineering.

Toy Fair

Each year in February, a toy fair is held for two weeks in New York City in which virtually every toy company in America (as well as most major foreign toy producers) show off their wares to the industry. Major department stores and other toy outlets attend the fair to obtain an idea of what will be available in the coming seasons. In addition, the toy companies get a chance to see what the competition is producing as well as to obtain some idea of what the market is interested in this season.

Sales and marketing attend the fair for the entire two weeks. In addition, each director of new product development attends for two to three days. Afterwards, the directors meet with their managers to review their current toy lines in the stores to decide which lines to expand and which to drop. This decision is based upon a combination of last year's sales and this year's current and projected orders. The director then meets with his counterpart, the director of marketing (not the VP), and marketing's three managers to discuss the conclusions reached. The marketing director reviews the conclusions of product development with his managers and comments on the results, providing a good idea of which areas to stress. The final decision on which areas in the different toy lines should be expanded is made by the marketing department.

As a result of these meetings, each product development director knows which product lines to expand and which to reduce. For example, the decision might be made to expand from the current three rattles to five. A designer who is working on rattles is then assigned to develop two new rattles. Fisher Price allows the initial parameters for new products (e.g., rattles) to be fairly broad because they feel that a good idea can always be modified.

The Creative Process

Every company has its own techniques for enhancing the creative process when solving problems or developing new products and services. At Fisher Price, once a product is assigned to a designer, he develops several ideas on paper (no models yet). Over a series of semimonthly meetings with his team, manager and new product development director, he will present his ideas to the group for feedback and refinement. After two to three such meetings, a manager from marketing might be asked to attend and provide feedback.

Following a sufficient number of these sessions to help crystallize some of the more promising designs, the designer will begin to work up models for them. These models and designs will continue to progress through a period of refinement, during which both marketing and product development engineering will be consulted, until a final design or model is selected.

Fisher Price feels that synergy is essential to the design process and acts to encourage and maintain that synergy throughout its design process. This is maintained not only through the semimonthly team show-and-tell sessions, but also through the continuous process of management by walking around. Designers are also encouraged to periodically walk around and see what the other teams and individual designers are working on. During these informal chats designers often help each other overcome minor design problems and generate new ideas.

Motivation

The management of Fisher Price has long felt that motivation is important to any creative effort. As a result, continuous feedback, encouragement, and support from peers and superiors are built into every facet of the company's policies. Overall motivation is promoted by:

1. Management's continuous close contact with staff, which provides plenty of feedback and support (management by walking around).

2. The directors of new product development, as well as their managers, regularly take designers (either individually or in small groups) out for lunch or dinner to discuss their work and offer support.

3. Regular show-and-tell sessions, both formal and informal, to provide praise and feedback from peers and higher-ups.

4. Intelligent compensation. When the budget is made each year, the managers recommend raises based upon two criteria:

   → Upper management guidelines (budget), and

   → The individual's overall performance. Note: A good director always fights for his people.

Summary

Fisher Price Toys has been and continues to be one of the most successful companies of its kind because it knows how to maintain an innovative atmosphere and manage one of its most important resources: its employees. More than any other company we studied, Fisher Price epitomizes the principles of managing innovative people so long written about by individuals like George Freedman, Thomas Peters, Peter Drucker, and a host of others.

Bibliography

Anastasi, A. *Psychological Testing*. 4th ed. New York MacMillan, 1975.

Arasteh, A. R. *Creativity in the Life Cycle*. Vol. 2. Leiden, Netherlands: E. J. Brill, 1968.

Bandler, Richard. *Using Your Brain for a Change*. Moab: Real People Press, 1985.

Bandler, Richard, and Grinder, John. *Frogs into Princes*. Moab: Real People Press, 1979.

———. *Reframing*. Moab: Real People Press, 1982.

Bennett, Dudley. *TA and the Manager*. New York: AMACOM, 1976.

Berne, Eric. *Games People Play*, New York: Grove Press, 1964.

Buhler, C. *Psychology for Contemporary Living*. New York: Hawthorn, 1968.

Buzzota, ct al. *Effective Selling through Psychology.* St. Louis: Ballinger Publishing Company, 1982.

Byrne, John A., and Miles, Gregory L. "Where The Schools Aren't Doing Their Homework." *Business Week,* no.3081 (28 November 1988).

Dilts, Robert. *Applications of Neuro-Linguistic Programming.* Cupertino: Meta Publications, 1983.

————. *Roots of Neuro-Linguistic Programming.* Cupertino: Meta Publications, 1983.

Dilts, Robert, et al. *Neuro-Linguistic Programming Vol I: The Study of Subjective Experience.* Cupertino: Meta Publications, 1980.

Drucker, Peter F. *Innovation and Entrepreneurship: Practice A Principles.* New York: Harper & Row, 1985.

Dunn, Paul H. *The Ten Most Wanted Men.* Salt Lake City: Bookcraft, 1967.

Eiduson, B. T. *Scientists.* New York: Basic Books, 1968.

Eliot, Robert S., and Breo, Dennis L. *Is It Worth Dying For?* New York: Bantam Books, 1984.

Freedman, George. *The Pursuit of Innovation: Managing the People and Processes that Turn New Ideas into Profits.* New York: The American Management Association, 1988.

Gardner, John. *aha! Insight.* New York: Scientific American/W. H. Freeman and Company, 1978.

Gretz, Karl F. and Drozdeck, Steven R. *The Effective Manager.* New York: Simon & Schuster/New York Institute of Finance, 1991.

Grinder, John and Bandler, Richard. *Trance-Formations.* Moab: Real People Press, 1981.

Guilford, J. P., and Hoepfner, R. *The Analysis of Intelligence.* New York: MacGraw-Hill, 1971.

Harper, James M., et al. "The Logical Level of Complementary, Symmetrical, and Parallel Interaction Classes in Family Dyads." *Family Process.* vol 16(2), (June, 1977), 199–209.

Holland, J. L. "Creative and Academic Performance among Talented Adolescents." *Journal of Educational Psychology* 6–7(1959):136-47.

Kroeger, Otto and Thuesen, Janet M. *Type Talk.* New York: Dell Publishing, 1988.

Linn, Louis. "Clinical Manifestations of Psychiatric Disorders." In *Comprehensive Textbook of Psychiatry / II,* edited by Alfred M. Freedman, vol. 1, 2d ed. Baltimore: Williams & Wilkins Company, 1975.

Maslow, Abraham H. *Motivation and Personality.* New York: Harper & Row, 1970.

————. *The Farther Reaches of Human Nature.* New York: Viking Press, 1971.

McClelland, David C. and Burnham, David H. "Power is the Great Motivator." *Harvard Business Review: On Human Relations.* New York: Harper & Row, Publishers, 1979.

Moine, Donald J. and Herd, John H. *Modern Persuasion Strategies: The Hidden Advantage in Selling.* Englewood Cliffs: Prentice Hall, Inc., 1984.

Niederland, W. G. "Psychiatry and the Creative Process." In *Comprehensive Textbook of Psychiatry / II,* edited by Alfred M. Freedman, vol. 2, 2d ed. Baltimore: Williams & Wilkins Company, 1975.

Perkins, D. N. *The Mind's Best Work.* Cambridge: Harvard University Press, 1981.

Peters, Thomas J., and Waterman, Robert H. *In Search of Excellence: Lessons from America's Best-Run Companies.* New York: Warner Books, 1982.

Raudsepp, Eugene and Yeager, Joseph C. *How to Sell New Ideas: Your Company's and Your Own.* Englewood Cliffs, N.J.: Prentice Hall, 1981.

Satir, Virginia. *Peoplemaking.* Palo Alto: Science and Behavior Books, Inc. 1972.

Scoresby, A. Lynn. "The Family as a Subsystem." *Journal of Employment Counseling.* vol. 10(3), (Sept, 1973), 127–135.

Watzlawick, Paul, et al. *Pragmatics of Human Communication: A Study of Interational Patterns, Pathologies, and Paradoxes.* New York: W.W. Norton & Comp., 1967.

————. *Change.* New York: W.W. Norton & Comp., 1974.

Weisberg, Robert W. *Creativity: Genius and Other Myths.* New York: W. H. Freeman and Company, 1986.

Yeager, Joseph. *Thinking about Thinking with NLP.* Cupertino: META Publications, 1985.

Index

305

C

Calming, 265-276
Carrot and stick, 207, 220
Challenge, 247
Change, 3
  preparation, 252-256
  stress, 260
Chunking, 127-128, 233
CLAPping, 270-276
Clarification, 270-274
Closure, 63
Coaching
  calming, 265-276
  employee, 263-286
  goal setting, 285-286
Communication, 119
  see personality traits, rapport
  effective, 133-199
  nonverbal, 153-162
  pacing, 155-156
  precise, 187
  speed, 163-165
  trust, 133
Compensation, 206
Competition, 3
Complementary
  see style
  interaction, 267
  style, 117-118
Control, 119
  see personality traits
  calming, 265-276
  goals, 123-124
  power, 211-213
Counseling
  see coaching
  employee, 263-286
Creative
  see motivation, personality traits,
    strategies, style
  abilities, 12-13
  definition, 7
  flashes, 84
  goals, 121-132
    steps, 122-126

increasing, 33-99
innovators, 4
outcome, 88-90
people/personnel
  administrator for, 28-29
  coaching/counseling, 263-286
  compensation, 206
  fame, 204-206
  goals, 121-132
  hiring, 21-25
  identifying, 17-20
  leader for, 29-31
  manager for, 27-32
  managing, 101-132
  motivation, 201-261
  nonjudgementality, 18
  originality, 19
  reality-based, 18-19
  recognition, 204-206
problem analysis, 11-12, 55
process
  characteristics, 8
  evaluation, 287-300
  monitoring, 287-300
productivity
  measuring, 289-294
resources, 86-88, 90
self-actualization, 18
solutions, 11-12
state, 83-92
  anchoring, 90-91
  control, 84-86
  installation, 93-99
thinking, 8-9
  submodality, 47-53
Creativity, 1-32
  anchoring, 52
  definition, 7-15
  innovation comparison, 13-14
  model, 55-71
  motivation, 13, 60
  strategy, 61
  stress and motivation, 239-245
  tests, 19-20
  verbal reframing, 73-81

senses, 44-51, 56
speed, 164
Innovation, 3-6
  creativity comparison, 13-14
  dictator, 136
Innovative
  company, 35-41
  departments, 28, 39-40
  environment, 35-41
  managers, 37-39
  personnel, 121, 203-207
  bureaucrat, 139-141
    measurement, 126-127
Innovators, 4
  fame, 204-206
  generalists, 21-23
  power-oriented, 211
  private language, 185-199
  quintessential, 277
  specialists, 23-24
Insight, 8-9, 11
Intelligence, 9-10
  quotient (IQ), 9
Interaction, 267
Interview, 185-190
Investment
  see ROI
Issues
  interpersonal, 73-75
  personal, 73-75
    verbal reframing, 75-78

K
Kinesthetic sense, 44, 65, 90
  terms, 172, 177-180

L
Labor Department, 207
Language
  calming, 266
  of thoughts, 171-183
  private, 185-199
  sensory oriented, 43-46
  undefined words, 192-193
Leader, 104-106, 109

Leadership
  nonverbal rapport, 153-162
  rapport, 161-162
  selling, 177
Leading
  personnel, 201-261
Learning strategy, 62-63

M
Management, 3
  appreciation, 206
  by objective (MBO), 290
  creative individual, 101-132
  innovative attitude, 37-39
  Japanese, 5-6
  observation, 292-294
  Ringi, 5-6
  stress, 247-261
Manager
  see communication
  administrator, 28-29, 117
  appreciation, 206
  criteria, 27
  dominating, 117
  effectiveness, 103-113
  innovators, 203-207
  leader, 29-31, 153
  overaccommodating, 117
  personnel measurement, 126-127
  projects, 204
  recognition, 204-206
  selecting, 27-32
Measurement
  built-in, 291-292
  creative productivity, 289-294
  employee, 126-127
  productivity, 296-297
Memory
  mental resources, 91
  strategy, 61-62
  stress reduction, 257-258
Million Dollar Round Table, 244-245
Mirroring, 156-158
Modality, 44
  submodalities, 47-53

About the Authors

Karl F. Gretz and Steven R. Drozdeck are the managing partners of Training Groups, Inc., an organization which specializes in team-building technology as applied to sales management, communication and leadership. Both authors were formerly with Merrill Lynch, Dr. Gretz as a senior training consultant, and Mr. Drozdeck as an assistant vice president and the Manager of Professional Development. They are also the co-authors of *Consultative Selling Techniques for Financial Professionals* and *The Effective Manager.*

Dr. Gretz received a Master of Education degree from Tufts University and a Ph.D. in Educational Psychology from Brigham Young University.

Mr. Drozdeck received his B.S. in Finance from the New York Institute of Technology and is a leading expert in neuro linguistic programming. He is also the author of *What They Don't Teach You in Sales 101.*

Other books by Gretz and Drozdeck:

Consultative Selling Techniques for Financial Professionals
The Effective Manager: Being the Best in Financial Sales Management

Also by Drozdeck:

What They DON'T Teach You in Sales 101 (with Yeager and Sommer)

For additional information regarding other books, tapes, lectures, courses and materials, contact:

Training Groups, Inc.
P.O. Box 996
Newtown, PA 18940
Phone: (215) 396-0501
or
(215) 639-1922